# Care, Socialization, and Play in Ancient Attica

# Care, Socialization, and Play in Ancient Attica

## A Developmental Childhood Archaeological Approach

*Maria Sommer and Dion Sommer*

Aarhus University Press |

*Care, Socialization and Play in Ancient Attica*



Layout: Anette Ryevad, Ryevad Grafisk

Cover: Jørgen Sparre

The book is typeset in Adobe Garamond Pro

Production: Narayana Press, Gylling, Denmark

ISBN 978 87 7124 297 3

International distributors:

Gazelle Book Services Ltd.

White Cross Mills

Hightown, Lancaster, LA1 4XS

United Kingdom

www.gazellebookservices.co.uk

ISD

70 Enterprise Drive, Suite 2

Bristol, CT 06010

USA

www.isdistribution.com

The publication of this book was made possible by a grant from Aarhus University Research Foundation

Aarhus University Press

www.unipress.dk

PEER REVIEWED

/ In accordance with requirements of the Danish Ministry of Higher Education and Science, the certification means that a ph.d.-level peer has made a written assessment which justifies this book's scientific quality.

# CONTENTS

List of Illustrations 7

Acknowledgements 11

**Part 1 15**

APPROACHES TO CHILDHOOD IN ANCIENT ATTICA – INTRODUCTION 17

Developmental childhood archaeology – an interdisciplinary approach 17

*A brief prologue* 17

*Childhood archaeology: Interdisciplinarity from the beginning* 20

*Developmental childhood psychology – main propositions* 22

Child perceptions in ancient Greece: Literary sources and material culture 33

Focuses of the book: Time, space, age and specific material evidence 37

*Content of the book* 40

**Part 2 43**

THE CARE AND SOCIALIZATION OF INFANTS AND YOUNG CHILDREN 45

Child-parent relationships in the household – the role of the mother and father 45

Beyond sentiment? High child mortality and infanticide 51

Multiple care, alloparenting and cooperative breeding 57

Infant feeding in the Classical period 64

The high chair-potty stool and its functions 69

Infant swaddling – evidence and explanations 75

Activating the infant – the rattle and adult-child relationships 78

Rattling in front of an infant 80

The exploring toddler boy 82

Sibling relationships 85

The religious world of the child – sacral actions and socialization 89

**Part 3 103**

YOUNG CHILDREN'S PLAY AND TOYS 105

The functions and meanings of play – a brief history 105

Did young children really play in ancient Attica? – the iconographic ambiguity 109

Children's play in Classical Attica 111

Toys in Classical Attica – the evidence 115

*Dolls* 115

*Rollers, push- and go carts* 123

*Other types of children's toys* 126
*Miniature toys* 130
*Children with pets* 131
Toys – objects to be used in many ways 139
Objects and toys – developmental perspectives 143

**Part 4 147**
CONCLUSIONS AND PERSPECTIVES 149
Conclusions 149
Interpretative validity? – discussion and conclusion 152
A repeated call for interdisciplinarity 154

Bibliography 157
Internet sources 165
Notes 167
Index 191

# LIST OF ILLUSTRATIONS


Fig. 1: Attic grave stele with mother, child and maid servant. *Dating:* Ca. 420-410 BC. *Exhibited:* Leiden Rijksmuseum, inv. no. I 1930/21.

Fig. 2: Attic red-figure hydria showing family scene. *Measurements:* H. 34.6 cm. Dia. 24.6 cm. *Dating:* Ca. 440-430 BC. *Exhibited:* Cambridge, Harvard University of Arts Museums, Arthur M. Sackle Museum, inv. no. 1960.342.

Fig. 3: Attic grave stele with mother, child and maid servant. *Measurements:* H. 1.5 m. W. 1.1 m. *Dating:* Ca. 370-360 BC. *Exhibited:* The Nat. Mus. Athens, inv. no. 3790. © Hellenic Ministry of Education and Religious Affairs, Culture and Sports /Archaeological Receipts Fund. Photo by Maria Sommer.

Fig. 4: The Ampharete stele showing grandmother with grandchild (boy). *Dating:* 430-420 BC. *Exhibited:* The Kerameikos Museum, inv. no. P695.

Fig. 5: Attic marble stele from Piraeus showing father (Euempolos) with his two children (boy in front, girl behind). *Measurements:* H. 54 cm. W. 41 cm. *Dating:* Late 5th century-early 4th century BC. *Exhibited:* The Nat. Mus. Athens, inv. no. 778. © Hellenic Ministry of Education and Religious Affairs, Culture and Sports /Archaeological Receipts Fund.

Fig. 6: Attic marble stele from Piraeus showing a father giving the characteristic departing handshake. *Dating:* Ca. 360 BC. *Exhibited:* Piraeus Archaeological Museum, inv. no. 46.

Fig. 7: Attic black-glazed feeding bottle with decoration. *Measurements:* H. 6.3 cm. Dia. 9 cm (including spout). *Dating:* The Classical period (source The Benaki Museum). *Exhibited:* The Benaki Museum, the Ancient Greek Collection, inv. no. 22477. Photo by Maria Sommer.

Fig. 8: Red-figure hydria with close-up depiction of breastfeeding mother. *Dating:* Ca. 440 BC. *Exhibited:* Berlin-Staatliche museum, inv. no. F2395.

Fig. 9: Potty stool in terracotta with red decoration found in The Athenian Agora. *Measurements:* Ca. H. 50 cm. Ca. 20 cm. in dia. on the top-bowl, the base of the stool is ca. 40-45 cm. in dia.. Dating: Ca. 580 BC. *Exhibited:* The Agora Museum, Athens, inv. no. PI18010. Photo by Maria Sommer.

Fig. 10: Red-figure chous with toddler on potty stool. *Measurements:* H. 12 cm. *Dating:* Ca. 440-430 BC. *Exhibited:* British Museum, London, inv. no. 1910.6-15.4.

Fig. 11: Attic red-figure and white-ground stemless kylix with mother and child on a potty stool (by the Sotades Painter). *Measurements:* H. 3 cm. Dia. 12.7 cm. *Dating:* Ca. 460 BC. *Exhibited:* Musees Royaux, Brussels, inv. no. A890.

Fig. 12: Attic marble grave stele with depiction of woman (mother) with swaddled infant. *Dating:* 375-350 BC. *Measurements:* H. 44.5 cm. W. 50.8 cm. D. 9.5 cm. *Exhibited:* The Museum of Fine Arts, Huston, inv. no. 37.25.

Fig. 13: Club-shaped rattle from Attica with white-ground and perhaps red paint. *Measurements:* H. 15 cm. Dia. 4.5 cm. *Dating:* The Classical period. *Exhibited:* The private collection of Argyriadi, the Benaki Toys Department, Phaliro, Athens, inv. 12. Photo by Maria Sommer.

Fig. 14: Owl-rattle from Cyprus made of terracotta with red decoration. *Measurements:* H. 11.5 cm. Dia. 6.4 cm. *Dating:* 4th century BC. *Exhibited:* The private collection of Argyriadi, the Benaki Toys Department, Phaliro, Athens, inv. 1093. Photo by Maria Sommer.

Fig. 15: Pig rattle from Cyprus made of terracotta. *Measurements:* H. 7.7 cm. Dia. of body 5.9 cm. *Dating:* 4th century BC. *Exhibited:* Leo Milden Collection, Zurich.

Fig. 16: Attic red-figure chous with children (girl rattling a rattle to infant brother). *Measurements:* H. 8 cm. *Dating:* Shortly after 400 BC. *Exhibited:* The Nat. Mus. Athens inv. no. 1258. © Hellenic Ministry of Education and Religious Affairs, Culture and Sports /Archaeological Receipts Fund. Photo by Maria Sommer.

Fig. 17: Attic red-figure chous with crawling male toddler (wears amulets). *Dating:* Ca. 420 BC. *Exhibited:* The Nat. Mus. Copenhagen inv. no. 10120. Photo by Maria Sommer.

Fig. 18: Attic red-figure pelike with crawling infant, mother and father. *Measurements:* H. 18.5 cm. *Dat-*

*ing:* Ca. 430-420 BC. *Exhibited:* British Museum, London, inv. no. E396.

Fig. 19: Attic red-figure chous with two male siblings playing with toy roller and chous. *Measurements:* H. 13 cm. *Dating:* About 420 BC. *Exhibited:* Nat. Mus. Athens, inv. no. 14509. © Hellenic Ministry of Education and Religious Affairs, Culture and Sports /Archaeological Receipts Fund. Photo by Maria Sommer.

Fig. 20: Attic red-figure chous showing boys playing ball. *Measurements:* H. 13.7 cm. *Dating:* Ca. 425 BC. *Exhibited:* The Metropolitan Museum of Art, New York, inv. no. 07.286.4.

Fig. 21: Drawing of votive relief from Echinos showing mother presenting her baby to Artemis. *Dating:* 4th century BC. *Exhibited:* Archaeological Museum, Lamia, inv. no. AE 1041. *Source:* Neils 2003, 145, fig. 6.

Fig. 22: Attic red-figure chous showing a father pushing a boy on a swing. *Dating:* Ca. 425 BC. *Exhibited:* Nat. Mus. Athens, inv. no. BZ 0319. © Hellenic Ministry of Education and Religious Affairs, Culture and Sports /Archaeological Receipts Fund.

Fig. 23: Votive relief from Brauron of family with child approaching Artemis. *Dating:* Ca. 450-400 BC. *Exhibited:* The Brauron Museum, inv. no. 1171. Photo by Maria Sommer.

Fig. 24: Votive relief from Brauron of family with children approaching Artemis. *Dating:* Ca. 350 BC. *Exhibited:* The Brauron Museum, inv. no. 1153. Photo by Maria Sommer.

Fig. 25: Votive relief from Brauron of family of Lycoleon with children approaching Artemis (Brauron). *Dating:* Ca. 340 BC. *Exhibited:* The Brauron Museum, inv. no. 1150. Photo by Maria Sommer.

Fig. 26: Votive relief from Brauron of family of Antiphates showing three generations sacrificing to Artemis. *Dating:* Ca. 350-330 BC. *Exhibited:* The Brauron Museum, inv. no. 1151. Photo by Maria Sommer.

Fig. 27: Marble dedicatory votive statuette from Brauron of crawling male infant. *Dating:* Early 4th century. *Exhibited:* The Brauron Museum, inv. no. 1196. Photo by Maria Sommer.

Fig. 28: Marble dedicatory votive statuette from Brauron of sitting infant/toddler boy. *Dating:* Early 4th century. *Exhibited:* The Brauron Museum, inv. no. 1160. Photo by Maria Sommer.

Fig. 29: Marble dedicatory votive statuette from Brauron of boy with ball, bird and himation. *Dating:* Late 4th century. *Exhibited:* The Brauron Museum, inv. no. 1164. Photo by Maria Sommer.

Fig. 30: Marble head of smiling girl from a dedicatory statue (missing) found at Brauron. *Dating:* Late 4th-century. *Exhibited:* The Brauron Museum. Photo by Maria Sommer.

Fig. 31: Corinthian terracotta doll with painted clothes and hat. *Measurements:* H. 12.3 cm. *Dating:* Early 5th century BC. *Exhibited:* The Metropolitan Museum of Art, New York inv. no. 44.II.8.

Fig. 32: Attic seated terracotta doll. *Measurements:* H. 18 cm. *Dating:* Ca. mid-5th century BC. *Exhibited:* The private collection of Argyriadi, the Benaki Toys Department, Phaliro, Athens, inv. 5. Photo by Maria Sommer.

Fig. 33: Attic jointed-doll in terracotta. *Measurements:* H. 19 cm. *Dating:* Early 4th century. *Exhibited:* The private collection of Argyriadi, the Benaki Toys Department, Phaliro, Athens. Photo by Maria Sommer.

Fig. 34: Attic seated terracotta doll with accessories. *Measurements:* 18 cm. *Dating:* Ca. 420 BC. *Exhibited:* British Museum, London, inv. no. GR 1906 3-14.1 to 5.

Fig. 35: Attic jointed doll in terracotta holding kroatala. *Measurements:* 32. H. 19 cm. *Dating:* Mid-4th century BC. *Exhibited:* Museum of Arts, Bowdoine College, Maine, inv. no. 1913.028.

Fig. 36: Hellenistic jointed doll from Tanagra. *Measurements:* H. 35 cm. *Dating:* Last part of 4th century. *Exhibited:* The Nat. Mus. Copenhagen inv. no. 3738. Photo by Maria Sommer.

Fig. 37: Attic jointed doll in terracotta with earrings, a "crown" and strongly wavy "mid-Classical" hair style. *Measurements:* H. 15.5 cm. *Dating:* Late 5th century BC, perhaps around 420. *Exhibited:* The Benaki Museum, the Ancient Greek Collection, inv. no. 30829. Photo by Maria Sommer.

Fig. 38: Attic jointed doll in terracotta with "late Classical" hair style. *Measurements*: Ca. 18 cm. *Dating:* Perhaps the second quarter or mid-4th century BC. *Exhibited:* The Nat. Mus. Athens, Room 56. © Hellenic Ministry of Education and Religious Affairs, Culture and Sports /Archaeological Receipts Fund. Photo by Maria Sommer.

Fig. 39: Attic marble grave stele with girl Melisto holding a doll and dove while playing with her dog. *Measurements:* H. 95.5 cm. W. 49.2 cm. *Dating:* Ca. 340 BC. *Exhibited:* Cambridge, Harvard University of Arts Museums, Arthur M. Sackle Museum Alpheus Hyatt Purchasing and Gifts for Special Uses Funds in memory of Katherine Brewster Taylor, as tribute to her many years at the Fogg Museum, inv. no. 1961.89.

Fig. 40: Attic Penthelic marble grave stele with youth with doll and goose. *Measurements:* H. 72.5 cm. W.

36 cm. *Dating:* Ca. 360 BC. *Exhibited:* The J. Paul Getty Museum inv. no. 82.AA.135.

Fig. 41: Attic Penthelic marble grave stele with female slave with doll. *Measurements:* H. 66 cm. W. 35 cm. *Dating:* Ca. 360 BC. *Exhibited:* The Nat. Mus. Athens, inv. no. 1993. © Hellenic Ministry of Education and Religious Affairs, Culture and Sports /Archaeological Receipts Fund. Photo by Maria Sommer.

Fig. 42: Up-close photo of hole in dolls head. Photo by Maria Sommer.

Fig. 43a & b: Attic Penthelic marble grave stele with Boy Mnesikles holding a toy roller. *Measurements:* H. 66.5 cm. W. 27.5 cm. *Dating:* Ca. 400-350 BC. *Exhibited:* The Princeton Art Museum, inv. no. y1986-87.

Fig. 44: Red-figure chous with boy running with chous and toy roller. *Measurements:* H. 10 cm. *Dating:* Ca. 430 BC. *Exhibited:* The Nat. Mus. Athens, inv. no. 1742. © Hellenic Ministry of Education and Religious Affairs, Culture and Sports /Archaeological Receipts Fund. Photo by Maria Sommer.

Fig. 45: Red-figure chous with boy dancing pirouette between festival gifts: A chous and a toy roller. *Measurements:* H. 11 cm. *Dating:* Ca. 425-420 BC. *Exhibited:* The Nat. Mus. Athens, inv. no. 1223. © Hellenic Ministry of Education and Religious Affairs, Culture and Sports /Archaeological Receipts Fund. Photo by Maria Sommer.

Fig. 46: Red-figure chous with girl pulling/playing with a toy roller. *Measurements:* H. 8,5 cm. *Dating:* End of 5th century BC. *Exhibited:* The Nat. Mus. Athens, inv. no. 1267. © Hellenic Ministry of Education and Religious Affairs, Culture and Sports /Archaeological Receipts Fund. Photo by Maria Sommer.

Fig. 47: Red-figure chous with child in push cart pulled by goat. *Measurements:* H. 9 cm. *Dating:* Early 5th century BC. *Exhibited:* The Nat. Mus. Copenhagen, inv. no. 1944. Photo by Maria Sommer.

Fig. 48: Black-glazed toy horse on wheels from a child's grave. *Measurements:* Ca. H. 15-20 cm. *Dating:* 950-900 BC. *Exhibited:* The Kerameikos Museum, inv. no. 642. Photo by Maria Sommer.

Fig. 49: Geometric horse on wheels from a child's grave. *Measurements:* H. 20.2 cm. *Dating:* 800-750 BC. *Exhibited:* Leo Mildenberg Collection, Zurich.

Fig. 50: Marble grave stele with infant with dove and ball. *Dating:* Second half of 4th century. *Exhibited:* The Nat. Mus. Athens, inv. no. 1040. © Hellenic Ministry of Education and Religious Affairs, Culture and Sports /Archaeological Receipts Fund. Photo by Maria Sommer.

Fig. 51: Black-glazed spin top. *Measurements:* H. 7 cm. Dia. 6 cm. *Dating:* Classical period. *Exhibited:* The Nat. Mus. Athens inv. no. 10451. Photo by Maria Sommer. © Hellenic Ministry of Education and Religious Affairs, Culture and Sports /Archaeological Receipts Fund.

Fig. 52: Attic black-glazed yoyo. *Measurements:* Dia. 5.3 cm. *Dating:* Classical period. *Exhibited:* The private collection of Argyriadi, the Benaki Toys Department, Phaliro, Athens, inv. no. 1098. Photo by Maria Sommer.

Fig. 53: Attic red-figure cup with youth playing yoyo. *Dating:* Ca. 420 BC. *Exhibited:* Berlin, Antikensammlung, inv. no.F2549.

Fig. 54: Knucklebones of bone and metal. *Exhibited:* The Nat. Mus. Copenhagen, in the Dionysos-festival collection. Photo by Maria Sommer.

Fig. 55a & b: Attic terracotta whistle from a child grave. *Measurements:* H. 4 cm. W. 1.7 cm. L. (with tail) 3.4 cm. *Dating:* Classical period. *Exhibited:* The private collection of Argyriadi, the Benaki Toys Department, Phaliro, Athens, inv. no. 13. Photo by Maria Sommer.

Fig. 56: Attic miniature altar believed to be a toy with decoration of child with a Hermes-stick (?) and other types of ornamentation, found in a child grave. *Measurements:* H. 10.2 cm. W. 5.5 cm. *Dating:* Classical period. *Exhibited:* The private collection of Argyriadi, the Benaki Toys Department, Phaliro, Athens, inv. no. 2722. Photo by Maria Sommer.

Fig. 57: Miniature terracotta pig (toy) with white slip and red paint on ears and snout. *Measurements:* H. 4.9 cm W. 3.5 cm. L. 8.5 cm. *Dating:* Classical period. *Exhibited:* The Benaki Museum, the Ancient Greek Collection, inv. no. 31077. Photo by Maria Sommer.

Fig. 58: Miniature terracotta turtle (toy) with white slip and red paint on feet. *Measurements:* H. 3.9 cm. W. 4 cm. L. 6.8 cm. *Dating:* Classical period. *Exhibited:* The Benaki Museum, the Ancient Greek Collection, inv. no. 31054. Photo by Maria Sommer.

Fig. 59: Miniature terracotta dove (toy) found in a child grave. *Measurements:* H. 6 cm. W. 3.5 cm. L. 10 cm. *Dating:* Classical period. *Exhibited:* The Benaki Museum, the Ancient Greek Collection, inv. no. 31079. Photo by Maria Sommer.

Fig. 60: Attic Penthelic marble stele showing two siblings Mnesagora & Nikochares with a dove. *Measurements:* H. 1.19 m. W. 74 cm. *Dating:* 420 BC. *Exhibited:* The Nat. Mus. Athens, inv. no. 3845. © Hellenic Ministry of Education and Religious Affairs, Culture and Sports /Archaeological Receipts Fund. Photo by Maria Sommer.

Fig. 61: Attic marble stele showing the boy Theokles with his pet dove and dog. *Dating:* The mid-4th century

BC. *Exhibited:* The Nat. Mus. Athens, inv. no. 3661. © Hellenic Ministry of Education and Religious Affairs, Culture and Sports /Archaeological Receipts Fund. Photo by Maria Sommer.

Fig. 62: Attic red-figure chous showing boy with starling. *Measurements:* H. 9 cm. Dia. 7.1 cm. *Dating:* 425-420 BC. *Exhibited:* The Museum of Fine Arts, Boston, inv. no. 01.8086.

Fig. 63: Attic red-figure chous showing girl chasing bird. *Measurements:* H. 6.3 cm. *Dating:* Ca. 420 BC. *Exhibited:* Worchester Art Museum inv. no. 1931.56.

Fig. 64: Attic Pentelic marble statuette of girl holding a pet bird. *Measurements:* H. 47 cm. *Dating:* Ca. 340-330 BC. *Exhibited:* The Nat. Mus. Athens. Inv. no. 695. © Hellenic Ministry of Education and Religious Affairs, Culture and Sports /Archaeological Receipts Fund.

Fig. 65: Attic marble stele of boy holding a dove and a ball (or pomegranate) playing with Maltese dog. *Dating:* Second half of 4th century. *Exhibited:* The Nat. Mus. Athens. Inv. no. 3249. © Hellenic Ministry of Education and Religious Affairs, Culture and Sports /Archaeological Receipts Fund. Photo by Maria Sommer.

Fig. 66: Attic marble stele of boy holding an exotic bird with a playful dog. *Dating:* Mid-4th century. *Exhibited:* The Nat. Mus. Athens. Inv. no. 748. © Hellenic Ministry of Education and Religious Affairs, Culture and Sports /Archaeological Receipts Fund. Photo by Maria Sommer.

Fig. 67: Attic red-figure chous with girl playing with stick and dog. *Measurements:* H. 8 cm. *Dating:* End of 5th century. *Exhibited:* The Nat. Mus. Athens. Inv. no. 1322. © Hellenic Ministry of Education and Religious Affairs, Culture and Sports /Archaeological Receipts Fund. Photo by Maria Sommer.

Fig. 68: Attic red-figure chous with dog jumping at a scared boy. *Measurements:* H. 8.3 cm. *Dating:* Ca. 420-410 BC. *Exhibited:* The Nat. Mus. Copenhagen, inv. no. 856. Photo by Maria Sommer.

Fig. 69: Attic red-figure chous with boy playing with dog. *Measurements:* H. 5.7 cm. Dia. 4.4 cm. *Dating:* Ca. 420 BC. *Exhibited:* Cambridge, Harvard University of Arts Museums, Arthur M. Sackle Museum Alpheus Hyatt Purchasing and Gifts for Special Uses Funds in memory of Katherine Brewster Taylor, as tribute to her many years at the Fogg Museum, inv. no. 24.1908.

Fig. 70: Attic red-figure chous with boys playing with dogs and sticus. *Dating:* 4th century BC. *Exhibited:* The Kerameikos Museum, show case 10. Photo by Maria Sommer.

Fig. 71: Attic red-figure chous with boy fetching a jumping hare. *Measurements:* H. 8.7 cm. Dia. 6.9 cm. *Dating:* Ca. 425-420 BC. *Exhibited:* The Nat. Mus. Copenhagen, inv. no. 344. Photo by Maria Sommer.

Fig. 72: Attic red-figure chous with boy kissing a duck. *Measurements:* H. 9 cm. *Dating:* Ca. 425-420 BC. *Exhibited:* The Nat. Mus. Athens, inv. no. 13261. © Hellenic Ministry of Education and Religious Affairs, Culture and Sports /Archaeological Receipts Fund. Photo by Maria Sommer.

# ACKNOWLEDGEMENTS

Holding a slim doll with articulating arms and legs that was played with nearly 2.500 years ago by a young girl; taking a photo of a wheeled horse, probably the toy of a young boy; shaking a rattle once used by parents in order to motivate their infant; seeing on a *chous* a toddler crawling around or a little boy sitting in a high chair potty stool kicking his legs and reaching up for his mother. Doing all this and much more, and being allowed into rooms stuffed with toys and playthings from Classical Athens has been a thrilling experience. The feeling is hard to deny – despite that we are millennia apart and living in different cultures – there is something deeply human here 'speaking to us'. It has been both hard work as well as highly enjoyable to collect, describe and interpret the rich material evidence with the intention to build a deeper understanding of young children's lives and childhoods during this period.

Collecting an empirical base and writing this book would not have been possible without generous help and enthusiasm from important people as well as support from institutions, particularly during the phase of collecting empirical data in Athens. Many must be thanked, and hopefully none will be forgotten. This book is dedicated to them.

Gratitude is due to the Danish Institute in Athens for a stipend awarded to Maria Sommer, which allowed her to collect empirical data in various museums in Greece. As a consequence, this book not only relies on previously published material, it also presents artifacts never before seen by the public.

Our special thanks go to Director Rune Frederiksen, Signe Riisager, Hanna Lassen, and Lone Gad. Their hospitality and help shall never be forgotten, and Maria will surely miss Parthenonos 22, room 4. Hope to see you all again.

We wish to express our profound gratitude to Dr. Nikolaos Kaltsas, former Director of The National Archaeological Museum in Athens, for his correspondence and interest, and for granting permission to take photos in the closed New Exhibition of dolls, toys, and choes in our portable photo studio. It was a great experience, and we much appreciate the help of Mr. Vivliodetis and the laboratory assistant during the photographing. Thanks are also due to Deputy Director Dr. George Kakavas for granting us the copyrights necessary for this publication.

It was a great pleasure for Maria to be at the Benaki Museum and The Benaki Toys Department at Phaliro, taking photos there of many 'children's objects'. A special thanks should go to Irini Papageorgiou from The Benaki Museum for giving us access to toys and choes in the Ancient Greek Collection. Our thanks are also due to Maria Argyriadi from The Benaki Toys Department, who made it possible to locate and photograph rattles, dolls, and other types of toys, not exhibited anywhere. The collecting of private photos of empirical data has been indispensable for this book. The photos originate from a catalogue created for Maria Sommer's master thesis "Children in Attica in the Classical Period" (July 2011).

Acknowledgement should also go to The National Museum of Copenhagen for the permission to use their children's artifacts in this book. We wish to express our profound gratitude to the head of the Collection of Classical and Near East Antiquities, Bodil Bundgaard Rasmussen, for her interest and for our correspondence on dolls and other child related objects in the museum (including the Geometric doll in room 308).

We also wish to thank associate professor Birte Poulsen, Aarhus University, for her inspiration and constructive feedback when discussing children's lives and conditions in ancient Greece. We hope to do further research together on children's lives in the ancient Greek world. Our heartfelt appreciation is due to Fredrik Fahlander at Stockholm University for believing in the initial and tentative ideas behind this research and for publishing a first article by Maria Sommer named "Toys, Play, and Swaddling – Indications of Early Childhood in Ancient Greece" in the anthology *Spåren av de små – Arkeologiska perspektiv på barn och barndom [The Traces From the Small Ones – Archeological Perspectives on Children and Childhood],* 2011.

Our special thanks must go to professor Armin W. Geertz, Aarhus University, for his enthusiasm right from the beginning and for stimulating our interest in the sacral world of children and their families in ancient Greece. We sincerely hope to do further research together on sacral topics. Warm greetings to Inge Marie Stilund (wife of Dion and mother of Maria) for professional assistance during the field study and the data-collecting phase including photo-sessions in Athens. We had an amazing time! Also many thanks to Eva Sommer (daughter of Dion and sister of Maria) for supplying a professional photo-tent with inbuilt lights as well as managing the picture processing in photo-shop. In fact this book is the result of a collaborative family project. It has also been great for the two authors, father and daughter – coming from two separate fields of study, childhood archaeology and developmental psychology – to present the interdisciplinary understanding of Developmental Childhood Archaeology.

Last but not least, a special thanks goes to the Aarhus University Research Foundation; their grant made it possible to produce this book. We also appreciate the archaeology and the psychology peer reviewers for their useful suggestions for improvements.

# Copyright permissions

A sincere gratitude to those who have given permission to reproduce copyright materials.

Every effort has been made to account for all the copyright holders. However, if any have been inadvertently overlooked the publishers will be pleased to make the necessary adjustments at the first opportunity

# PART 1

# APPROACHES TO CHILDHOOD IN ANCIENT ATTICA – INTRODUCTION

## Developmental childhood archaeology – an interdisciplinary approach

The age-group selected for in this book will be 0-7 years old. The reason is that our main aim is to focus on the most 'invisible' people in archaeology: The infants, the toddlers, and the pre-school girls and boys. Another very important point to make clear is that 'the children' in this book will be from the aristocratic and upper-middle classes. This is due to the very nature of the material and written sources. In fact little is known about the majority – for example, poor children and slave children. This book is heavily founded on evidence. In essence it is an archaeological study based on a collection of material relating to childhood in ancient Attica, dating back to 480-300 B.C. That is, various types of toys, iconographic evidence of children on vases and graves steles, primary written sources on children's lives, and their view on children in the Greek Classical period. However in order to understand and interpret the rich material evidence, a theoretical framework is needed. Here we will propose a new interdisciplinary approach called Developmental Childhood Archaeology.

### *A brief prologue*

Before the discipline of childhood archaeology appeared, theorists from other disciplines than archaeology were very influential in shaping the understanding of children. Below we have selected some particularly influential thinkers for evaluation in the light of recent understandings.

The concept and understanding of childhood in the modern world has been discussed in various fields for centuries. The psychoanalyst *Sigmund Freud* (1856-1939) had an enormous impact on the study of children in the 19th and 20th centuries, claiming that the child is a sexual being that undergoes three stages of development.[1] His theory on the Oedipus complex emphasized the focus on sexuality in childhood. His influential theory on children has, for example, been used to explain the portraits of nudity, the Greek 'pederast' interests in young boys' bodies.[2] Freudian theory, however, has long been discarded in psychology, and is today seen as one of the grand, universal theories of the 20th century.[3] The French historian and medieval expert *Philippe Ariès* (1914-1984) claimed that the concept of childhood did not exist until after the 17th century.[4] In his book *Centuries of Childhood* he argues that childhood is purely a social construction, and the biological and mental development of the child was not important. He claimed that the view of children was positively progressive, and advanced with the technological and economical development in the western world. Ariès argued that the parents' attitude (or the attitude of adults in general) towards children created a childhood. Before the industrialization a childhood did not exist (perhaps only in the upper class) because of the high child mortality rate, which resulted in parent's decreased attachment to their children.[5] This was echoed by *Edward Shorter* in his *The Making of the Modern Family.* In a strictly sociological way he theorized that sentiments between parents and children were the sole product of societal development, and a rather late historical phenomenon[6]. The big transformation that allowed intimate and personal feelings between spouses, parents, and their children took place around 1750, and the causal effect was attributed to the rise of market capitalism. Increasingly families were transformed from extended units to the isolated nuclear family. Until recently such theorizing was influential, and meant that intimacy, parental love and devotion in ancient Attica were out of the question. On the basis of both material and literary evidence this book will document that this theory has been proven wrong. Moreover, it will present a new theory that will provide an explanation as well. Concerning the 'invention' of childhood, Ariés became famous by his remark that in the Middle Ages a childhood feeling did not exist because of an adult centric perception of children. This idea dominated many disciplines for a long time and the understanding of when in history childhood was accepted in society as a genuine period in itself. Ariés' conclusions have since been criticized by historians and archaeologists, and do not represent the leading conduit to the history of childhood[7]. *Lloyd DeMause*, an American social philosopher, and 'psycho-historian' has had a highly negative impact on the study and understanding of childhood in the ancient worlds. In his book *The History of Childhood* he proclaims, inspired by Freudian thinking, that all ancient societies treated their children horribly.[8] He divides the societies' treatment of children into six stages:

1. Infanticidal
2. Abandoning
3. Ambivalent
4. Intrusive
5. Socializing
6. Helping [9]

From stage 2 the society is no longer infanticidal and ancient Greek society is placed within the first two stages. He also uses the theory of positive progressive development of childhood and argues that modern society provides a good childhood. According to him, all children in antiquity did per definition have a horrible childhood and no parents had feelings towards their children, because the society was not 'modern'.[10]

Recent archaeological research tells a very different story, which will be documented in this book. DeMause's framework of understanding history was rooted in a so-called 'teleological enlightenment belief' that all types of development, societies, cultures, and humans temporally progressed stepwise from lower immature ('un-enlightened') stages to an optimal final stage of maturity and rationality. However, the influence of such top-down theorizing – 'documenting' childhood with handpicked nicely fitting examples – has faded and the paradigm has shifted towards a much more material, evidence-based, inductive approach.[11] After her comprehensive evidence-based investigation of the main theories of the history of childhood, Sandra Pollock (1983) concludes in her PhD thesis that "the area in fact bears the hallmark of sloppiness".[12] In addition the claims have proven false that 1) there is no conception of childhood before the 17th century. 2) There was a formal, indifferent parent-child relationship; parents were distant beings and children's demands and needs were not met. 3) Children were (until the 18th century) mostly brutally exploited and subjected to cruelties difficult to imagine today.[13] Pollock deals with the historical period from 1500-1900, but the three conclusions have been disproved much further back in time as evidenced by childhood archaeologists. This book will also document in detail and in various ways that these three views are generally unsubstantiated. To sum up, the selected but highly influential theorists produced a general negative view on children and their childhoods in ancient and past cultures. The further back in time they looked, the worse conditions for children were, they assumed. Or for some, childhood did not even exist in ancient times, as it was a later 'invention'. Such an outdated linear teleological idea will not be in line with the thinking in this book.

As seen in the subtitle of this book *Developmental Childhood Archaeology*, the phrase 'childhood' is placed in the middle. This emphasizes that childhood will be the main unifying concept – bridging archaeology with psychology and evolutionary developmental theory. But naming this work *Developmental Childhood Archaeology* does not imply that there is only one type of childhood, so some clarifications are needed from the outset. On the one hand the very concept of childhood indicates some similarity within a special period in the human lifespan that differs from later phases in life (for instance adulthood). Childhood will in this work be seen as a meta-individual concept that relates to children in historical time and cultural place, for example children in contemporary society or children in ancient Attica. The coming of age of the discipline 'the archaeology of childhood' or 'childhood archaeology' represents an enriched understanding, spelling out many features. However, the phrase 'childhood' and not 'childhoods' can be misleading, inadvertently claiming a monolithic understanding. For example, there are quite different slave and upper class childhoods; there are sacral and not so sacral; there are urban and rural; there are different Athenian and Spartan childhoods; there are male and female childhoods. Looking at age within the same culture we can identify different childhoods for infants, toddlers, and young children, as well as for older children.

In addition various theories reflect their particular versions of childhood, as the understanding of children is 'in the eyes of the beholders'. So various theories both within and across disciplines can have each their interpretations of the 'same realities'. But they also hold promising potentials to enrich our knowledge, in terms of our research being produced by more than one approach. Dealing with the whole range of possible childhoods, would be an impossible task in one publication. (In Part 1 it will later be specified what childhood we are dealing with regarding historical time, cultural space, and age group). But first the childhood-specific approaches from archaeology, and developmental and evolutionary childhood psychology will be outlined for the purpose of suggesting a specific interdisciplinary framework.

*Childhood archaeology: Interdisciplinarity from the beginning*

Children have for more than hundred years been the main object of study in psychology, but this has been far from the case in archaeology. In this discipline the child is metaphotically speaking in its infancy. Moving from the study of males towards females via the feminist impulse in the 1970s, the archaeologists of the 1980s began to turn their interests towards children and childhood. According to Baxter (2005), children were for many years considered peripheral to traditional interests of archaeological research:

> "Archaeological literature prior to the 1980s included few references to children and showed little theoretical or methodological interest in considering children in archaeological analyses" (Baxter 2005, 8).

In her latest review of the field, Beaumont (2012) continues the momentum with her view of the present state-of-the-art: It is only since mid 1980s that a critical mass of scholarship has come to be produced specifically on children and childhood in ancient Greece[14]. But what is childhood archaeology and how did it evolve? This question shall not be answered here as Beaumont (2012) has already made a very informing up-to-date review of that[15]. Another way to go that has not been tried out before is to evaluate some of the most important childhood archaeological publications from the start in the mid-1980s until today, asking: 1) How are their approaches to and uses of interdisciplinary theory? 2) What specific theory and research do they refer to outside archaeology?

As a start – after having scrutinized the literature – we can conclude that it is mainly the 'childhood' part of the concept that seems to need explanations from theories drawn in from beyond archaeology. And this book is not the first attempt to go inter- or multidisciplinary, combining childhood archaeology with other disciplines. In her final conclusion Beaumont (2012) points out that there is a future need for multiple perspectives:

> "There is also a broader need for scholars to explore the study of past childhoods in a multidisciplinary, diachronic and cross-cultural context in order to develop more refined and sophisticated ways in which we can access the youth of bygone days" (Beaumont 2012, 210).

However, it is fair to say, that interesting suggestions have already been made, in fact from the very start of childhood archaeology: In 1986 *The Norwegian Archaeological Rewiew* published an article by Lillehammer called "A Child is Born", introducing what must be considered the birth of childhood archaeology. Her new concept "a child's world" defined the child as a living subject in its world, not an object to be studied. In addition this approach opens up the possibility that children can be inventors of culture, and that culture can be not only transferred to and from adults, but also among children themselves. Such an understanding was drawn from new paradigms within social and cultural theory, arising at that time. In *Children and Childhood in Classical Athens* the first book in English on the subject, Golden (1990) to some extent uses attachment and sentiment theories from psychology as interpretative tools. Although this is not followed by many subsequent scholars, this shows the potentials of a developmental approach. In Part 2 of this book new attachment research explaining multiple care and socialization in families in ancient Attica will be introduced and used.

As the child is literally a new member of society, Lillehammer (2000) advocates for the "archaeological need for the development and application of social theory in order to understand society's recognition or rejection of the new, both in terms of the birth of the individual and his or her subsequent behavior and achievements within that society"[16]. She specifically, but briefly addresses recent psychology research that criticizes 'ageism' in psychology, indicating that chronological (biology organized) age is becoming a poorer and poorer indicator of the way people live and, one could add the way children develop.

In Derevensky's (2000) *Children and Material Culture* contributions come not only from archaeologists but from anthropologists and a psychologist as well. In her introduction of theoretical perspectives, contemporary childhood sociology is applied and there are references to recent critical developmental psychology. Kamp (2001b) in a highly important paper "Where Have All the Children Gone?: The Archaeology of Childhood" also points out that archaeology itself cannot solve that question. She draws not only on ethnographic and historical literature, but also on important child concepts imported from contemporary childhood sociology. When dealing with learning and teaching, which archaeology has paid little attention to, she applies cultural anthropology, educational theory, and psychology. For example, when dealing with play, psychology is used interpretatively. However, her call for *recent* psychology has hardly or only sketchyly been addressed in the major publications that followed.

Neils and Oakley (2003) in their groundbreaking *Coming of Age in Ancient Greece* deals with the study of childhood by referring to historians as well as, in terms of developmental psychology, the outdated perspectives of Sigmund Freud and Erik Erikson. In the prologue of the same book Korbin (2003) – in her definition of what childhood is – again builds on contemporary childhood sociology.

In order to establish a new understanding of what a child is and how to interpret archaeological artifacts, Baxter (2005) in *The Archaeology of Childhood* effectively uses anthropology in combination with apprenticeship and situated learning theory, gender and socialization theory. In addition, key conceptions stemming from contemporary childhood sociology – for example the active child paradigm- are used. In childhood archaeology this work is a particularly rare and remarkable example of a comprehensive use of recent theory. The socialization approach for instance not only opens new ways to understand the cultural construction of childhood, but also interprets the hidden functions established in the material culture and artistic representations of children.

In Cohan and Rutter's (2007) *Constructions of Childhood in Ancient Greece and Italy*, the introductory chapter is inspired by the works of the anthropologist Margaret Mead, and to some extent also by social constructivism, psychology, and a range of childhood historians. In an in-depth introduction to archaeological perspectives on childen and childhood, Fahlander (2011) draws on an extensive knowledge-base within and not least outside archaeology. Among other approaches he uses demography, history, ethnography, anthropology, childhood sociology, and to some extent psychology. Beaumont (2012) in her scholarly work and rich interpretations mainly sticks to archaeology, although, as mentioned above, she ends up calling for future interdisciplinary work, for example bio-archaeological and ethnographic perspectives. Recently *The Oxford Handbook of Childhood and Education in the Classical World* was published (Grubbs & Parkin 2013), showing the maturity of the subject.

In conclusion, it is quite safe to say that the emergent discipline of childhood archaeology from the very beginning in various ways has been oriented towards interdisciplinarity, avoiding a narrow focus on archaeology. On the other hand – apart from the work of Baxter and Grubbs & Parkin, but also to a certain extent Kamp and Fahlander – the outlines seem suggestive and rather sketchy. They function mostly as a kind of sparsely elaborated 'theory scaffolding'. Therefore the imported perspectives are used in limited ways or not at all, when it comes to interpretations of, for example, specific iconographic material. Till now, especially the integration of recent developmental and evolutionary psychology has been very limited. This is probably because this wealth of new knowledge is not well-known beyond the field of psychology. But as developmental psychology represents a considerable span divided into diverse subdisciplines, a selected perspective is necessary[17]. This will be presented in the next section.

### *Developmental childhood psychology – main propositions*

More than a decade ago childhood archaeology was blooming, as were the many suggestions for interdisciplinarity. However, in 2001 Kamp concluded:

> "Archaeologists have not attempted to systematically reconstruct a detailed picture of childhood in any single prehistoric culture or relate these studies to the broader literature that is available from cultural and biological anthropology or other disciplines such as history and psychology."[18]

More than a decade later this seems to be an acceptable approach, however, Kamp is right concerning psychology. Having scrutinized the relevant literature within the field of childhood archaeology concerning types of interdisciplinarity, we can conclude the following: Some authors hints at old-fashioned developmental psychology. Freud may be obvious (and devious), seeing pederast iconography nearly everywhere, but lacking in explanatory power when other interpretations of iconographic child nudeness may be more appropriate. Apart from anthropology (with a cultural and evolutionary focus) no one has till now introduced *recent* evolutionary approaches to either human development or an evolution of childhood approach[19]. By acting on Kamp (2001) and Beaumont's (2012) calls for interdisciplinarity, we will attempt to remedy this situation – not only introducing our paradigm, but actively using it throughout this book.

First six governing contextual theses will be presented. Then we introduce a conceptual model showing children's integration in society and culture, ranging from macro to micro levels. The model's specific connections to ancient Attica will be established by examples. Since this book will deal with care, socialization, and play in the juvenile phase in ancient Attica, an introduction to those concepts and how they are understood will be outlined. In the following parts 2 and 3 these approaches will be applied to the archeological evidence in order to prove their interpretative value.

### *A contextual approach*

A characteristic focus of developmental psychology is human ontogenetic change over time, for instance observing and explaining how an infant learns its first social co-operative skills in relationships with parents. The toddler increasingly develops by actively exploring his or her immediate surroundings, and in that phase humans begin to know the symbolic world, learning the first words and constructing sentences. In addition the *phenomenology* of the child, that is the subject's way of experiencing and making meaning of its world, is a genuine object of study. In this respect developmental psychology differs from for example childhood sociology, as well as ethnographic and cultural approaches to children. Here a child and children are interpreted in relation to for instance their position and meaning in and for society, their ethnic groups and culture. In this book the phenomenological approach will to some extent be used in interpretations of various types of material evidence. But this is far from enough, because there is no such concept as the isolated child in Developmental Childhood Archaeology. The child will be defined in its contextual world and this includes the following six governing principles:

- *Contextualism*: Any 'trace' of human activity shall be understood in its historical, societal, cultural, physical, social, normative, and ideological dimensions. Childhood and what it was like to be a child then are time-space dependent. Developmental Childhood Archaeology describes and interprets traces of human activity, for example children's artifacts and written sources about children.
- *Functionalism*: All recurrent human activity and its material and non-material products carry manifest and/or latent cultural functions. For example, toys, potty stools, feeders, votive statues, and grave steles of children had not been made if they did not fulfil some kind of need or task in society. The intention of Developmental Childhood Archaeology is to identify and explain various potential functions.

- *Embeddedness*: Children grow up in a complex of developmental and socializing arenas each with their specific routines, normative systems, and human relationships. Concerning small children in ancient Attica, one arena will be the *oikos*[20], another the street where the child plays in the company of peers. A third arena can be the temple where the child is involved in sacral rituals with the parents.
- *Meaning*: Humans generate signification, and culture is among other aspects a composite of *meaning* systems. Thus, human activity – relevant to children in a given prehistoric culture – carries explicit, but most often implicit meanings. Developmental Childhood Archaeology intends to reveal and explain such underlying cultural meaning systems.
- *Children's cultural acquisition and socialization.* These processes take place through both ritual and routine types of social interactions that gradually enhance the child's ability to read and manage cultural systems of meaning in specific everyday situations. Adults mediate culture to children who are involved as active meaning makers. When children for example through play actively process cultural and societal information, it will be called self-socialization.
- *Cultural differences as well as panhuman similarities.* A dichotomy between nature/culture, evolution/culture will be discarded in favor of a 'that depends' approach. Differences are obvious and exist contingent on for example different historical, geographical, and ecological conditions. However, some 'common denominators' also exist in the sense that we belong to the same species (cognitively and socially advanced; using symbolic functions/language; we are tool-users and -inventors; we have a long helpless childhood; we avail ourselves of 'institutionalized' care, and socialize the next generation). However, some panhuman similarities across vast historical periods are not necessarily species specific. They can survive if there is a 'need' for them. For example, when comparing modern parenting with parents in ancient Attica, 'protecting strategies' for the small ones can be evidenced. Prehistoric parents gave their toddlers protecting amulets to wear (obviously this did not enhance their survival rate!). In our times we 'protect' the toddler by taking such precaucions to ensure that he or she does not get into dangerous situations for example, by regulating the childs whereabouts.

### Children's integration into society and culture – a reciprocal level perspective

Children grow up in specific practical contexts that place definite manifest and latent demands on them. Centuries ago generations of children were raised by illiterate, 'unenlightened' adults with no knowledge of either academic theories about children's development or legislation intended to regulate parental behavior. Instead, adult-child relations were probably guided by religion, strong cultural beliefs, and indisputable local morals. Everyday social life is a crucial arena, because this is where the young child meets its societal and cultural 'integrators' and 'socializers' in relationships. But activity on more distal levels is potentially important as it also affects children's lives. Regarding the relationship between society, culture, and the young child, four conceptually distinct, but intrinsically related levels are illustrated in Table 1.

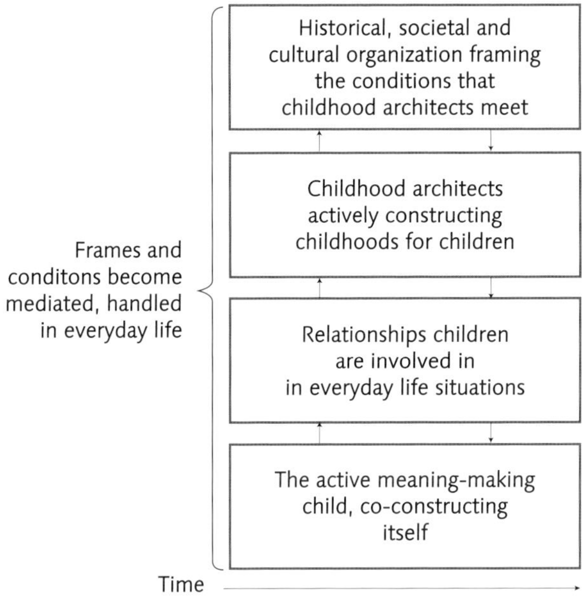


**Table 1.** *A level-specific perspective of the child's integration into society and culture*[21].

If one wants to know what children are influenced by, it is important to know the particular historical time, society, and cultural group of which they are a part of. The macro-level denotes conditions that influence culture and society, conditions which also frame the child's cultural group and childhood in important ways. This framing is two-fold in that it restricts some possibilities, while expanding others.[22] At the macro level, however, a host of conditions do not impinge on children or interfere with their life. On the other hand many macro factors frame the conditions that adult childhood architects meet. The Peloponnesian war, for instance, placed big burdens on Athenian families, when fathers had to go to war as soldiers. This in turn influenced the relationships in the family, for example important decisions that the mother, now as leader of the household, nurture, and upbringing, had to take. In other words, this macro level condition alters the mother's latitude in some families. However, this situation did not pertain to all families, because in some instances older males were probably not going to war.

Macro conditions do not affect a child directly; they have to be *mediated* in order to be transferred into the child's life world.[23] Specific adults can be involved in care and upbringing, thus shaping childhood in ways that are particularly essential to a child's cultural acquisition and socialization. As specific childhood makers, these adults modify, utilize, and transform given conditions that frame (not determine) the meaning and function of interactions in which the children become involved. Thus, at birth a child enters and performs on various already set-up developmental arenas. In such arenas cultural and societal macro conditions are mediated – that is transformed and converted by skilled adults into *culturally attuned affordances*[24]. The Greek culture was very demanding to grow up in. Early and young childhood were to some extent exceptions compared to the demands on older children and adolescents. However, in spite of that there was a clear awareness of what was expected from a little girl and boy. For example, girls were expected to be mothers and boys were meant to become politicians and warriors, and thus both socialization and early skill training were seen as important.[25]

These constructs lead to specific child conditioning mediated by adults in the attempt to guide young children. This is achieved by 'childhood-architects actively constructing childhoods for children', i.e. various adults who shape the conditions under which children grow up. This can be observed in multiple ways, but just to give one example: The physical environments of the family house in Athens were actively constructed by a house planner (the space, location, and functions of rooms) and erected by professional builders. In addition, parental rules for behavior in the house, and 'what-to-dos', etc. influenced the children. The parents as childhood architects choose that the *oikos*' life takes place in a particular house that is reasonably adapted to needs and purposes. The spacial and material realities combined with decisions and regulations made by various distal and close adults vis-àvis a child, frame behaviors and regulate the possibilities for interaction. This will be the consequence also when arrangements and decisions are not necessarily meant for children, but are mere necessities or received culture among for example the elite, upper class Athenians 2,500 years ago.

The parents also structured their young children's daily lives by giving them toys such as balls, dolls, spinning tops, horses on wheels, and a miniature altar which they were allowed to play with. But the 'active meaning-making child' obviously used the toy objects in its own preferred ways. The childhood-architects actively structuring early and young childhood for children in ancient Attica, could be all extended family members living in the *oikos*; for example parents, nurses, pedagogues, and slaves. However, also professional craftsmen making toys and other objects meant for children can be counted in this group, as well as legislators, planners, priests and others more or less directly involved in the physical, special, and mental shaping of children's worlds. The entire society was not a part of children's worlds, only the people who directly or indirectly influenced the child's life.

However, affordances, external expectations, and possibilities are only one side of the coin, because external information needs to be processed by the protagonist. By being an 'active meaning-making child', infants and young children participate in the co-construction of themselves. Thus, young children make essential contributions to their own socialization and development.[26] In written sources it can be difficult to trace the active child. But on many *choes*[27] and vases there are portraits of children depicting movements and inferred intentions, alone or in interaction with others that will be difficult to understand with a passive-receptive model of the child in mind.

As seen in Table 1 to the left, the model is about how 'frames and conditions become mediated, and are handled in everyday life'. In this book everyday life is understood not only as what actually is supposed to happen on a micro level among agents, i.e. 'what people do', but also as 'lived and practiced culture'. This is difficult to depict, given the few glimpses we have of ordinary life in ancient Attica, but some inferences can and will be made later in this book. Routines, whether daily or special ritual celebrations and culture, are two sides of the same phenomenon. Without routines and rituals, there is no culture, because culture can be seen as complex systems of habits shared by many. Routines have these meanings, among others:

- Routines can be 'pure ritualization' for example as seen in religious procedures, events and activities that are built on strictly conventionalized and repetitive habits. As we shall demonstrate in this book's section on sacral actions and socialization, the ancient Greek culture is rich in thise practices, even when it comes to young children.
- Routines can also be 'customized behavior' that is connected with various ways of doing things in a culture. Customs can be spelt out in various behaviors and are thus not ritualized. For example, the divided roles of a father/male and a mother/female in the ancient family that organize gender specific expectations and behaviors.

What are the functions of daily routines, including ritualized sacral and other events? As humans are the most non-instinctual species, routines, rituals, and social customs become a necessity to develop and transmit and reproduce culture.[28] Cultures can even be identified by their specific routines and rituals. Recurrent activities in ancient Attica were at the time in many respects very different from what characterizes contemporary modern Greek culture. They even varied in ancient Sparta and Athens though these cities were not geographically far apart.[29] Routines and rituals also have a personal identity dimension: Without customized behavior regulating and giving meaning to social life and one's place in it, it will be difficult for a citizen to know and feel at home in a society and a culture.

As mentioned above if one wants to study children, it is important to know the society and cultural group of which they are a part of. To sum up, Table 1 highlights the indirect impacts of cultural and societal organizations and events on micro levels where children live their everyday lives. The model highlights the importance of mediating processes and cultural affordances which are enacted by adult childhood architects who spend time with children. In addition, the young child's involvement is often based on routines and customs that the child has not been involved in negotiating. However, young children use their options to reshape and modify relationships to their childhood makers. Children engage in creating social interactions and 'negotiate' direction and content of the relationships in their everyday life. This model is based on the principles about context and embeddedness that were presented earlier.

Last but not least *time* permeates all levels. Very little in society, culture, care, and socialization constitutes unchangeable constants seen in a temporal perspective. We concentrate on an historic time period 2,500 years ago in ancient Attica, where the inhabitants did not have the strict monochronic time experience that characterizes modern society. Nevertheless, unforeseen changes occurred that could make both the present and the future problematic. For example, the Peloponnese war (431-404 BC) came abruptly and changed many things for a prolonged period in Greek society and culture. As previously mentioned, this changed adults' opportunities and sequence of actions which would have consequences on an everyday basis. The time arrow at the bottom of Table 1 indicates that all systems from macro, through the intermediary, to micro levels are influenced by time. Time is also a prevalent factor when considering the ontogenetic changes in the human lifespan. As will be documented in a section below, the ancient philosophers obviously knew that, and in fact discussed ontogenesis in terms of phase-specific age differences.

### Approaches to 'care'

Care basically refers to the protection of the vulnerable child from danger, thereby ensuring the survival of the species. In terms of development, care is also of the utmost importance. In infancy, early, and young childhood, the family (broadly or narrowly defined) is considered to be a principal societal and institutional locus of care. The family, including the extended family, is a complex evolved system that evolutionarily and ontogenetically promotes protection of the ones who cannot take care of themselves. It enhances their development in such ways that they can grow up and function in their society and culture.[30] In this book 'care' will be defined in these ways:[31]

- *Physical care*: Providing food/feeding; cleaning and dressing. (For example, infants in ancient Attica were either breast fed or fed by a feeder. At least in the upper classes various types of evidence indicate that children were kept clean and tidy).
- *Emotional care*: Providing sensitive attuned nursing in stable relationships. (Small children in the family were surrounded by mothers, wet nurses and other carers to ensure the child's emotional needs were being cared for).
- *Social care*: Involving children in relationships. (For example placing the toddler in a potty stool in front of his mother, so they could communicate).
- *Planning/organizing care*: Adult actions on behalf of the child that ensure its protection, presumed well-being or social involvement. (For example, regulation of infants' sleeping periods; involving children in planned activities in the family and in sacral rituals).

Although women give birth to children and thus become mothers, what happens thereafter in relation to care has not been clearly defined in the history of mankind. Motherhood, namely, is constructed by culture and highly ecologically sensitive. In the history of mankind mothers have been one of many (and sometimes not at all) nurturers.[32] Archaeology is very important in relation to this because it can document and show women in roles other than the primary nurturer and break down 'universal' constructions of motherhood (one can add that the same goes for understanding the vicissitudes of fatherhood).[33] As will be shown in Part 2, the role of the mother was greatly idealized and worshipped in ancient Attica. But if we step over the doorstep into an ancient Attic *oikos* to see which inhabitants would typically have been in contact with children as potential carers, the idea of the biological mother as the exclusive figure will fail. She was just one among other significant persons that practiced multiple care.

Until recently, developmental psychology was packed with theories about *the mother-infant* relationship as the first and profound dyad, indicating that this is the prototypic (and right) relationship. But in order to explain the nursing and care of infants, toddlers and young children in the family context in ancient Attica new conceptualizations must be introduced. This book will build on new conceptualizations like *alloparenting, cooperative breeding* and *multiple care.* This is a theoretical framework based on developmental research after the so-called paradigm shift, combined with recent evolutionary evidence.[34] We present this new knowledge in the hope that it is seen and regarded as a way towards understanding such a complex cultural construction as the family in ancient Attica, and not as absolute explanations of child rearing and caring practices.

In the Classical Attic family, mothers were seemingly available for the children. However, stopping here would be like presenting a 'family picture' where many other important persons in the child's life were missing. The child in ancient Attica was not simply a passive appendage to women/mothers, and children clearly had or developed multiple relationships with carers and socializers in the *oikos.* A contemporary investigation of caring practices in many industrialized and non-industrialized contexts shows that the mother is the exclusive child carer only in few cultures.[35] Interestingly the paradigm shift in developmental psychology as well as in evolutionary theory has invoked a growing emphasis on the consequences of multiple attachments, cooperative breeding, and alloparenting that has in fact been very frequent during the history of mankind.[36] Such new conceptualizations have caused recent child psychology to move away from the once pure 'mother-centric' stance.

As a consequence we will present a wider social unit than the mother-child (or father-child) dyads when dealing with the ancient Greek *family* and *oikos* (family unit). Within this unit, relationships with the young child in particular will be in focus, which includes children from 0-7 years old. Archaeological books exist on the ancient Greek family, but the subject of infants and young children's care and socialization is seldom treated independently or in much detail.[37] Here we will focus on the child's social world in the Classical Attic household: Who did the child interact with on a daily basis? What was its relationship to its co-inhabitants?[38] Supported by empirical evidence, we know now that in principle, infants and small children are capable of building meaningful and differentiated relationships to many people at the same point in time.[39] This research accepts that children then grew up in complex everyday face-to-face caring and socializing units that were much broader than, for example, the nuclear family of today.

### Socialization – some clarifications

The understanding of socialization has a lot to do with the fundamental question: What is a child? The choice of the *type* of socialization concept can be seen as a more or less latent answer to that question. So, before it is used in this book some important clarifications have to be made. We are in concurrence with some childhood archaeologists that appreciate the idea of the active child. For example, Baxter (2005) says that a child is "...not a *tabula rasa* on which infinitely diverse meanings are ascribed".[40] And she outlines an interesting program using socialization theory; an approach that allows archaeologists to study children as 'active participants' in past cultures. But there are some inherent semantic problems as well as underlying child-views hidden in the very notion of 'socialization'. Its two basic elements 'social' and '-ize' mean *to make social*, which is ensured through socialization that is an externally induced process. What is a *child* here? Coming into the world it is essentially a non-social human being. Only through the primary and secondary socialization processes will a child become social and culturally knowable. But this does not fit well with the paradigm of the active child, because in micro-cultural human relationships *being an active participant presupposes sociality*. So, it becomes tricky to use the socialization concept because the concepts traditional connotations creep in. Perhaps this is why it is seen in Baxter (2005) when she explains female gender socialization: … "a young girl is socialized not only *into* her role as a child, but also *into* roles that are *culturally determined* to be feminine".[41] The preposition *into* shows a "from-outside-in" process, and *determined* means that the cultural world with its gendered affordances is pre-set.[42] This is problematic and makes it necessary to 'modernize' the concept of socialization and bring it in accordance with new academic ideas about the active, participant-child.

Let us start with the following approach: The young of the cultural group do not simply imitate the practices of, or internalize the prescriptions of those who are more competent in the culture. Children mentally process and are able to recreate these practices and affordances by *engaging in them*. Sometimes what is enacted can be close to the intended adult purpose, and other times it can be markedly revised. Where do we see this? Play is a relevant example, as this is what children from early childhood are engaged in. By observing girls in play with dolls it is obvious that make-believe and fantasy are what characterize their play. Therefore, a strict "from-outside-in" imitation of, for example, mothers or other females, is rarely what is happening. Rather, young children use their experiences in everyday life not as 'detailed manuscripts' but as 'props' for play. Another example could be having a toy altar (which they had) to play with. (See more in the section 'The religious world of the child – sacral actions and socialization', and under 'miniature toys'). This particular toy makes it possible not only to rehearse ritual scenes, but also to identify with the gods – 'being a god'. Or maybe imagining being an adult participating in religious rituals? Even the chubby but apparently joyful crawling toddler seen in his 'snap-shot' movements on a vase 'exploring' his world is better explained having the active participant-child in mind than the passive *tabula-rasa* one. Exploring means that the child makes his own observations and experiences underway. In sum, this leads us to the understanding that socialization in many ways turns out to be the active child's *self-socialization*.[43] This means the child's contribution to its own integration in culture. In Part 3, which deals with play, there are many examples of how children during locomotive, symbolic and fantasy play operate on and with toys in ways where they learn and socialize in self-governed processes. In order to connect the child's socialization with society and culture the definition will be as follows:

"Socialization entails the social human being's active gradual mastery of the society and culture in which it grows up" (Sommer 2012, 78).

However, despite this room for influence it is naïve to think that every child invents cultural and social customs anew. As seen previously, adults are in many ways very influential using affordances to frame the direction of socialization. Children, depending on age and individuality, 'process' and actively engage in this. In this book this understanding of socialization will be exhibited in many ways, but especially within the ancient child's involvement in the sacral world where it was proven useful. We have therefore construed the concept 'sacral socialization' to understand the wide ranging consequences for a forthcoming generation to be involved in the world of gods and spirits, which was an integrated part of growing up in ancient Attica. The families were very often involved in cult activities, many of which evolved around the children themselves.[44] Thus, early involvement in religious actions and rituals was an important part of the next generation's enculturation process. But again it should be emphasized that the young child – using these experiences as 'plots' – could actively participate, and thus self-socialize.

In order to fully grasp the child's socialization into its culture it is important to differentiate between *explicit* and *implicit* socialization. Explicit means, for example, that children are told and take in 'what to do' and 'how we do it' through direct instruction. But probably most knowledge and mastery of culture is learnt not by instruction, but indirectly, as the child's cultural learning process takes place in everyday routines. (See earlier part on routines). On this cultural micro-level people in ancient Attica strove to make their everyday life function. In some parts of this adult life children became actively involved and most socialization occured by observing and enacting the 'what-we usually-do' procedures.[45] This implicit socialization becomes to a high degree equivalent to self-socialization.

### *Approaching play*

This book's functionalist approach to culture favors the idea that if an artifact or an activity has existed for a considerable period of time it must have some underlying important functions. If, for example, there is 'no need for play' this activity will be frowned upon and not allowed in a culture, meaning that toys will not be produced, and 'play-space and -time' will be denied or highly restricted. Apart from the lower classes and slave children, ancient Attica actually favored children's play. We know that this culture had an organized, almost factory-like, mass production of toys made by professional craftsmen, and over many generations adults provided children with toys that they were allowed to play with.[46] This tradition seems to reflect a deep cultural value that it is 'worth the effort'. In other words there is a meaning behind all this, and some latent functions to be inferred. In the growing discipline of childhood archaeology there has been interesting examples and documentation of children's play, games, and toys, but on the whole, however, mostly in descriptive ways. There has been less emphasis placed on discussing what significance play may have had for the child, its development and socialization process in the specific culture it grew up in.[47] In ancient Attica, knowing how to behave and what is expected of adult males and females required years of learning. This society and culture, seen even from a contemporary viewpoint, was highly sophisticated demanding complex knowledge and experience. Therefore, a prolonged time of preparation of the next generation was necessary. With regard to older boys and girls, this was systematically done through the institutionalized educational system designed especially for them. When it came to infants and young children there seems to have been a more relaxed attitude to the specific training of (at least) the children from the upper classes. Play with and without toys may then have been a training opportunity for young children to create and recreate what has been experienced in everyday life.

Several types of playing activity existed: Language play, fantasy and pretend play, object play, (e.g. with toys or animals), physical activity play, and then, for instance, mentally stimulating 'board'-games and puzzles, etc.[48] When objects are created for the sole purpose of being played with, the object changes into a toy. In the material records of Classical Attica only specific object-related play can be traced: Play with toys, animals and various games (both physical and mental) are portrayed in the iconographic evidence. However, imaginary pretend play most likely also occurred even though it is not directly visible in the material culture.[49]

Usually play is defined in opposition to work, because play has an intrinsic value in itself for the child and is not done for reward purposes. Seemingly the child has to be in a special 'play humor' most often governed by positive and joyful feelings. One cannot claim that a crying or upset child is "playing", as more positive expressions would be expected from a playing child:

> …"both phenomenological and neurobiological evidence strongly suggest that emotional states during play are positive, pleasurable and rewarding. Positive emotions like joy, pleasure, satisfaction and happiness grade into each other" (Konner 2012, 511-12).

What emotions filled a young playing Attic child more than 2,500 years ago? We cannot say for sure, as nothing has been found in the material record that may give us a hint. But despite many iconographic examples showing playing children no evidence exists of a child crying or showing clear negative emotions in play scenes. On the other hand it is also difficult to spot really happy faces and the children depicted on *choes* do not seem overly excited.[50]

In order to 'read' the toy/play evidence an interpretative structure has been made in Developmental Childhood Archaeology. Based on what we know, and presented in detail in Part 3, we have depicted a forceful institutionalized 'cultural and adult structuring' of young children's opportunities to play. This in turn indicates a kind of 'appreciation' or 'being in favor of' toys and play because otherwise it would not have been worth the rather impressive financial, professional and other investments in producing and using toys in ancient Attica. This appreciation does not necessarily mean, however, that it was consciously or verbally expressed, but to some extent we can assume that it could have been a part of the cultural cognition at that time.

We can characterize play *as a primary child-driven activity*. Adults could structure and appreciate what was important, but it was the child itself that was involved in play with all its self-socializing and developmental consequences. Therefore young children themselves in ancient Attica were probably highly engaged in play activities. Following these ideas the framework for understanding the characteristics of toys and play will be the following: Toys and play are

1. *Structured and appreciated by culture*: Toys were professionally made. The ancient Attic society had many production facilities and shops, with skilled craftsmen constantly engaged in making toys for children and selling them.[51] In addition markets were spread around the Mediterranean, which could indicate (although not precisely documented) that toys as well as other commodities probably were carried in vessels.
2. *Structured and appreciated by adults*: Parents (and other adults?) were buying and bringing home toys and giving them to children; seemingly allowing young children play-time and play-space in or outside the family. (Although social play is portrayed on images, we do not know for sure whether this was with siblings or peers). As Plato mentions: Play is of utmost importance in children's societal process.[52]
3. *Appreciated and used by young children themselves in their self-socialization*: As mentioned earlier we are in line with Baxter (2005) who claims that children are not "tabula rasa on which infinitely diverse meanings can be inscribed".[53] She instead claims an archaeology that opens the study of children as 'active participants' in past cultures. Turning to play objects, this indicates that young ancient Greek children actively played with their toys and thus created their own fantasy world, – influenced by the actual world in which they lived. Socialization is then turned from being 'out-side-in' becoming an active self-socialization process.

## Child perceptions in ancient Greece: Literary sources and material culture

Understanding children in ancient Greece from a modern point of view could be misleading. So, it is essential to go back in time and learn how the ancient Greeks themselves perceived and understood children. As will be shown in this section child perceptions were not stable but changed considerably over a long period in ancient Greece. This section not only covers the Classical period, but describes the changes in attitudes towards children from the Archaic to Hellenistic period as expressed in the material culture of children. This is done in order to give an understanding and knowledge of the shift in the perceptions of children over a longer time span. This will help to create a better comprehension of the Classical period with regard to the changes that occur in the socio-historical context during this period of approximately 140 years. When working with children in an archaeological context it is important to realize that changes in social structures and cultural constructions, e.g. laws, wars, plagues and demographic changes etc. are reflected in the expression of children in art.[54]

The interest in and value attributed to children in ancient Attica underwent several stages from being less visible in, for example, the archaic times, to being more pronounced in for example the middle-late Classical period. Children seem to be featured more frequently in art, at times when they are more important to ancient society, for example, during or after wars and plagues. Views on children were often linked to views on women, and therefore the increased focus on children followed the increased importance of women (and the ability of childbirth). The increased importance of women and children socio-historically is not only witnessed in the written sources but also affected the material evidence of children.[55]

When it comes to the division of life stages the ancient Hippocratic physicians had ideas quite similar to the modern understanding of childhood phases and stages.[56] In Hippocratic literature these three stages concern children:[57]

- Stage 1 was called παιδίον (paidion) and referred to children age 0-7 years.
- Stage 2 was named παίς (pais) and covered age group 7-14 and the last stage in childhood.
- Stage 3 was μείρακίον (meirakion) age 14-20.[58]

Various words for child existed in the Classical period, and no standard terms were used.[59] The word νήπιος and βρεφοσ (*nèpios/brephos* ) referred to a baby and was used in Greek poetry and τέκνον (*teknon*) was used for a young offspring in literature.[60] However, it is clear that boys and girls did not follow the same social path and both sexes had different life cycles and stages. Girls were believed to mature faster than boys, as we also acknowledge today. But females were considered to be adults at the age of 12 to 14,[61] which is not the case today.

In contemporary European societies age is more specified: 0-2/3 is considered to be the period of infancy followed by the toddler period age 2/3-3/4 and age 5-6 as the preschool age. Age 7-10/12 is the school age for smaller children which is followed by puberty (which is a part/stage in childhood). Childhood ends at the age of 18 when the child legally and otherwise enters adulthood; however, the term adolescence is used for older children age 13-18. Interestingly the modern view on specific childhood periods separated from, for example, adulthood is relatively similar to the antique ideas when it comes to boys. Girls, on the other hand, are not allowed to marry at the age 12-14 in modern society. It appears, however, that whereas we today have a stage of puberty, in Classical Greek society this was perceived instead as a stage for marriage. For example a 12 year old girl was seen as a young adult woman, which corresponds with the reproductive maturation of girls.

But other interesting understandings of childhood were sketched as well in ancient Attica, indicating that the 0-7 year's age span mentioned by Hippocrates was not necessarily perceived as a blurred undifferentiated period. According to Golden (2003), Plato and Aristotle operated with an age-bound sequence of five distinct stages, each period with its own psychological and physical characteristics.[62] Here we will concentrate on the first three stages that cover the selected age group of this book:

- Stage 1. *Babyhood*: From 0 to about 2 years of age, until the child is weaned and able to speak.
- Stage 2. *Early preschool*: From about 3 until 5 years of age. A phase for independent play and with growing physical activity.
- Stage 3. *Real preschool:* Until 6 or 7 years of age – here children establish their own social (peer) networks.[63]

Here cautions must be taken as it should be remembered that the various age periods are not nearly as 'chronologically stiff' and definite with regard to the individual as witnessed in contemporary Western societies. They should rather be seen as age-periods *relative* to those around them in the culture where, for example, sameness of age, plus or minus some months, was important for ritual or domestic purposes[64]

For a child psychologist of today this (although sketchy) plan looks surprisingly similar to some developmental stage theories claiming the 'teleological principle', i.e. that human development progresses stepwise from immaturity (specified by infant and young childhood phases) towards maturity as the end goal (adulthood). The progressions were for example in the highly influential Piagetian theory – influential in developmental psychology – seen as governed by age-bound inner physical and cognitive maturation principles. External stimulation, learning and socialization were not the creator of the sequences, but well adapted to a given stage could be of vital developmental importance.[65] Interestingly, Plato was also in favor of the idea that the purpose of a child was to become an adult, fulfilling important roles in society.[66] For example, Plato saw role- and fantasy play as having direct preparatory functions where future adult roles were to be rehearsed.[67]

We do not have the above age distinctions from a learned pedagogue living together with children in the family, but from philosophers. This could otherwise have explained the apparent relative practical validity (usability) of the concepts. The pedagogue (as well as other persons in the family) had direct contact with children of various ages and could by observation and extended experience have come up with such meaningful distinctions. In comparison Plato and Aristotle may probably have been male 'ivory tower' philosophers rather detached from the everyday world of babies and young children, and therefore not able to observe their behavior. So, one could wonder how these stage distinctions as outlined by Plato and Aristotle for babyhood and early childhood outlined by Plato and Aristotle could be so telling. Their thinking in this regard could of course have been due to a number of 'lucky punches' constructed out of the blue, for example to prove or suggest a point in an ongoing philosophical argument. But this seems unlikely, because of the apparent validity of what specific psycho-social and physical competences children are expected to master at the specific ages. Although we do not know, perhaps Plato and Aristotle did have some knowledge of "real" babies, toddlers and young children – knowledge not only created by their own direct observation, but from conversation with other informants.

In the early Archaic period (Ca. 700-580 BC) children were seldom represented in art with the exception of the *kourotrophos* (a terracotta or clay figurine often showing an infant or toddler in the arms of a mother or nurse).[68] The *figurines with children* were mostly of a votive character (often sacrificed to Artemis and many from Boeotia) but are also found in women and child graves.[69] Depictions of children on vases are rare with the exception of heroes as babies (e.g. Achilles).[70] When children do appear on vases, boys are represented more frequently than girls – and always as miniature adults. The most commonly known 'child-representations' are the *kouros* and the *kore*, which were free-standing sculptures of older children placed as a funeral marker or as a votive sculpture in a sanctuary.[71] The lack of infants, smaller children and girls in the art of the Archaic period has been attributed to the social system of Archaic Greece.[72] The Archaic Greek society was male-oriented with a focus on aristocratic origin and rivalry. However, a change in views on children from 480 BC is recognized in art and burial customs, perhaps as a result of the Persian invasion.[73] The war against the intruding Persians may have cost many male lives, resulting in an increased focus on the importance of childbirth (focus on women's position) and thus ensuring the next generation of Athenian citizens (with increased focus on the importance of children). But the change can also be ascribed to the introduction of 'democracy' by Kleisthenes making it easier for non-aristocratic males (men of a good *oikos* or Athenian tribe) to become citizens of Athens creating an increased focus on family origin and family-values.[74]

Children became more visible in art and on graves from the late part of the Archaic and early Classical period.[75] Here, children appear more frequently and in a wider pictorial context, and although boys are regularly represented, this is not as marked as earlier. In the early Classical period the different childhood stages also become visible. Children of different ages, and the infant, are now more clearly observed on vases.[76] The child is more naturally painted or sculpted following the general tendency towards the idealized naturalism of the Classical period (no more miniature-adults). Domestic scenes, e.g. of parents/nurses/pedagogues with a child become increasingly popular from around 450 BC. The socio-historical explanation for this change of focus on women and children is connected with the changes in the Athenian citizen laws from 451/450 BC.[77] Now the child could only become an Athenian citizen if both parents were citizens (not only the father as earlier). This created an increased importance in the status of the mother and therefore also the status of the child.[78]

Once again the socio-historical impacts are visible in the material evidence on children. Children are now seen in friezes,[79] painted in different life stages on *choes* from the Anthesteria-festival[80], depicted on grave steles individually or with family members, and shown on white-ground *lekythoi* found on or in graves. During the middle and late Classical period the child has gained a more central role in art. The increased attention to children in Greek art is ascribed the Peloponnesian war, and the plague in 429 which cost several Athenian male citizens their lives and decreased the total population drastically. The plague epidemics during and after the war killed both women and men but especially struck a more vulnerable part of the population: The children. The war created an increased focus on children, especially in funerary monuments erected by the parents of a deceased child.[81]

After the Peloponnesian war, an increased focus on wealth and the display of power rose in Athens. This resulted in the erection of permanent children's monuments by families in honor of their children. The monuments were not only erected for deceased children but also for living offspring, and were often bought from merchants. From the early 4th century expensive free-standing sculptures were made as votive offerings showing both infants and young children and this tradition became well-established by the 330s. The sculptures are reminiscent of the *kourotrophos* from the Archaic period, except that now the child is not merely a supportive element, but sculpted independently.[82] In general, the Hellenistic period showcased a tradition in free-standing sculptures of children with emphasis on the so-called Hellenistic pathos. However, despite the increased focus on child sculptures, children are under-represented in the bio-archaeological record in two distinct cemeteries of Athens.[83] This tendency would correspond with the material evidence of the votive free-standing sculptures and the less represented funerary steles. In the Hellenistic period, the focus was on sentimentalized sculptures of children with emphasis on cute childish behavior and chubby realistic anatomy.[84] Children in the Hellenistic period were often compared with and depicted as the god Eros as a child: Angelic, cute and innocent, but also mischievous, weak and dependent.[85] The tradition can also be assigned the expression of Hellenistic style of art.[86]

The expression of children in art undergoes a considerable change from the Archaic to the Hellenistic period.[87] These changes are often linked to specific socio-historical events in the history of Athens (or Greece in general). The Classical period was marked by the Peloponnesian war and numerous changes in the citizen law (and other laws) which influenced the view on children (and women). This change in the socio-economic and demographic structure made an impact on the children's art. Children were made more visible in art – probably reflecting a higher cultural acceptance of their importance – in some periods of the ancient Greek past.

## Focuses of the book: Time, space, age and specific material evidence

Apart from a few steps back to the Archaic period, the *focus will be primarily on the Classical period*, dating from 480-300 BC. This period begins after the Persian invasion, and ends in 300 BC. However, the timelines should not be seen as absolutes because stylistic overlapping exists in the transitional periods – from late Archaic to the early Classical period and in particular between the late Classical and early Hellenistic period. Grave steles and dedicatory votive statues of children from the late 4th century are used in the book even though some may argue that they are early Hellenistic. Artifacts that lie outside the Classical period are used either to show a chronological development or whether a specific artifact is unique.

*The geographical area will be Attica*, since many child-artifacts are found in this area. However, objects from outside of Attica are also included to illustrate that children's artifacts also existed outside of Attica.

As mentioned at the beginning, the selected age-group will be 0-7 years old. A main aim of the book is to focus on the most 'inconspicuous' children: Infants, toddlers and pre-school. Another very important point worth mentioning again is that the 'children' referred to in this book are aristocratic or upper-middle class. This is due to the very nature of the material and written sources. In fact little is known about the majority – for example poor children and slave children.

With regard to children older than 7 years, and youths, some specific artifacts might suggest that older children also played. Perhaps, though, a particular object was only represented in the presence of older children/youths. Infancy, toddlerhood and young childhood have been selected for the following reasons:

- They are still underrepresented and less well known in Classical archaeology, although rich material and iconographic evidence exist relating to this age-group.
- We are able to address new research issues that for the most part have not been dealt with before or only in brief terms, for example early care and early play.
- It will be possible to produce new knowledge about complex care (for example multiple care and alloparenting) and primary socialization (for example sacral socialization), not focusing on more well-researched child topics such as education and schooling.
- Developmental psychology can contribute to childhood archaeology with an in depth research base dealing with ontogenesis in early and young childhood. Selected theory and research can be implemented in order to interpret and understand the material evidence. In addition an updated childhood evolutionary research approach makes a 'dual interpretative framework' possible: On the one hand human commonalities can be traced across time and space; on the other hand significant historical and cultural differences can be acknowledged. In sum, this dual interpretative framework will go together in this book's interdisciplinary Developmental Childhood Archaeology approach.

*The material evidence:* Together with selected literary sources from the period (for example, Plato and Aristotle) the specific material base evidence used in this book will be the following:

- *Grave steles with children*: Such steles give important iconographic evidence in the understanding of children in ancient Greece. For example, the Ampharete-stele with both picture and inscription depicts a grandmother sitting with her dead grandchild revealing deep distress. The steles, taken together, can among other things, show changes in the perception of children from the Archaic to the Hellenistic period.
- *Grave gifts for children*: For example, dolls from Cyprus, Attica and Corinth. These artifacts seen together with vase paintings indicated that children did indeed play.
- *Care items meant for children*: Found in a domestic household context in Athens, Agora, and Corinth are professionally made ceramic pots, potty stools and feeders. This indicates that the primary needs of infants and young children were seen to.

- *Votive offerings and gifts to the Gods*: For example, statues of children in sacred places; and gifts as various toys, for example dolls in the Brauronia.
- *Votive reliefs showing families with children and grandchildren* when making offerings to the Gods. These reliefs show children's specific roles in the ancient sacral world and this kind of children's socialization in a polytheistic society.
- *Vases showing scenes of play, potty training, adult-child interactions and children in motion*: For example, crawling toddlers can tell about young children's ability to move freely.[88]

*How the material evidence is 'used'*: Taken together and put in various contexts this material evidence can give a rich understanding of how children lived in ancient Attica and how they were perceived. The various artifacts selected constitute the fundamental evidence base in this book. Approaching the material evidence has been guided by Developmental Childhood Archaeology's basic principles stated previously. Perhaps needless to say, the artifacts are not 'naked truths', so they have to be interpreted in order to understand their function and meaning, and that is why a specific theory approach was argued for earlier in this introduction. But it is also fair to say that within childhood archaeology the understanding of how to interpret the iconographic the evidence is not the same. Some researchers, would not consider this evidence as proof of the "real" life of children.[89] It is important to be aware of different decipherings of the same vase or *chous*.

Nonetheless, it must be stressed that no artifacts have been deemed as non-options just because they did not fit into a pre-established idea. Nor have any artifact been 'handpicked' in order to fit in and illustrate an already construed interpretation. Therefore, few top-down deductive approaches have been practiced in this book; instead it all started step-wise beginning with the sometimes tedious work of categorizing and describing the several artifacts and placing them in their respective temporal contexts. Then the eventual functions and meanings of each object were tried out making various cautious bottom-up inferences. Each object, for example a doll, could at the same time have had important sacral, domestic and play functions, in which case, each specific function is followed by explaining and spelling out these functions.

Realistically painted vase scenes can be seen as 'frozen here-and-now-episodes' that should not only be understood in a sacral context, although it can also be so in many cases. For example, what do vase paintings (as well as grave steles) tell us about the child itself as well as its relationships? We have been inspired by this clearly archaeology-psychological approach:

> "Athenian vase painters developed a sophisticated language of gestures to allow their figures to communicate. In the absence of [sometimes] facial expressions, and within the constraints of a small format, gestures prove to be an economical and effective way to display graphically the reactions and personalities of characters in a scene, and to indicate their communication with each other." (McNiven 2007, 85)

So, the iconographic evidence conveys invaluable and rich information about the ancient Attic representations about children and their developmental relationships. Exploring the 'silent language' hidden in the material evidence, putting as many fragments together as possible can give us at least some sense of ancient beliefs about children as well as the actual worlds of young children. The observation of humans in action has proven especially useful in the study of pre-verbal humans in developmental psychology. The basic principle being that every act by the infant facial, motoric, gestural *means* something, and are intentional expressions.[90] A present-day example could be observing an infant or young child reaching up to its mother, while at the same time they look at each other (this is also evidenced in the iconography from ancient Attica). It is inferred from this that the child's intentions are 'I want to be picked up' and 'I want my mother'.

Inferences can also be made that the mother is known and recognized, and is therefore being remembered from previous interactions. This in turn means that the child has a mind based representation of the particular parent. In developmental attachment research this construct is called an 'internal working model'.[91] Contingent on that its content is associated with mainly positive emotions this representation functions as a developmentally important social-emotional cognitive structure. Methodologically important such a mental feature is constructed from the observation of external behavior – for example a snap-shot picture of mutual adult-child gestures. The observation of preverbal infants and toddlers used in developmental psychology will be tried out as one of a range of interpretative ways into the material. In addition there is an important cultural layer to be understood also. The scenes depicted, and thus the important episodes to be observed, reveal a specific cultural way of presenting the life of infants and young children in ancient Attica. Several examples are at hand in the material evidence of 'frozen scenes and episodes' representing infants, toddlers and young children 'doing something', in locomotion, in play, alone or together with important others.

### Content of the book

Part 2: *The care and socialization of infants and young children* will focus on infants and toddlers, two age-groups which are rarely studied in depth in Classical archaeology. Children's relationships with their co-inhabitants in the ancient Classical family (*oikos*) will be examined, especially concerning the relations to mother and father. Dealing with early care this section will introduce and elaborate on new research on alloparenting, multiple caring and cooperative breeding. Whether love of the child was probably experienced by mothers (and fathers) will also be discussed. On the other hand infanticide was practiced and probably culturally accepted. How, therefore, can sentiments to one child go together with killing another child? This question will be addressed combining actual evidence from this period and psychological evidence about microsocial 'humanization/ dehumanization' processes. Part 2 will also present and discuss the functions of different types of material evidence of early care and nursing practices: Feeders, potty stools and the rattle, the earliest type of toy. Iconographic representations of nurses/mothers caring for the child will be analyzed along with nursing objects. Written sources will be used in order to interpret the ancient view on infant and toddler nursing. The topics cover different themes such as: Infant nursing, breastfeeding and the use of wet nurses; other nursing practices such as potty training and how common the tradition of swaddling was in ancient Greece. Adult activating of infants by the use of rattles stimulating sensor-motor development will be dealt with also, as well as the images and importance of the 'exploring, crawling toddler boy'. Did young children in ancient Attica interact with their siblings? If yes, in what ways? These questions will be answered also. The last section in Part 2 deals with the religious world of the young child and how sacral actions and socialization happened.

Part 3: *Young children's play and toys* focuses on the age group 3-7 (toddler age – preschool age) – an age group rarely described in depth in archaeology. By handing a toy to a child to play with, a special relationship is established between a child's self-socialization activity and an adult-organized cultural process. Part 3 will be organized around topics based on various types of toys, iconographic materials, e.g. vase paintings and grave steles of children playing (sometimes with toys). The themes in Part 3 are selected to show the variation in children's toys and play, gender divided activities and the (self-) socializing aspects of play, which in turn indicates how the ancient Greeks viewed children and understood child's play. First, a brief history of theory about the functions and meanings of play will be reviewed and evaluated in relation to recent understandings. But did young children really play in ancient Attica or does the iconographic evidence only hint to sacral functions? The iconic ambiguity about how to answer that question will be addressed and a conclusion reached. This is followed by an evidence-based section about children's play in Classical Attica, based on Classical philological, ancient written sources and recent understandings of play. After that the specific evidence of toys will be presented: Dolls, rollers, push- and go carts; other types of toys; miniature toys and children with 'toy' pets. Finally, toys as the specific objects they are will be considered in their developmental and functional perspectives using new developmental and evolutionary research.

Part 4: *Conclusions and perspectives.* In part 4, the main conclusions will be derived from the foregoing Part 1, 2 and 3. A discussion about interpretative validity will also be taken up, because the various ways that childhood archaeologists interpret the material and iconographic evidence vary considerably. On the one hand there seems to be a 'realist wing' considering artifacts as reasonable (albeit often idealized) 'evidence' of some sort of underlying reality. On the other hand, there is an 'ideal wing': When it comes to the interpretation of iconography this is in essence not about reality but serves idealization's spiritual and religious purposes. In that discussion we wish to make the standpoint of Developmental Childhood Archaeology clear. Finally, some future perspectives will be dealt with, i.e. the focus of the importance of interdisciplinarity.

# PART 2

# THE CARE AND SOCIALIZATION OF INFANTS AND YOUNG CHILDREN

## Child-parent relationships in the household – the role of the mother and father

The following section will discuss the Child's relationship to it's cohabitants, ie., mother and father. This is done to show the roles of parents in connection to their offspring, and to illustrate that sentiments existed between parents and children.

The *biological mother* has seemingly taken great part in the raising of her children, as Xenophon tells us about the important role of the mother.[92] Mother and child representations in art are numerous, and women are often seen with children on steles and vases from the Archaic period-Hellenistic times (fig. 1, 2, 3).

The numerous iconographic representations of mother and child may once again suggest that biological mothers in the Classical Attic *oikos* engaged in the daily rearing of her children. But they may also be inferring that women were connected to children and vice versa, and thus children can be seen purely as attributes to the female identity. However, written evidence on motherhood highlights the importance of mothers in the upbringing of children: It was not only a mother's prime responsibility to teach children polite manners and discipline them, but also to provide joyful moments for them, for example take them to visit the neighborhood, temples and festivals.[93] These activities and visits would help the child in its developmental and socializing process, and it was a mother's role to oversee that the development both mentally and physically progressed in the proper direction.[94] The mother's influence on the child's development appears to have been of psychological, moral, cultural and social importance.

*Human sentiments*, positive as well as negative, are often traceable when looking at iconographic representations of mother and child. The mother is depicted sometimes smiling at her offspring, while the child is either smiling back or reaching out for its mother (fig. 3).

However, the sentiments depicted may also be sad when appearing on grave steles and funerary monuments (fig. 1),[95] indicating the sorrowful situation of an untimely

**Fig. 1.** *Handing over the child to sitting mother. Attic marble stele, Ca. 420-410 BC.*

**Fig. 2.** *Handing over the child. Attic red-figure hydria, Ca. 440-430 BC.*

death of either mother or child (or in some cases both).[96] Yet, these touching scenes may perhaps illustrate that interaction with children was a joyful activity for mothers, and that with death the mother was denied the joyous engagement and contact with her child. The mother had special responsibility in educating her daughters: She taught them how to raise children by giving them responsibilities in the care of younger siblings, she taught them how to make wool, weave and participate in religious activities

**Fig. 3.** *Maidservant reach child to smiling mother. Attic grave stele, Ca. 360 BC.*

**Fig. 4.** *Grandmother and grandchild. The Ampharete stele, Ca. 430-420 BC.*

**Fig. 5.** *Father (Euempolos) with his two children. Attic marble stele from Piraeus, Ca. late 5th-4th-century BC.*

etc.[97] The mother thus instructed her daughters in how to run a household (with family members, co-habitants, slaves etc.).[98]

Besides motherly love, evidence of cross-generational sentiment is seen on the Ampharete stele showing a mourning grandmother with her little grandchild (fig. 4).[99] The stele bears this touching inscription:

> *"I hold here my daughter's dear child, whom I held on my lap when we were alive and saw the light of the sun, and now being dead, I hold it dead."*[100]

Graveyards with their many objects conveying symbolism can be seen as *a cultural place of grief*; this means the special ritualized and materialized 'customs' that a society invoke in order to cope with the loss of the dear ones. According to Hewlett (2007) grief can be seen as a 'cry for survival' and a time where corollary social networks, kin and other carers, even a whole society becomes involved. Seen in that perspective funeral inscriptions can be read as 'statements meant for the living' and for the community as a whole.

Sometimes grief is manifested in farewell messages, other times with reflection on happy times spent together. The inscription in Figure 4 clearly bears witness of both, showing the affection and close ties over three generations.[101] This grandmother's grief over her daughter's little child is strengthened by the antistrophes' life versus death: … "when we were alive"… (…) … "now being dead, I hold it dead".

Besides the material evidence, written sources also show sentiments between a grandparent and a grandchild, for instance in a Euripidean play, where the old Cadmus mourns the loss of his grandson Pentheus, who protected him from insults.[102] Another play of Euripides tells that a grandson Orestes remembers his grandparents with much affection and states that his grandfather: "raised me when I was small, and often kissed me as he carried me about in his arms".[103] Even though grandfathers are almost invisible in inscriptions, they are mentioned in literary sources.[104]

While mother-child-relationships are relatively often depicted with sentiments and love, the relationship between *father and child* is (sometimes) illustrated differently. When fathers are depicted with children on grave steles it is most often in the company of a male child, *almost* never a daughter.[105] An example is a grave stele found in Piraeus, which shows a father with two children, a son in front and a daughter behind (fig. 5).[106]

Fathers almost never smile in these depictions but appear very serious when looking at their offspring. This may indicate that depictions of sentiment between father and child were not acceptable or 'appreciated' in grave iconography, and that the father was mainly illustrated as the patriarchal *Kyrios*. Fathers are also portrayed giving the characteristic farewell handshake to young male offspring indicating that the child is seen as an adult and not as a child.[107] This type of handshake is never performed between mother and child, but mostly between adult family members of same kin. However, in the case of handshakes between father and son it may illustrate that the son is seen as the new head of the household, the *Kyrios*, who assumes all legal responsibilities after his father's untimely death – thereby the child is placed in an adult sphere. Sons are identified (and distinguished from slaves) by their clothing or by inscriptions (fig. 6).[108] The child departing from his father on grave steles is often an older child, around the age of 5, and fathers are seldom, if ever, seen with infants and toddlers.[109]

Yet, on some vases male adults are shown interacting with toddlers, for example, on an Attic red-figure pelike from 430-420 BC (see fig. 18). However, it is often difficult to know whether the male adult is the father or a male pedagogue. A written source (Aristotle) indicates that children were expected to behave with respect, loyalty and obedience towards their father.[110] Respect for the father is mentioned by Aristotle in *Politics*, where it is written that the father rules the mother like a magistrate rules a fellow citizen, and rules his children like a king. Aristotle mentions in another work, the relationship between father and sons as being rather one-sided, with the son bearing all responsibility for a good relationship.[111] He writes that a relationship between father and son is not a friendship of equals: He points out that the obligations of a son to his father overrule any claims the son may have, stressing that no one can ever give his father the honor he deserves.[112] In an interesting analyses "Father and sons, men and boys", of the ancient greek gods and heroes' (prescriptions) for such relationships, (Shapiro 2003) portray the father role as both absent, disengaged and, when in contact, filled with tensions and drama. Although the gods and heroes clearly are exaggerated characters not taken out of real life, probably the heroes in particular, being male, provided an important cultural gender message as fatherhood role models.[113]

**Fig. 6.** *The farewell handshake. Attic marble stele from Piraeus, Ca. 360 BC.*

However, a milder version of father/son-relationship is stated in Euripides' play Antiope, where some fragments proclaim that "a father who is mean to his children heavily weighs down his old age" and that "it is sweet for children to find a mild father and not to be hateful to him".[114] These fragments may indicate that a good relationship between father and child was desirable for both parties. What supports this is the established norm in Classical Athens that *philia* (affection) should be considered and distributed between the generations. Respect and obedience towards the older one was important, but there was more to it than that. For example a father's *philia* was to be towards both his father and his son, and vice versa.[115]

Relying on archaeological evidence and not only on written sources it becomes difficult to observe the relationships between fathers and children, because fathers are simply not portrayed as often in the company of their children as mothers. This could have been because the main responsibility for raising offspring was probably with the mother. However, it may also have to do with the fact that male-dominant societies did not accept 'soft' male values such as parenting. It was not well-seen for a man to engage in child nurture, even less to be shown engaging in child interaction in iconography.[116] That was not an accepted male role in a society that was built on male aesthetics and male ideas of moral standards and ethics. Yet, we do not know what actually happened in the *oikos*, when the father was alone with his family. Perhaps, some fathers did engage in daily contact with their children, for it is hard to believe that *all* fathers totally ignored or were non-involved in their offspring and, as we soon will see, some evidence suggests that some fathers were not.

Recent research has documented the importance of fathers in child development – both involved and absent fathers.[117] Fathers involved in the care of their offspring are not a recent phenomenon: Far back in human history fathers have seemingly been involved in the care of young children. When prehistoric fathers helped with child care, this male 'investment' in their offspring could lessen the burden placed on mothers, thus allowing more births and ensuring reproduction.[118]

But involvement in care is highly dependent on context. During human history and across various cultures fathers were (and are) not necessarily involved in the care of the next generation:[119] For example, if others took the burden and assisted in the caring of the offspring – for example other females, older siblings and grandparents. As seen, the above analysis of the written sources addresses male ruling and the emotionally distant father in the *oikos*.[120] Seen in relation to the relatively many, predominantly female carers available in the *oikos*, the involvement of fathers was not as necessary as in earlier hunter-forager cultures. Obviously the role of the father is related to a vast complex of temporal and cultural ecological factors. There could though be more in it than a 'numerous births investment' and cool reproductive pay-off strategy – perhaps a 'psychological investment'? Interestingly written ancient Greek sources support and document that *some* fathers in fact expressed close sentiments towards their children:

> "Aristophanes provides a glimpse of a new father's joy, which is so intense that it makes him easy to deceive (…).[121] Another father commandeers his son from a nurse, feeds him from his own mouth, making kissing sounds, and calls him a pet name, 'daddy's little rascal'" (Golden 1990, 90-91).[122]

These (exaggerated) fatherly affections were frowned upon by ancient Greek philosophers such as Theophrastus.[123] They were considered to be inappropriate and folly and were used as bad examples of how males should not behave. But the actual behaviors, testify to a fondness for children and were as significant (and perhaps more widespread) as an old male philosopher's moral prescriptions.[124]

In general, however, balancing the evidence it is fair to conclude that mothers and fathers had relatively sharp and distinct roles in a child's life. The role of the mother was even idealized to a degree that can be labelled *mother-centricity*.[125] The father is often connected to older male children, while the mother is engaged in both sexes of all ages. Nonetheless, the Athenian family was idealized and held high in the Classical period, and affections were developed within the family and through generations. Aristotle adds to our understanding discussing the importance of affection (*philia*) within a family: He states that philia originates from the affection of parents (seemingly not only mothers) for their offspring, and that parents believe that children are a part of themselves.[126] If the latter should actually be a fundamental parental belief then 'meshing identities' will be the consequence. Today, not being able to separate one's identity from another (parent being symbiotic with her child) would be a sign of mental pathology.[127] This is obviously not the case here. The phrase 'children are part of themselves', should not been taken too literally, but rather – just as we say today – my own 'flesh and blood', i.e. as a declaration of a 'blood-bond' relationship meaning that the child is a part of us, our family, our stock and lineage.

Aristotle writes further about the nature of affiliation in children, for example that children love their parents as the source of their being, yet parents' feelings of affection are of longer duration than a child's, since the child does not start loving its parents before it develops understanding and perception.[128] Here Aristotle almost sounds like a child psychologist's calculation of the importance of perception and cognition for the age-bound development of sentiments in children. Parents, according to Aristotle, love their children from birth, but he concluded that parents love their children more than children love their parents. However, because children were in more close daily contact with the mothers, they developed stronger feelings for the mother than for the father. In addition, mothers tended to live longer than fathers, thereby surviving until their offspring reached maturity. They could follow the child into adulthood – once again creating closer mother-child attachments (as illustrated in art e.g. on vases and steles).[129] The ancient Greek family was a complex unit as will be demonstrated later, and further research on especially the father-child relationship is needed to determine similarities and differences in parental roles and practices in the Classical period.

Thus, if mothers loved their offspring and mourned when they died, how should we then explain the evident practice of infanticide in ancient Attica? So there was another more sinister side to this that must be dealt with in order to obtain an understanding of parenthood in ancient Attica. Many children died naturally at an early age, however some were caused by infanticide, which was practiced and appeared culturally accepted.

## Beyond sentiment? High child mortality and infanticide

This section will focus on high child mortality and the practice of infanticide. A tradition of infanticide may indicate a lack of emotion towards the youngest, yet it may also show a more complex side to the demographic, economic and social problems, which were to be solved according to the practice of the specific period.

Societies with high child mortality rates were more prone to practice the tradition of infanticide than societies with low child mortality. But why kill your own baby? Why 'voluntarily' kill babies in a society where a great deal of parents experienced the sudden death of their infant or young child? This paradox has been discussed and debated for years, and has for example resulted in the conclusion that past societies did not mourn their children when they died.[130] This deduction is strongly questioned, however, by the fact that human parental love is an evolutionary, beneficial sentiment.[131] But a society with high child mortality may not necessarily contradict the practice of infanticide and moreover, infanticide may not necessarily show a society lacking in emotion and empathy towards children. The ancient Greek infant mortality rate was high, perhaps around 25-30 percent in the first year of life.[132] Until the age of 7, the risk was higher than in youth, and death was always close by – a fact to be expected. Infants were especially at high risk, and perhaps therefore epitaphs on grave steles almost never stated that a child's death was 'untimely' when the deceased child was under 2 years of age.[133] Smaller children were almost never commemorated, but were allowed to be buried inside the city walls and beneath domestic houses. These burial customs have been interpreted as the adult's disinterest in infants; however, the tradition may on the contrary indicate that parents were not ready to be separated from the baby after death.[134] It has been claimed that families with many children did not mourn the loss of newborns, because they already had a large family.[135] In addition, grief would be worse for a first-time mother upon losing her newborn child. Of course, it is impossible to know what parents in ancient Greece actually felt in these situations, but perhaps it may be possible to gain an insight by looking at anthropological studies of high mortality societies and their attitudes towards the death of children.

At some point in the history of mankind mothers began to bear offspring too precious to rear by themselves. This made a mother's commitment to any given child contingent on her admission to social support.[136] This was especially necessary in high mortality societies where the threat of many children being lost could be counteracted by many infants being born thus heightening the burden on the mother. Social support meant that children had many individuals around them, who either helped or took over the nursing and care of the infant. Child rearing was not always the sole responsibility of the parents, but was shared to some extent by other family members, e.g. siblings, older children and grandparents. Losing a child meant that the loss was more widely shared than in cultures with exclusive maternal care. A set of strict nursing rules and practices were followed to ensure the optimal care of the child.[137] If the child dies there is less of a burden on the parents, because these rules and practices were followed.[138] This practice may be built on defence mechanisms ensuring the mental stability of the parents upon child loss. Another tradition, which may also be ascribed to defence mechanisms, is the culturally widespread burial and ritual practices connected to child mortality.

Often traditional cultures with high child mortality rates (or high mortality in general) have specific *ritual practices, which help parents to cope with the grief*.[139] Eschatological beliefs are often combined with these practices assuring the parents that the child will live happily in the afterlife.[140] It should be remembered that having or losing a child in ancient society was intimately interwoven with both spiritual beliefs and fatalism; individuals were not creators of their own lives – what happens is prescribed and governed by external forces. The influences and powers exerted by evil spirits, for example, were part of ancient beliefs. So, who could prevent an inevitable fate, the will of supernatural powers, if protective amulets, sacrifices and rituals could not save one's child from death? It was definitely out of the hands of the parents.

The generally negative view held about childhood in past societies, together with the argument on the lack of paternal emotions towards children, has been an explanation for the high child mortality rates (and infanticide) of ancient cultures. Theorists such as DeMause argued that parents of earlier centures did not have any emotions towards their children.[141] It was also stated that children were typically abused, not raised with care and sometimes killed, because the parents were not interested whether the child lived or died. In other words, the longer we go back in history the worse the fate of being a child was, if compared to modern humanized times. However, anthropological studies and recent studies from childhood archaeology paint quite a different picture.[142] In addition several anthropological studies of high child mortality societies show that parents and caregivers were extra attentive towards infants. The infant is almost constantly being nurtured and cared for, and is the center of attention in the family.[143] Some traditional societies even perform a distinct infant stimulation program.[144]

Some evolutionary-based theory argues that in normal circumstances parental love and devotion is the rule, not the exception.[145] Another evolutionary approach, however, the so-called 'parental investment theory' claims a more cool and calculative point: Parents provide physical, social and psychological care to infants, allocating effort and resources to their offspring that could otherwise be devoted to their own sustenance and acquisition of resources. Thus, although a parent probably always wants the very best for their child – healthwise, etc. – many aspects such as economic hardship, and the support or otherwise of other people, all influenced the amount of investment that parents were willing to devote to any offspring.[146] This approach explains why in special circumstances parents accepted a child's early death, or were even driven to kill a child. But on the other hand, it also explains that if circumstances were favorable, they invested in the protection, love, devotion and education of offspring. It seems highly plausible, therefore, that parents in the Classical Athenian society showed positive emotions for, and payed special attentive behavior to their infants – especially when they had been officially welcomed into the family some days after birth.[147]

Children's lack of a clear societal role in Classical Athens has been attributed to the high mortality rates degrading small children to non-members of society (not necessary in the family). However, the exclusion may be of practical character: If the child did not hold a position in society, the child's death would be less of a problem to the public system, since its role should not be refilled by another person. The 'only' problem that several child deaths could pose to society was of demographic character, e.g. after wars, when the Athenian population had dramatically decreased. Nonetheless, these societal views of children may not have been the case within the family in Greek households. In addition small children appear figuratively, both individually and in family groups, on funerary monuments throughout the ancient Greek period (more frequently in the early 4$^{th}$ century BC). Steles with individual children indicate deep grieving and sorrow over the death of a beloved child.[148]

To turn back to the *house burials of infants*, these burials have been connected to small children's lack of societal importance – meaning no burials in public graveyards.

But these unimportant creatures were not treated as garbage when they died. Could it have been a parental empathetic and sympathetic gesture? Why then was this home burial ritual a culturally established domestic practice that obviously was worth the 'effort'? Going through this burial procedure may indicate that children were welcome in the family, and that the parents wished to have the deceased child with them in the *oikos*.[149] Unfortunately we cannot depict the exact age, in days, of the buried infants, in order to ascertain if they were from *before or after* the *amphidromia* ritual. (Here the child, some days following birth, was welcomed into the family. The father literally ran around with the baby in the house, followed by other family members, 'showing' the house to the baby). Before that ritual the baby may have been in a type of 'no-man's land', considered to be a 'not one of us' organism. (The important *amphidromia* ritual will be discussed later in this section in relation to the exposure and infanticide of infants). This particular transition ritual could be important for the parents in order to make some sort of demarcation line for when exposure and infanticide was acceptable. If this interpretation is valid that the baby first had to be 'officially' welcomed in the house, and thus become a part of the family (allowing parental emotions to intensify), then the house burials of infants were probably not for those who had just been born or only a few days old.

A *medical explanation* for the high child mortality rate in ancient Greek society is ascribed to the lack of antibiotics and other types of medication.[150] However, by examining the nursing practices and artifacts, it is possible to obtain a clearer picture of the risks that infants and smaller children have in Greek Classical society. As elaborated later in the book, swaddling can cause different, serious, side effects such as hyperthermia in cold weather, overheating in warm weather and respiratory infections, such as asthma. Children may well have died from this swaddling practice without parents knowing it. Another serious illness may have been child diarrhea, which could have been caused by unsterilized feeding-bottles and other insanitary items. Today this can be treated, but 2,500 years ago it could have been fatal. Children in Classical Attica were exposed to many risks, some being fatal, mainly through illnesses or accidents. Yet material evidence suggests that parents did try to prevent accidents from happening, for example, by giving their offspring protecting amulets.

The *fear that a child might die* is clearly expressed through material, iconographic evidence and written sources. Parents did what they could to protect the child from harm and children wore protective amulets, which are shown on vases.[151] These depictions are most often seen on choes, showing crawling children with amulets (see fig. 17).[152] The function of these amulets was to ward off evil spirits, that were believed to be the cause of illness and accidents.[153] Feeders and rattles are sometimes interpreted as having an apotropaic and protective value, like the pig.[154] Why produce these objects and, for example, put a protective amulet on a child's body if 'child indifference' was widespread?

It was also the ancient Greeks that created the medical discipline of *pediatrics* especially devoted to ensuring the health of children.[155] In mythologies and in epic stories the death of children, for example the untimely and brutal death of Astyanax, is mentioned to bring pathos to the reader and to underline the tragic event of the death of a child. In general, it is reasonable to believe that parents in the Classical Athenian society mourned their children, also when they died at a young age.[156] Mourning the consequence of broken ties to a child, is also expressed in funerary arts, where children were depicted with sentiment and empathy.[157]

Turning to *infanticide*: This practice has been rebuked by researchers for centuries. It has been claimed that past societies detested children and threw them to the wolves if not needed. However, studies of the tradition of infanticide have revealed another side of the coin. Living in past cultures, with no birth control or organized abortion systems, families had to deal with the burden of too many children. Modern research on the attitude towards abortion may shed some light on the subject. Such research shows that abortions are related to women's lack of stable life situations e.g. financially and emotionally.[158] Most often abortions are not carried out because of a dislike of children or a negative attitude towards children in general. Interestingly, surveys show that 65-69 percent of women wish to have children later in life, and follow-up studies show that they do have children and care for them like any other mother. Moreover, the reasons for abortion are most often to provide a better environment for the children they already have or might have in the future.[159] In addition, studies from early modern Europe show that in societies, where infanticide was illegal, children were very often mistreated, neglected and abused. Yet, past societies that permitted infanticide, could just as well want children, care for them and love them.[160]

> "Among some Greeks exposure of newborns could coexist with, and even be caused by, care for other children" (Golden 1990, 89).

This practice is explainable using the 'investing in children' approach earlier mentioned. In this case the death of newborns can have many causes; but too many mouths to feed, for example, the burden of having too many children and the lack of social support may be possible reasons.

It is reasonable to believe that newborns were exposed in the Classical period, especially girls. Golden (1981) suggests that around 10 percent of all newborn female babies were exposed. A so-called 'marriage squeeze', meant that parents with many girls could look forward to paying huge dowries once their daughters got married, often at a young age. Girls, then, were a considerable future economic burden, whereas sons were more prosperous, receiving marriage portion. This is an example of how cultural rules can influence parental decisions about life and death. If female infants were not exposed then too many girls would never marry due to the lack of men: More females survived infancy than the vulnerable males. Furthermore, it was more expensive to raise a girl, because of the marriage dowry.[161] Infanticide was obviously a widespread tradition. Sparta was known to throw infants off a cliff, when exposed after birth.[162] The exposure of infants does not necessarily correspond directly with child-murder. Exposure was a tradition linked to infanticide and took place when Greek families in various ways wished to get rid of unwanted infants – for example, leaving a living baby in a desolate place in nature, where perhaps the gods could take it (or the wild animals). Not being a 'direct' killing, this was a more passive act resulting in the subsequent death of the child, being, as it were, out of the hands of the adults. Whereas in present-day societies child exposure is punishable by law and considered to be on the scale of 'negligent homicide', which will result in a prison sentence, in Classical Attica the exposure of children was legal and thus culturally and morally accepted.[163]

Literary evidence indicates that this practice was carried out before the *amphidromia* (literally, a walking around) where the household head accepted the child into the family and before the name giving on the 10th day – the *dekatê*.[164] This information is highly important for our understanding of parental decision, because it indicates that before 'acceptance' and name-giving, infants were not seen as 'real' human beings or as being a part of the family i.e., not transformed into 'one of us', which may correspond to the modern view of an aborted fetus. This view on newborn and unnamed infants could explain why parents were emotionally capable of exposing of their newborns.[165] Until deciding whether a child should be kept or killed, parents seem to have been capable of being in a state of an 'emotional standby'. Another point is that some children were most likely illegitimate, physically weak or were born with defects.[166] Yet, healthy children may also have been killed, because of economic problems or simply because they were unwanted at a time when birth control was not at hand. Infanticide and the exposure of children can, as seen earlier, be ascribed a 'too many mouths to feed' theory: Due to lack of food and poverty in general. But although this may have been the case with the ancient Greek lower and middle-classes aristocratic families also practiced infanticide. Researchers have claimed that the ancient Greeks preferred small families, and had a relatively small number of children in the family.[167] Aristocratic family values in the Classical period were very important, which is clearly illustrated in art, e.g. funerary monuments, where the family is never large. There are never a lot of children shown on either family commemorative reliefs or on sacral reliefs with Athenian families. Perhaps this ideal concept of 'the perfect family' and the right number of children had an impact on the death rate of children. The reason may also have been of economic character: Wealthier classes may have been more concerned about a diminishing estate, once again linking female infanticide to the 'marriage squeeze' and dowry. However, it was also a problem with too many boys since sometimes the estates were 'inherited' not only by the oldest son but by all male offspring in the family, thereby dividing and splitting the family wealth and estate. Therefore, the aristocratic family could not uphold their wealth if too many children were born and this may explain why it was the wealthier classes that were criticized for their extensive use of infanticide and their refusal to raise children.[168]

Nonetheless, children were also an economic asset and help to the family, especially in poor families. The cost/benefit balance of raising a child in the Classical period could be less than the economic value of the child's labor, once it was out of early childhood. Therefore, the key question may in some families have been whether the child was wanted or not.[169]

Little information exists as to how this tradition was practiced, and moreover, to what extent children were exposed. But the material and iconographic evidence demonstrate that love and care of 'wanted' children could coexist with the practice of infanticide in order to create better living conditions for the other children of the household. This practice could exist because unnamed infants of less than 10 days old were viewed as *non-humans*, which would thus emotionally 'allow' the adults to dispose of the child. *De-humanization* has been a well-known 'strategy' in human societies for creating a sharp boundary between 'us' and 'them'. Various constructions follow such divisions.[170] This opens a door and legitimizes indifference or even cruel acts towards the constructed non-humans without investing much regret or emotional pain – they even may deserve it. [171] Also today such practices are evident, for example in rural Africa, where infants born with defects, are expelled or laid down to die. But before the mother ceases to care for her baby it is de-humanized by the mother, the village elders and the witchdoctor. The abandonment is rationalized when the baby is considered 'bewitched' or born with an alien 'evilness' that can even be seen in its eyes.[172] The anthropologist Scheper-Hughes (1992) reports similar cultural cognitions from a field study in the poorest quarters of Recife in Brazil. Here infant mortality is close to 50 per cent. It was observed that mothers sometimes withdrew from some of their most fragile babies as if to protect themselves from eventual emotional shock and mourning. A weak and physically vulnerable baby was in accordance with cultural ideas of children labeled "an angel that wants to die" or "ghostlike".[173] The de-humanizing labels – 'angel', 'ghost', i.e. a non-human – starts a self-fulfilling process where the mother withdraws and the baby's chances for survival diminish.

The withdrawal of maternal (and paternal) emotions and exposing the child (getting rid of the evil spirit, or letting the angel go) – supported by a whole community's belief systems – becomes a necessary defensive act and is not acted upon as murder. By the same token, many of these mothers are sensitive carers that both practically and emotionally invest in their other children.[174]

## Multiple care, alloparenting and cooperative breeding

In Part 1 the basic understanding and definition of care was introduced. It seems that in human evolutionary history and in many cultures the isolated nuclear family with a mother, father and child has not been prevalent. Instead multiple care, i.e. the child was raised and nursed by many agents besides the mother, has been the norm.[175] Moreover recent developmental attachment theory and research have changed dramatically from the 'mother-centric' position of John Bowlby and Mary Ainsworth towards 'multiple attachment' – i.e. investigating the real everyday socio-emotional relationships children are involved in. Recent research has confirmed that more secure attachment relationships are more developmentally healthy than a relationship only to the mother.[176] In the *oikos* (an important arena for care) in ancient Athens, many people were around and therefore probably a part of the child's 'social horizon' early in life. It is likely that a child will have encountered the following people quite often:

| *THE SOCIAL NETWORK OF THE* OIKOS<br>*Children 0-7 of age*<br>*Potential relationship partners* [177] |
|---|
| *Mother* |
| *Father* |
| *Siblings (older/younger; brothers/sisters)* |
| *Wet nurses (not always slaves)* |
| *Other nurses (not always slaves)* |
| *Grandmothers (often the father's but sometimes from both lineages)* |
| *Grandfathers (often the father's but sometimes from both lineages)* |
| *Servants (mostly slaves)* |
| *Slaves (adults)* |
| *Slaves (children)* |
| Paedagogus *(mostly but not always slaves)* |

**Table 2.**

At least two important consequences can be drawn from Table 2. In the first place growing up in the *oikos* involved many people. Looking at the array of potential relationship partners in the *oikos* it becomes clear that they must have had different roles and functions vis-a-vis the child, as well as sometimes overlapping roles. If we, besides a mother and a father, tentatively estimate the amount of siblings in the *oikos* to be between two to four; up to four grandparents;[178] wet nurses, servants, slaves and pedagogues (number dependent on wealth and circumstances) the face-to-face social network may well have been about fifteen to twenty adults and children living or coming in the *oikos*. This does not even include persons that could be in contact with the household: Occasionally visiting guests or friends (*xeno*i) and family. In addition, because of death and remarriage, step-parents and their eventual children could sometimes be counted in, as well as divorced or widowed daughters returning home. Moreover there could also be both adopted children and 'free' children (not slaves) that were allowed to come to the household for protection and care. Golden describes the interesting 'circulation of children' phenomenon.[179] For various reasons (for example war), parents gave their child to another family for protection and care. This was even seen as a 'ritualized friendship' (*xenia*) which could be life-long (*xenoi*). A bond of solidarity was expected to develop between, for example, a boy entrusted-into-care and the boy in the family.[180] Perhaps this was done in order to teach boys 'general basic trust' toward non-kin, based on friendship to peers in the *oikos*? A basic trust in others could later in life prove helpful in building a relationship after having left the family.

In the second place, although we know that many different people surrounded the child on a daily basis, we know little about the nature of the relationship they had with the child. For example, did the aristocrat's children and the slave children of the *oikos* play together? Possibly, but we do not know. Adult slaves, however, in their different roles and functions, were clearly associated with the children in the *oikos*, for example as nurses and pedagogues.

Anyway we do know that the family unit was an extended one compared to the contemporary nuclear family. In addition, its boundaries were quite fluid and shifting over time, some people stayed for longer periods, others for shorter. Using the system and developmental approach presented in Part 1 it can be said that the relationship of one part of a 'face-to-face' group always has direct or indirect consequences for all other parties. As an example, the mother-child dyad (as portrayed as a unit on idealized iconography and steles) or other dyads are not to be seen as 'closed units' separated and developmentally privileged over the child's relationships with others. This reciprocity is precisely captured in this dynamic square dance metaphor:

> "Households are not made up of neatly defined reciprocal pairs related only to each other in a precisely choreographed slow waltz; rather household members engage in a square dance, with alliances constantly shifting, groups forming and reforming in response to the actions of others" (Golden 1990, 163-64).

Defining the *oikos* as a family unit that consists of members that are solely related by kinship would be too limiting. If we focus on reproduction, this is greatly enhanced by multiple caring and alloparenting, socializing and learning from various developmental agents in infancy and early childhood.[181] In order to fulfill its many functions the *oikos* must have been a basic 'cooperative unit'. Its several agents with their different and similar roles vis-a-vis the child, presumingly had their share of impact on the child.

After having dealt with the complex potential array of persons in the Classical Attic household, some iconographic evidence is now presented. The following is a short presentation of the artistic representations of the Classical Greek family, which should be seen in relation to the socio-historic impact on art in ancient Greek society as visible in the iconographic evidence, for example on grave steles, dedicatory monuments and reliefs. Families are also shown on vases and, as mentioned previously, parents are seen in the company of children.

Often it is not the entire family that is represented in iconography, but rather specific members e.g. father/son, mother/child, mother/father, siblings, etc. The family is most often seen together on votive reliefs from the 4$^{th}$ century, commemorated by wealthy aristocrats.[182] On grave steles the child is often seen with its mother, perhaps indicating that the mother died in childbirth, but steles with father and child do exist, as mentioned earlier.[183] Besides the members of a nuclear family: Mother, father and children; nurses, pedagogues, servants and slaves are also portrayed in connection to the ancient Greek family.[184] Often servants/slaves are seen on grave steles accompanying their master/mistress and are frequently portrayed as smaller in stature or wearing simpler clothing. Sometimes a female servant/slave is handing an object to her mistress, for example a jewellery box, a necklace, a mirror or even a child (see fig. 3).[185]

Servants never perform the characteristic farewell handshake (*dexiosis*), which is seen on steles when two people (or more) depart with the dead. The servant may have been considered a mere attribute to the deceased, indicating the wealth of the person. Interestingly, though, it is very likely that servants/slaves were part of most ancient Greek households.[186]

Societies with high child mortality often used multiple care, meaning that a child after weaning may have continued to have contact with its nurse until schooling began. This meant that girls would learn how to do female chores like weaving, sewing and wool-making, which may have been taught by the mother, but perhaps also by female slaves/servants, who may have been in charge of the daily household affairs.

Boys were expected to start school at the age of seven and they were left in the care of a male pedagogue and teachers. However, before that boys were probably most often in contact with female carers. Wet nurses were of course females, and boys dined with the women in the *gynaikonitis* until the age of seven.[187]

Research on the layout of domestic houses built solely on archaeological evidence from excavations in Olynth, indicates that *there probably were no strict gender boundaries in the oikos*.[188] Women were not restricted to the *gynaikonitis* but were 'allowed' to move freely in the *oikos* (except when the male household *kyrios* had other male visitors). Most likely children were also allowed to move freely between the household rooms, and were therefore not restricted to a specific gender sphere.[189] This also means that children had the opportunity to meet other persons living in the household.

Therefore, beyond the mother, father and child relationships it seems that children in the Classical Athenian *oikos* engaged in wider relationships with the household's other co-members, and recent developmental research has repeatedly demonstrated that children's development prospers in multiple-caring relationships.[190] The infant develops important internal 'working models' according to the various functions of its multiple caring persons. This socio-emotional competence seems to be panhuman,[191] and has probably been of evolutionary importance, since prehistoric infants could not always 'rely' on the primary care of the biological mother. The ability to 'co-work', 'cooperate' and attach to multiple carers has probably been a survival mechanism. This relatively new knowledge of infants and young children's ability to attach to multiple carers has, among others, resulted in the empirical substantiated concept of *alloparenting* (co-parenting).[192] *Cooperative breeding* is a related concept that refers to any species with alloparenting assistance in both the care and provision of the young. Human babies are prepared for close communication with anyone who will be attuned to their needs which is quite smart considering the potential high risk of maternal death during human history.[193] Cooperative breeding is the 'extra' that human babies look for, because

> "…lumping together various interactions with sibs, cousins, fathers and other adults, nearby caregivers are more likely to speak to babies in 'motherese' and entertain them than their mothers are" (Hrdy 2009, 112-113).

If 'nearby carers' did that *more* than mothers in the oikos, we do not know. But 'motherese' is a specific attuned way of speaking to babies using simplified vocabulary, melodic pitch, and slow deliberate tempo. It is a communicative way to establish and sustain a close relationship to the infant. Because nearby carers other than mothers use motherese, this phenomenon has also been called child-directed speech. Fathers, however, were probably not so close to infants in ancient Attica, but as seen in Table 2 many others were potentially so. This evolutionary idea is supported by anthropological and biological research of multiple caring systems in different human cultures and societies and is also observed in the animal world (e.g. among birds, mammals and in specific primates). Alloparenting explains that infants are able to function and grow up in such a caring context without being mentally or physically disturbed, and seen in a long historical perspective it has been the rule and not the exception.[194] This idea will be pursued and implemented as a hypothesis to gain a more complex insight into caring systems in the ancient Greek culture that were probably more than just father/mother and child relationships. It is suggested, not claimed, that the concept of alloparenting can be implemented to analyze and interpret caring practices of the Classical Attic household. A society practicing alloparenting must meet these three criteria:

1. People live in groups with overlapping generations.
2. Care must be provided by more persons than the parents.
3. Reproduction is regulated to such a degree that many care-givers never reproduced (or did not do so at the same time as the rearing of a family child). This made the allocarers more efficient as carers. [195]

The ancient Greek household does meet the two first criteria, and to some extent the third. Turning to the first criterion, it is evident that overlapping generations co-lived in the *oikos*. As witnessed on the Ampharete-stele (fig. 5), *grandparents* could have had deep feelings towards their grandchildren (and vice versa). Children have also been fostered by their grandparents, probably grandmothers, which may have functioned as an alternate and/or co-caring caregiver to the mother, slaves and nurses.

Interesting evidence has shown that the 'truism' that only women in the reproductive age have real importance for survival of the species is not necessarily correct. Biologists and anthropologists of today alike have long taken for granted that the function of women was to bear and rear a man's child. From this perspective, women past the childbearing age were deemed irrelevant and of no interest. Yet a demographic analysis has revealed that, for example, a forager-hunter individual who survived up to age 15 had a good chance (approximately 60 %), of living further to 45 years old – and perhaps even to old age – if grandparents have been involved in his care and upbringing.[196]

Why then are women made to live more than 70 years (the right conditions in place) if the last decades are functionally in vain and they thus become a burden on society? An answer lies in *the grandmother hypothesis,* proposing that post-reproductive life spans are enhanced when grandmothers are a part of the mothers' caretaking support system.[197] Although we do not know specifically how grandparents were involved in child care in ancient Attica, their mere presence in the *oikos* and living and meeting in the same rooms could feasibly have invited to building relationships of some kind.[198] Generally, therefore, if grandparents provided physical and emotional care, and invested time in the children's well-being, they could forge special attachment relationships with their grandchildren.[199] Such relationships could help protect children from adjustment problems, even under conditions of great hardship. Thus having grandparents around in the *oikos* could have been an important resource in the care and upbringing of children. Interestingly, Golden refers to ancient scholars that use the word *mammothreptos*, which means not only 'reared by grandmother', but also referring to spoiled children![200]

As shown in Table 2, many people lived in and were part of an ancient Greek household and probably had contact with the infants and young children in the *oikos*.[201] This indicates that multiple care was practiced in Classical Attica, which also corresponds with the evidence from high child-mortality societies (as mentioned earlier, they often practiced multiple care to compensate for maternal death and reduce the risk of infancy death). Turning to the criterion 3, reproduction-control may have been practiced to some degree in Classical (upper class) Greek society, where the socially and economically advanced women relied on assistance from slaves, poorly-paid wet nurses and nursemaids.[202] As a consequence, this is where the third criterion may apply, the wet nurse's own baby suffered the high probability of bad health or death, when there was not enough milk. In addition, prolonged lactation suppressed ovulation thus creating sterile and almost constantly lactating wet nurses. If female slaves were used as wet nurses, it may have prevented them from becoming pregnant, thus solving a potential demographic (and economic) problem in the upper class household.[203] By using this type of child rearing practice, upper class parents ensured and controlled the prime conditions and care for *their* infants, while by the same token, solving the problem of having too many slave children born in the household.[204]

To sum up: It is very likely that alloparenting was practiced in the Classical Attic *oikos*. The children were probably raised by numerous caregivers ranging from the biological parents, grandparents and siblings to nurses and slaves (slaves may have functioned as wet nurses, nurse maidens, and perhaps also as teachers, play friends, and may have been the primary nurses of upper class children). Children in upper class families seemed to have had better odds for survival than poor children due to the use of wet nursing. Children will function normally if their primary needs are attented to and they are cared for and loved. This may have been accommodated by alternating or co-caring persons and alloparents (grandparents, siblings, slaves and nurses). Perhaps some upper class children and slave/nurse relationships evolved into an almost child/parent-relationship? This can be witnessed by the dedicatory inscriptions created by grown-up children from the upper classes to their deceased nurses. [205]

**Apollodorus the immigrant's daughter Melitta, a nurse.**

*"Here the earth covers Hippostate's good nurse,*
*and Hippostate still misses you. I loved you*
*while you were alive, nurse, I love you still,*
*now even below the earth, and now I shall*

*honor you as long as I live. I know that*
*for you below the earth also, if there is*
*reward for the good, honors will come*
*first to you in the realm of Persephone and Pluto".*

(4th century inscription from Peloponnese; Fildes 1986, 21).

Yet, in general, it is difficult to trace slaves and slave children in the material record as well as in iconography.[206] Most often it is children from the aristocracy and upper-middle classes that are visible in the material record, yet they are a minority group. As it was well-off children that were buried with fancy toys, and portrayed on vases, elaborate steles, funerary monuments, dedicatory monuments and sculptures, it creates an incorrect and one-sided picture of children's lives in ancient Greece. Due to the lack of evidence it is not clear whether slaves and slave children engaged in the care of aristocratic infants, and therefore if they were a part of alloparenting.[207]

Humans have a prolonged juvenile period because we are not equipped with instincts and inner programs that direct us how to manage our environment. In particular, infants and young children are totally dependent on care and nursing from adults,[208] they have not yet developed the psychological and behavioral skills to master their own survival. In evolutionary thinking the basic function of early care and nursing carried out by parents is simple survival:

> "Few things are as crucial to a child's well-being as parents. A child's very survival depends on the nurturing received from his or her parents, extending well past infancy and into the juvenile period and perhaps beyond" (Bjorklund & Pellegrini 2000, 219.)

If we extend the phrase 'parents' to include other important caring persons this nurturing has been practiced in millennia.[209] Humans, compared to other species, have a remarkably extended period of dependency. Without protection, feeding, care and nursing by others, any infant and young child will die. But there is more to it than basic survival. It is a well-established fact in developmental research that during early care and nursing special emotional and social ties between the nursed and the nurse develop depending on the quality of the relationship. And it is seemingly not, as previously thought in developmental (Freudian) theory, the hunger need that 'drives' the child into the mutual cooperative process of nursing, but the need for a close relationship with another person.[210] In addition, as a basic human *need for protection* the attachment process growing out of nursing and early care seems to be relatively independent of both history and culture, although *type* of relationships and their emotional quality are highly dependent on actual context, history and culture.[211] So, culture and history demonstrate the various ways in which to care for and nurse the very small ones.

## Infant feeding in the Classical period

In this section we will discuss primary nursing, breastfeeding of infants and the feeding tradition in Classical Greece, including the seemingly widespread use of wet nurses and feeding-bottles. Feeding infants is of course inevitable for the survival of the next generation. The glimpses we obtain from the material record of feeding can be a 'window' into not only the type of nursing depicted but also, in some instances, the relationships between the 'giver' and the 'receiver' can be observed. And even eventual idealized images of mother-child may signal and derive from some kind of practice. For example, as seen in fig. 8 of the *breastfeeding* mother, the way she holds her child is very much like the way a real mother will feed her child.[212] Although feeding can be associated with a mother breastfeeding her child, this 'natural' relationship was far from being the only one in history. Perhaps the breastfeeding person on the vase is not the biological mother, and maybe the infant is only partly, or not at all, breastfed but nourished in other ways with different kinds of food. For example, in Classical Attica some children were probably fed on goats milk from purchased feeders/feeding bottles made and sold by professional craftsmen.[213] Although depicting breastfeeding mother-child as an idealized pair, the fact that feeders were made in vast numbers and used indicates a cultural acceptance of this sometimes preferred practice.

Various types of archaeological finds that have been discovered indicate the tradition of infant nursing in ancient Greece. Several Bronze Age *feeding bottles* have been found on Cyprus as well as toys, especially rattles from a later date, which would indicate a production area on the island for children's artifacts dating from the Helladic period to the Classical period. Considering the geographical position of the island, Cyprus may have been an ideal place for the production, distribution and shipping of children's nursing- and play objects to the Mediterranean/Aegan area. [214]

The feeding bottle is a typical nursing object found in Classical Attica, indicating an alternative feeding practice to breastfeeding.[215] Numerous feeding bottles have been found in the ancient Greek material record from the Archaic to the Hellenistic period.[216] In the 4$^{th}$ century feeding bottles are often of Attic or Cypriote origin and distributed throughout the Mediterranean world, which indicates at least two craft and distribution centers.[217] This makes it very likely that a mass production of feeding bottles took place, and that they were transported over long distances to reach customers in many places. One could assume that a cargo ship loaded with the usual basic and luxury commodities, as described in archaeological literature, also carried specific 'infant gear' like feeding bottles and toys. This shows that feeding practices other than breastfeeding were widespread in the ancient Mediterranean world and not only in Attica. A skilled craftsmanship was developed and a complex distribution system was in place as well. In other words there was, at that time and even in earlier times, a profound societal investment in making tools and cultural objects that were beneficial for the nourishment and health of infants, as well as freeing mothers of the time, consuming duty of long-term breastfeeding. Objects made by professionals, specifically for children, (toys) have probably been widely distributed as well.

**Fig. 7.** *Attic black-glazed feeding bottle with ornamentation. The Classical period*

What did these feeding bottles look like? Different types and forms exist, however, no typology or chronology have yet been made.[218] But the Classical feeding bottle is often very skilled and nicely made, glazed and sometimes with ornamentation.

The feeder (fig. 7) is a typical example of a Classical type and it measures H. 6.3 cm. Dia. 9 cm including the spout, which is normal size for Classical feeders.[219] At first the feeders were interpreted as oil lamps, but the finding context in primarily infant graves has changed this interpretation. What does the feeder imply about the caregiver? Obviously that it was accepted that breastfeeding was not the only way to nurse an infant. In addition feeders may have been used as an alternative solution to wet nursing, although they may also have been standard nursing equipment used by nurses. Feeders could perhaps also have been used if a sick infant was too weak to suckle, but interestingly they have also been interpreted as adult feeders used for sick elderly. Nonetheless, since they are most common in child graves they are likely to be associated with child nursing.[220]The grave context indicates moreover, that feeders were viewed as the personal belongings of the individual child and buried beside the child to take into the afterlife. Parents probably only selected objects that were symbolically important for them (and their child), so why a feeder? A feeder put in the grave with the child could perhaps have represented symbolic food for the afterlife, or perhaps a soothing substitute object for caring.

Apart from the breastfeeding mother (fig. 8) material evidence suggests that infants born into the aristocratic elite in the Classical period were not nursed by their biological mother, but is this true? What does other evidence tell us?

The logographer Lysias (ca. 445-380 BC) writes in his first speech that his wife suckled their infant and she often slept with the baby downstairs to breastfeed it when it cried.[221]

However, in mythologies, breastfeeding is a savage tradition practiced by animals and humans of lower status.[222] These varying ancient views on primary nursing may have influenced caring traditions in the Classical period. The lack of iconographic evidence

Fig. 8. *Breastfeeding mother. Red figure vase, Ca. 440 BC.*

of nursing mothers is puzzling. Corresponding with that, Beaumont also points out that the image of the young child nursing at the female breast is almost non-existent in Athenian iconography. She concludes that the nursing motif was probably taboo.[223]

However, where there is a rule there will also be an exception: Iconographic evidence of child nursing by aristocratic mothers does exist, for example on a red-figure vase from 440 BC (fig. 8).[224]

On this vase, an upper class mother is breastfeeding her male child. He appears to be around 3 years old. A man stands in the background observing the child. Due to the woman's fine clothes, the scene is interpreted as a mother (not a nurse) and her child, because a nurse or slave would not wear this type of clothing. The scene is set in a domestic sphere in the *oikos*; however, it could also stem from a mythological context, since domestic breastfeeding scenes are very rare.

By taking a closer look we can observe that the little boy is sitting on her lap and seems actively engaged in sucking. The mother is holding her son close to her body one arm holding him and with her open hand and fingers sheltering his head. Probably the watching male is the father, so this scene seems to portray an intimate family feeding episode held in the *oikos*. In Part 1, the 'active child' paradigm was presented.[225] This fundamental view is also shared by recent childhood archaeologists.[226] Being a 'still-picture' depicting a temporal phase in the breastfeeding process, we do not know what came before and what comes after. But the scene clearly visualizes the both participatory and engaged role of the child: He is evidently not bouncing around but sitting still on his mother's lap. He is leaning forward engaged in the sucking process itself and as he seems to be around 3 years old, is probably skilled in 'doing his share' cooperating in the feeding process. Child psychology stresses the early developmental importance of such (and other) obviously recurrent intimate social-emotional episodes (intimacy can be evident in other episodes than breastfeeding as well). Basic trust in both self and others and the gradual building of mental representations of such experiences are vital milestones in early human development.[227] The boy's mother also does her share in making the scene a mutually beneficial event, allowing it, bending towards and holding her boy, although she is not looking particularly amused. Why did the artist prefer to portray that expression of hers? Could it be accidentally? Probably not, because representations showed on vases (events, gestures) usually carried a symbolic message, thus meaning something. Is the intention to show that breastfeeding is a duty and a burden for mothers? We do not know. But seen as a whole we can observe a 'coordinated-action', and if this is a recurrent event for infants and toddlers, it inevitably leads to the development of close ties between child and mother and vice versa. In addition, the infant begins to develop 'affect attunement', understanding the other as different from itself, but at the same time one with whom you can share feelings and understandings.[228] Development of close ties between child and caregiver is not restricted to breastfeeding. Intimate feelings can also arise during other feeding practices, for example using a feeder, in a being together context that is similar to breastfeeding. The quality of feeding as a socio-emotional activity is highly important in the early self-other development between humans.

On the other hand, breastfeeding and other types of early feeding practices are not always happy and cooperative. Instead they can be filled with conflict and negative emotions which will lead to reciprocal 'affect mis-attunements' between the nurser and the nursed.[229] Should a wet nurse (as was the experience of many infants in Classical Greece) have breast-fed a child on a daily basis, then exactly the same socio-emotional and self-representations will develop if it was the mother. This is because it is the caring *relationship* (and its qualities) itself that is crucial for early development, not a specific person, for example the biological mother.[230] As mentioned in some instances breastfeeding can be the conflicting issue between mother and child. This sometimes leads to finding alternative ways of feeding the baby by substituting milk in a feeder.

Miniature statuettes have been found with breastfeeding mothers or nurses. However, the figurines are rare and perhaps connected to a sacral sphere rather than a domestic context.[231] These figurines rarely appear in the material record from the Classical period, which again indicates that the upper class women may not have breastfed infants while it was not an event that should be idealized. While the lack of nursing-figurines and other breastfeeding representations in art combined with the numerous feeding bottles might suggest that breastfeeding was not prevalent in the upper class in the Classical period, other types of evidence show that infants were breastfed, but not necessarily by the biological mother.[232] Ancient written sources mention the practice of breastfeeding and the quality and nutrition of human milk.[233] The Hippocratic corpuses tell about breastfeeding and children's corporal development in the section on Dentition.[234] Plato mentions the benefits of good nourishment and exercise for the mother during pregnancy and after the birth of the child.[235] Aristotle briefly writes about methods of infant feeding, and describes the change in infant excrement when breastfed.[236]

It is commonly known that *wet nurses* were used as primary feeding- and nursing substitutes for the biological mother.[237] This might have been a way to ensure breastfeeding of the infant without the use of the biological mother and/or the feeding bottle. Using a wet nurse could have obvious advantages for the mother. Just to mention a few: To uphold a high fertility level or to maintain her youthful appearance.[238] When these elite women had their babies breastfed by other women, it enabled them to give birth with intervals of approximately 1½ years without compromising their health and the survival of their young. It also enabled them to maintain a handsome body for a longer time, and this was not unimportant considering the high value – and thus cultural pressure – of having and maintaining an esthetical appearance in ancient Attica. Therefore, to be 'slim', also after child birth, is obviously not just a recent trend. This was a female ideal for the upper classes in Classical Greece which included wearing sophisticated hairstyles and clothing, and not least, displaying well-bred manners, being a presentable representative for the family, the center of the *oikos*. Interestingly, all Greek goddessess, besides their important sacral function, where also portrayed as icons of beauty with their 'aristocratic' appearance to be seen in many places. None were depicted as plump, fat, short, old, or wrinkled, with unelegant clothing and hairstyles. The Greek *Aphrodite* is clearly made with slimmer limbs and hips compared to the Roman *Venus*, indicating some secular and cultural changes in the 'standardization' of ancient female beauty. In addition (as will be dealt with in Part 3 about play and play objects), the dolls given to girls in the ancient Greek period were not baby-dolls, as many are today, but represented adult females, almost never males. The dolls were rather similar in appearance – slim and almost Barbie-like in shape. Thus, long before maturity and motherhood – giving birth, and perhaps handing the infant over to a wet nurse – young girls probably played with gendered objects of beauty that they could identify with.

A wet nurse could be a slave or a free woman earning a living by nursing aristocratic infants.[239] The service was often required for two years and contracts were made between the nurse and the biological parents of the infant (if the nurse was not a slave). If the contract was violated, the nurse had to pay back the wages and could be fined.[240] However, as mentioned earlier, epitaphs on grave steles suggest that wet nurses became an important part of the Greek *oikos*, and followed and participated in the child's development until adulthood.[241] Some nurses were even responsible for the total care of the child and early education, and did not end their function as carers after the weaning of the infant, but continued their role until marriage.[242] Research has now proved the human child's early capacity to form attachments to the *actual person* who takes care of it.[243] Biological mothers (and fathers) do not establish themselves as important attachment figures if they are not in a consistent caring relationship with their child. Therefore, there is seemingly no inherent 'blood bond' to ensure connectedness between children and adult biological relatives. Building close bonds and affection grows out of practice. It seems highly likely that the prolonged relationships between wet nurses and children, even sometimes as primary carers for years, as previously mentioned above must have established the wet nurse as the primary 'parent' and attachment figure for such children. If culturally acceptable and practiced and not overruled by the idea of mother-centricity, i.e. that the mother must be the only carer, such types of surrogate arrangements will not have negative consequences for children's short and long term development.

The ancient Greek material record and written sources suggest complex and differentiated feeding traditions in ancient Greece. The aristocratic classes in the Classical period may have used wet nurses as well as the mother herself, who may have nursed the infant. But some written sources and the sparse iconographic evidence does suggest that some high ranking mothers did. Though, it was also believed to be negative if the biological mother was not able to produce milk herself.[244] The lack of maternal milk symbolized a less productive woman, which was considered one of the worst fates of women.[245] Breast milk production is connected to the menstrual cycle so nurses that were either menstrual or pregnant could not be used as wet nurses since it would spoil the milk and thus make it unsuitable for the child.[246] Breastfeeding began the first day after birth and ended after six months. But according to Wileman (2005), some ancient writers suggested that the child should be weaned at the age of 2-3 years, and the iconographic evidence, fig. 8, suggests the same.[247] If the biological mother chose not to breastfeed her own child – perhaps for aesthetical reasons or tradition – she may also have had the option of using a wet nurse or slave until the infant was six months, followed by the use of a feeding bottle (but, fig. 8 does not indicate this).[248]

## The high chair-potty stool and its functions

Besides breastfeeding, small children of course needed other types of care. Training (for example, potty training) was seemingly just as important at that time as it is today. This was in a culture where it was not considered good behavior if children after the toddler stage were still not able to go to the 'right place at the right time'. The history of potty training shows that the ways used to induce the child also reflect basic values in how to treat a small child. For example the shift could happen rather fast: In the 1930's a harsh and disciplinary style was seen, which conformed with the view that the will of the child had to be broken. At that time the following idea was suggested to mothers by a leading Danish pediatrician: "In most cases, with thorough training from birth, one can in reality make the child accustomed rather quickly to a steady and quiet way of living, where everything runs like clockwork and where no untimely screaming betrays that there is an infant in the house".[249] Not surprisingly, Svenn Monrad recommended strict potty training based on strict time-schedules and not on the needs of the baby. Some parents even tied the child to the pot until it has finished. Some decades later

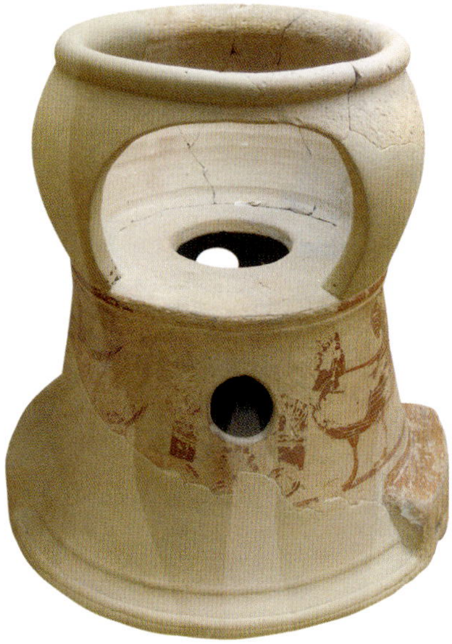

**Fig. 9a.** *High chair-potty stool.* **Fig. 9b.** *Close-up of decorations.*
*From the Athenian Agora, ca. 580 BC.*

this strict training practice was abandoned, which corresponded to more humanistic ideas about the child and its needs.

We do not know what kind of potty training that was practiced in the *oikos* in ancient Attica. But the iconographic evidence, the specific construction and functional use of the ancient potty stool, opens for some inferences. There is little doubt that potty stools were used to habit-train the toddler, as such a stool has been found in the Athenian Agora dating to the 6th century (c. 580 BC) (fig. 9a & 9b). [250] Compared to a contemporary chamber pot this one is much higher. This means that it must have had more functions than potty training: 1) like our present-day chamber pot, and 2) as a high sitting-stool, also like the ones in use today. The higher chair lifts the little child up into a position to 'converse' with adults (see fig. 11). For practical reasons it was probably also used when feeding the toddler. And, what comes in must come out. Observe the round hole in the middle of the seat in fig. 9a. When the naked child sat on the chair the waste matter from his body could drop down to the lower level without causing a mess. This procedure makes the process easy without 'assistance' or pressure from the adult. So, no diaper-changing routines were needed when the child was placed on its stool. Eventually a servant or slave would clean up after the baby. In addition, we can observe on *choes* that small children sitting on their stools usually look happy and engaged, either shaking a rattle or swinging their legs, and perhaps chatting with an adult. This indicates that strict habit-training in the upper classes was not on the upbringing agenda in the *oikos* or at least was not the ideal as inferred from the cultural vase painting message.

The high chair-potty stool (fig. 9) is the only one found in Greece (in a well) and is in many ways of exceptional archaeological value.[251] Therefore a rather detailed archaeological description and discussion of its possible functions will be relevant. The stool measures ca. H. 50 cm. and is around 20 cm. in diameter on the top-bowl, where the child was seated, while the base of the stool is ca. 40-45 cm. in diameter.[252] It fits perfectly to any child of one or two years old. The seat could in principle have been shaped in different ways that would be more or less comfortable to its user. But it has been nicely adapted to the bottom of an infant, indicating some kind of 'child perspective'. With its perfect round forms, the high chair-potty stool is made of pottery drilled by a skilled craftsman and is nicely decorated. If we look closer it has obviously been constructed with a 'belt' to stop the child from falling off. In addition the stool is not constructed 'top-heavy'. The circular, broad base seems sizable and heavy enough – seen in relation to the other proportions of the stool – to prevent eventual tilting should the toddler throw its body energetically from side to side. Should this not be sufficient the two pierced lugs at the base (fig. 9b) have seemingly been used for preventing the stand from tumbling. The small holes seem to show traces of wear on their lower sides which indicates that a rope were threaded through them.[253] These specific constructions are highly interesting because they clearly show certain safety precautions were enforced to protect the child. Deliberate care was taken in ancient Greece to avoid unnecessary harm to young children.

The two round holes in the lower part facilitated lifting, according to Lynch and Papadopoulos in their very detailed description of this high chair-potty stool.[254] In their description of how it could have been lifted and carried we can nearly see it happen: An adult puts two or three fingers in the carrying whole, with the other hand gripped in the rim behind the back of the child and lifted both the stool and the child to another location. This high chair-cum-potty stool cannot have been an incidental construction; clearly there has been expert design behind it, based for example on the previous practical use of high chair-stools and/or knowledge about how small children behave in chairs like these.

No high chair-potty stools have been found from the Classical period. But iconographic evidence clearly shows that this type of stool was also used in the 4$^{th}$ century BC (fig. 10 and 11).[255]

An Attic red-figure *chous* from c. 440-430 BC shows a scene of a male child in a high chair-potty stool (fig. 10).[256] The baby toddler is sitting in a deep bowl placed on a conical base, and his legs stick out allowing free movement. Comparing high chair-potty stools, fig. 9 shows evidence of one large hole for the child's legs, whereas fig. 10 shows two holes in the bowl. But both give the child enough space to allow free movement. Despite this difference, the fig. 10 high chair-stool is quite similar to the real one found in the Agora, and may indicate that the high chair-potty stool on the vase is of the same terracotta type – perhaps a standardized shape. The child is holding a rattle in his hand with a stretched out right arm, looking – from the child's position – to the right. Perhaps gazing at the rattle, or maybe even an unpainted adult? He is surrounded by other boyish artifacts: A *chous* and a toy roller indicating a domestic scene in the *oikos*. The *choes* originates from the Athenian festival of Dionysos, the Anthesteria, where

**Fig. 10.** *Baby boy in his high chair-potty stool waving a rattle. Red-figure chous, 440-430 BC.*

children were given small pint size vases (choes) with pictures of children performing different activities (both of domestic and ritual character).[257]

Another portrait of a child on a high chair-potty stool is witnessed on an Attic red-figure and white-ground stemless kylix from around 460 BC, which depicts a rare 'time frozen' scene of mother and child sitting opposite each other close enough to have a 'conversation'. They are clearly engaged in an activity of mutual social alertness (fig. 11).[258] This scene is filled with developmentally important relationships when a psychological interpretation of body language is used: The gesturing hands of both parties indicate an ongoing one-to-one mutual, social communication. The posture of the child's upper body and the outreaching hands indicate an intention showing a 'pick-me-up' gesture. Here the high chair function is very clear, lifting the child up into a position that facilitates social-exchange communication. In addition, it is observable that the infant's legs are not passively hanging down, but 'moving out-of-synch' with each other, thus expressing motor activity, free movement and agility. Interestingly, though, high chair-

**Fig. 11.** *Toddler in a high chair-potty stool interacts with his mother. Red-figure kylix, Ca. 460 BC.*

potty stools are not, as they in principle could have been, without holes for the legs which could restrict movement, but instead there is enough room for free movement. If, on the contrary, gross motor activity becomes restricted, the sensor-motor active toddler will react with negativity, becoming agitated. The existence of large hole(s) indicates that the spontaneous energetic kicking that is so characteristic of infants and toddlers was welcomed by both the high-chair-potty stool constructors (they deliberately carved out the hole(s) in the clay) and the adults/parents that purchased it (accepting its specific construction) and used it in the *oikos*. Why, we do not know, but perhaps to avoid too much incoherent and negative behavior that disturbed the obvious positive relationships that had also been seen on vase paintings, for example in fig. 11. Here mutual eye-to-eye contact can be observed – a developmentally important, universal human activity between a parent and her child. Focusing on the infant it is evident that he (a boy) is gazing upwards with his head raised slightly backwards. The mother – not looking to the right or left – is looking directly towards her child, smiling.

This kylix was found in a rich grave attributed to a young woman who died before marriage. The kylix was, among other artifacts, found with another kylix also with a depiction of a domestic scene: A woman spinning her top, the two kylices being a set.[259] This sentimentalized mother-and-child scene perhaps shows what the deceased woman never experienced: The joys of motherhood. The mother and child face each other while reaching for one another, and the mother, sitting on a finely carved wooden chair, is clearly smiling at the squirming baby. Despite the fact that this may be a highly romanticized portrait of a mother-toddler relationship, it seems unlikely that an artist has made this scene up as a pure imaginative invention with not the slightest root in reality. The scene looks much too 'realistic' for that and too many details are right. A suggestion here is that actual high chair-potty stool scenes where children are habitually seen together with various female adults besides the mother have, although somewhat idealized, functioned as 'positive relationship prototypes'.

The mother's social status is identified by her fine clothes, which indicate her aristocratic or upper class descent. Therefore we also know that she is not a servant or a slave. The scene is set in a domestic and private context in the *oikos*, which is witnessed by the house-furniture (the wooden chair).[260]

The high chair-potty-stool resembles the design of the one found in the Agora and the one seen in fig. 9, which indicates that a standard type of high chair-potty stool had probably existed. This sentimentalized mother-and-child scene is of great importance and tells seemingly that not all infants in the aristocratic household were solely cared for by nurses. It infers that some aristocratic mothers did nurse and interact with their offspring or at least that this was favored by society. The scene also depicts positive sentiments between mother and child showing that this potty-training-interaction is not (this time) a negative duty for the mother (in contrast to the depiction of the breastfeeding mother on fig. 8). The reasons why nursing mothers are rare in ancient Greek iconography are unknown, yet domestic scenes are in general under-represented in the pictorial context. Domestic scenes may not have been selected since they had no mythical or historical value, or perhaps they were just 'boring' since they depicted 'everyday common life'. The most common depictions on 5$^{th}$ and 4$^{th}$-century BC vases are those of heroes, myths and wars, which contain dramatic scenes, which are more interesting than 'ordinary lifescenes'.[261] So, one possible reason for the lack of domestic scenes may simply be that everyday-life was uninteresting for both the painter and the buyer. One could therefore speculate that vases with domestic scenes were private orders from a specific buyer.[262]

In sum, the 'high chair-cum-potty stool' obviously fulfilled various important caring functions: For example to ease the 'potty training' process; to facilitate social reciprocal exchange in infancy and early toddlerhood. Supportive evidence for the last function is given by Lynch and Papadopoulos.[263] They argue that some high chairs probably were not always potty stools, noting that on a specific lekhytos the child is wearing clothes while sitting in his high chair.[264] Other obvious functions (but not yet evidenced) could be the feeding of the upright positioned child, and with age, the toddler is perhaps allowed to learn how to feed itself? In human cultures self-feeding without spilling too much is a

**Fig. 12.** *A swaddled infant.*
*Attic marble stele, Ca. 375-350 BC.*

necessary skill to reduce the 'many-mouths-to-feed' workload of the adults. Learning the basic hand-mouth coordinative competencies behind this is quite complex and has to be practiced. Growing up in the upper classes of the sophisticated ancient Attic culture probably add specific expectations about how to eat in an aesthetic and proper manner. Perhaps the first steps in this kind of socialization began in the high chair-potty stool? Another possible practical function of the high chair-potty stool could be to keep the child safely seated and located in a particular spot when the adults, responsible for the care of the child, had other necessary domestic duties to perform in the *oikos*.[265]

## Infant swaddling – evidence and explanations

The following section is about the restraining of infants by the tradition of swaddling, which may have affected the high child mortality rates in the Classical population. Swaddling is included in order to give a more complex presentation of child nursing practices and traditions in the ancient Greek household, and the discussions on restrainment and mortality risks should be seen in connection with the previous sections on high child mortality and child activation.

Turning to the evidence, *swaddled infants* occur on grave steles from the Greek past, although in small numbers. The earliest archaeological evidence of swaddling dates to the Geometric period and includes terracotta figurines showing children swaddled in the arms of a female carer.[266] However, representations of swaddled infants from the Classical period do exist. Moreover, the tradition of swaddling is not only an ancient Greek practice, but may have been employed for thousands of years. Today swaddling is still a widely used practice in different cultures around the globe. In present-day Nordic countries swaddling has been exercised until the 18th century but is now an extinct practice. Remarkably, however, in some countries such as USA, swaddling, although not widespread, is still used to some degree to the regret of physicians.[267]

Evidence of swaddling exists on an Attic marble stele from around 375-350 BC (see fig. 12).[268] The child appears to be newborn and is swaddled tightly in clothing with no possibility of moving its arms and legs. The infant's head is not swaddled and it wears no cap as seen on some steles.[269] In general, young infants (newborns) are frequently seen swaddled as tight as in fig. 12.[270] However, older infants are most commonly 'swaddled' lightly for instance in its mother's dress or in a loose blanket with the arms free to move.[271]

Ancient written sources indicate that the practice of swaddling was used only to some extent in the Classical Greek society.[272] Swaddling was believed to straighten the limbs and ensure correct growth of the child. Swaddling would result in good posture and a straight back. However, there was some disagreement as to how long the child should be kept in swaddling clothes. Plato suggests that children should be swaddled up to the age of two and that they should be carried by nurses until the age of 3 years due to the lack of strength in the child's legs.[273] Aristotle recommends that the child should be swaddled as soon as possible after birth to prevent deformations to the infant's body.[274] However, he does not state the length of time the child should be swaddled. Soranus of Ephesus, contrariwise, suggests that the child should be unswaddled after 4 days, depending on physique.[275]

In general, the infant was believed to be helpless and in constant need of care during the first 40 critical days. Massaging the child and wrapping it in woolen clothing was considered to have been the practice in the Greek past.[276] However, it should be stressed that the ancient written sources are all written by men with perhaps no daily contact and knowledge of infants. Therefore it is essential to take the material evidence into account when interpreting cultural practices. When looking at material and iconographic evidence swaddled children do not appear more often than unswaddled. However, it also seems that it is only the youngest infants (newborn) who are swaddled, perhaps indicating that the mother died in childbirth, or to show the age of the deceased child (which perhaps died with the mother).[277] Children after the age of six months do not appear to be swaddled tightly. Older infants can be lightly swaddled e.g. in the scarf of the mother or a nurse.[278] Toddlers are never swaddled, but are engaged in activities like playing and exploring. Swaddling, therefore, can be seen as an age-indicator of the child portrayed on the steles or vases.[279]

Why was swaddling practiced on smaller children in the Classical Greek society? The tradition may have resulted from the necessity for the child to be dormant for a longer period of time. Perhaps the Greeks believed that a quiet infant was a happy child, mistaking passive behavior for calmness and contentedness. Besides the benefits of a sleeping child, another practical function may be attributed to the fact that a child wrapped tightly in clothing did not move, which enabled the carer to do other chores while still having the baby nearby.

A later written source mentions that infants were viewed as being 'plantlike' (a passive organism), and Aristotle addresses infant care in his *Historia Animalium,* placing small children within the animal context.[280] Perhaps when children were old enough to become part of the household, swaddling was no longer necessary,[281] but Plato's statement concerning swaddling to the age of two contradicts this idea, including the fact that a child became a member of the family after two days (or sometimes after 10 days with the name-giving ritual). Important to consider, however, is that Plato gives an idealized portrait of swaddling, and it may have been practiced because of the believed physical benefits (improved growth and straightening of limbs), of which there is no (modern) evidence.[282]

Moreover, the ancient Greeks probably did not realize the possible serious side-effects of the practice. Hyperthermia, if the infant's wrapping cloth is not applied properly in cold weather, or the risk of overheating in warm weather. The latter is not irrelevant when one considers the climate with its hot summers in ancient Attica. Furthermore, there is evidence of respiratory infections related to the tightness of the clothes, and wrapping even increases the risk of SID (Sudden Infant Death).[283] Perhaps therefore the tradition of swaddling contributed to the high mortality rate in the ancient Greek past?

Today swaddling is generally not welcomed and no longer a widespread practice in Western individualistic culture where it is considered an 'old-fashioned' practice. In addition, swaddling does not go well with humanistic and commonsense ideas of self-actualization. When a main goal of upbringing in an individualistic culture, in contrast to a traditional collectivistic culture, is to foster autonomy and an early independent self, then a child must not be constrained but have the right to act freely.[284] The ancient Attic society had many similarities to collectivistic cultures where the ethos of upbringing was predominantly to foster interdependent selves. The next generation, according to the ancient written sources, must not be selfish, but must learn and obey the established cultural customs and practices. 'Being different from' previous customs would be a threat to social order.[285] To 'fit in' by adapting collectivistic rules is expected, and respecting traditions and the authorities are important virtues. Following this line of reasoning it becomes understandable that infants may be perceived as passive moldable organisms (as, for example, fragile plants) and thus swaddling will not be seen as a negative restriction of the child but rather as a protection. As can be inferred from the evidence, the *swaddling period* was short and even infants were activated by adults, as we shall see in the next section. In addition, it does not necessarily have to be either 'swaddled or not swaddled'. As adults and older children probably did not wear the same clothes in the daytime as when sleeping, why should a baby? Although we do not know for sure, on a 24-hour basis there may well have been times when the baby was naked (boys more than girls?), for example unswaddled in order to be washed, and other times when the baby was put into tight clothing by its carers for various unknown reasons.

But what does empirical research tell us about the consequences of swaddling? Recent pediatric studies have shown that children sleep longer, arouse less and the REM-sleep is deeper when swaddled.[286] The infant does not cry as often or as much when wrapped in clothes and is more passive than free-moving infants. Swaddling a crying infant can soothe it and calm it down.[287] Preterm-born infants benefit physically from swaddling and show improved neuromuscular development, better motor organization, more self-regulatory ability and less physical stress.[288]

It can thus be concluded on the basis of various types of evidence that some children were wrapped in cloth in the Classical period, especially newborn infants until the age of six months. Moreover, the iconographic evidence states that children were most likely not swaddled after the age of two, which was recommended by Plato. In addition, infants are not always depicted as swaddled, which leads us to believe that the swaddling tradition was only practiced by some. Research on swaddling shows both the benefits and otherwise for the infant.

## Activating the infant – the rattle and adult-child relationships

The next section will deal with the activation of infants (age 0-1), and should be seen in connection with and as an antithesis to the previous section on swaddling. This section is included to illustrate that children were not only restrained in early years, but were also activated and stimulated by adults, which may have been part of primary nursing in the Classical Greek household. A culture that invested in skilled labor to produce for example rattles, and parents who bought them for their infants, signals some kind of interest in small children. Rattles can be seen as toy objects and can therefore be dealt with in Part 3. But as it can be documented that many rattles were not only used by the infant itself, but by adults and older siblings in order to interest and activate the child, it will be more relevant to discuss the main function of rattles in this section.

Just like today, a favorite Greek toy in ancient Greece was the *rattle*. Rattles were probably made for the youngest children to play with (until the age of 3 or 4). Various types of rattles have been found and are all made of terracotta.[289] As applied to the feeders, no typology or chronology has yet been made, but various types of rattles exist including *the club-shaped rattle*, which is perhaps the most common.

A rattle found in Attica (fig. 13) dated to the Classical period (found in a child's grave dated to this period) is a typical example of a club-shaped rattle.[290] It is white-ground terracotta with perhaps remains of red paint, which indicates decoration. The handle has a hole at the end, perhaps to put a string through, so that the rattle could be worn around the child's wrist to avoid being shattered if dropped in play. This type of rattle is also seen on an Attic *chous* from ca. 440-430 BC (see fig. 10). The club-shaped rattle is also made today and is a favorite toy for young children from the age of 8 months.

Other rattles formed as animals were also common like *the owl-rattle* (fig. 14).[291] It is made from terracotta and has remains of decoration with red paint.[292] It is conical shaped with 'ears' and two holes as eyes, but no beak. The terracotta owl makes a rattling sound when shaken due to the clay pebbles inside. The owl rattle has a handle on

**Fig. 13.** *Club-shaped rattle. Attica, the Classical period.*

**Fig. 14.** *Owl-rattle. Cyprus, ca. 4th century BC.*

its back, where it was probably held by the child. These types of rattles are not seen in iconography.[293]

Larger rattles, for example formed as pigs also existed, but they were too heavy and large for the child to carry and may have been used by the adults activating the infant. Shaking a noisy rattle in front of the child may have been for pure fun, but no matter what the reason the child will start to develop a process of early physical and mental skills. The rattles are attuned to the spontaneous movements of the arms, and the child is rewarded with an instant rattling sound when shaken. This evokes a reaction in the child's brain and mind connecting the movement to the sound of the rattle (action and result). In addition, the rattling sound is important since it stimulates and coordinates vital sensori-motor faculties.[294] This knowledge was not known in the ancient world, although, parents and nurses may have sensed that an active infant was vigorous and looked happy. The club-shaped rattles and miniature figurines were used by children themselves, yet as mentioned some rattles were too big to be used by the child, and were therefore employed by adults.

A pig rattle belongs to this type of *large rattle* (fig. 15).[295] The rattle originates from Cyprus and is dated to the 4th century BC.[296] The pig's body and snout is wheel made, while the ears, legs, tail and spinal ridge are molded by hand. The pig has pierced holes, which prevent the rattle from exploding during firing. It contains either seeds or clay pellets which make a rattling sound when shaken. The diagonal stripes on the body indicate hair.[297] This pig measures H. 7.7 cm. L. 13. 2 cm. Dia. 5. 9 cm. Numerous similar rattles have been found in Cyprus, and indicate the existence of a specific production centre. The size would indicate that the rattle was used by caregivers when playing with and activating the child. Aristocratic children in Classical Attica were thus activated through play from early in life (by mother/father or nurses/pedagogues). This is in concordance with our idea of multiple care in the extended Classical Greek family.

A *chous* from shortly after 400 BC shows a young girl shaking a rattle to a male baby, which may indicate that larger rattles were also used by older siblings to play with the infant (fig. 16).[298]

## Rattling in front of an infant

Rattling in front of an infant is probably just done for fun, getting an enthusiastic response from the infant. Adults (and older children) are in their everyday interaction with infants doing many 'developmentally appropriate' things that they are probably not aware of. This applies also in this case. Rattles, when moved, are producing both visual and auditory stimulation and the developmental function of a rattle is to be an important 'attention attractor'. Perhaps this is why rattles are found in numerous cultures in history, and are still today a preferred activation object in families with an infant. What is going on in the rattling scene on fig. 16? How does the activation influence this infant boy? The answer is obvious: When we cannot even look into the minds of today's preverbal infants, it is a much more difficult thing to do from a scene depicted on a *chous* 2,500 years ago.

In developmental infancy studies, however, there is a well-established tradition for making *inferences* on the basis of observations i.e. that external behaviors can reflect inner states. For example, that a smile (observed in real life or in a picture) correspondents with a feeling of joy and not sadness, anxiety or anger, and that looking at an object as well as reaching out for it is a sign of an inner wish to get it – also called an 'intentional act'. This approach has during the last few decades revolutionized our understanding of the minds of infants. Although they cannot speak they are able to communicate, but they need other people to share meaning with. Contrary to previous thinking that culture does not enter into the minds of children before the development symbolic understanding and language, infants are from the beginning cultural beings.[299] For example, specific objects used in social exchange are culturally made and used with attached meanings and functions.

Maybe this developmental/cultural approach can give important suggestive information (not proof whatsoever) on the 'magical' influence of the act of rattling on an ancient infant boy? If we take a close look at Fig. 16 it can be observed that the little boy is clearly attentive and focused on what is going on. He looks towards the rattle (and his sister) slightly lifting his right arm as if he intends to reach out for it, and at the same time keeping his upright position and balance by supporting his left arm on the table.[300] This Classical period scene proposes that using an activation tool will not only start a chain of coordinated movements and focused attention, but also (assuming that he reaches out for the rattle) can be interpreted as an intentional act. But it has other important consequences as well. From very early in life not only persons but objects are very interesting. When children reach one year old and can sit up they begin to point at *things*. Pointing (and reaching) is a communicative signal to adults. Infants know that they can use other people to get to know more about the world. In the rattling scene the cognitive developmentally important 'eternal triangle' (person-object-person)

**Fig. 15.** *Pig rattle.*
*Cyprus, 4th century BC.*

**Fig. 16.** *Activating her little brother?*
*Girl with rattle.*
*Attic red-figure chous, Ca. 400 BC.*

is enacted: The infant boy and his sister are rehearsing an interaction with the object 'in their middle'. Why is activation and the eternal triangle so important, as humans in essence are active beings, and not a passive object that has to be 'set in motion' by external stimulation? The answer is that if this basic propensity for activity is not nourished by the environment it will fade out. For example, infants with depressed mothers eagerly try to 'activate' their mother by using various gestures and facial expressions. But if they do not get much response in return, sooner or later the infant gives up, looking sad, being unengaged and inactive.[301]

Recent research demonstrates that activation of infants is important, since the lack of contact through human touch and activation can cause severe brain damage, mental sickness or even death if the infant is massively neglected from an early age.[302] This evidence was not known in Classical Attica, although, adult caregivers may have sensed the importance of not only primary nursing (such as breastfeeding and potty-training) but also the active play of the young child. The importance of interaction through play is mentioned by Plato.[303] So, the give-and-take relationships, as well as the emotional regulation functions inherent in social play may have been sensed by Plato.

Not surprisingly, both the material and written evidence clearly contradict the predominant theories of neglect in past societies.[304] Various types of material and iconographic evidence show that children were taken care of, cared for, activated and played with and nursed by primary caregivers. Yet, when it comes to the well-being of the ancient Greek child it is less important, whether it was activated and nursed by the mother or a nurse. As seen on the Attic red-figure and white-ground stemless kylix (see fig. 11), some aristocratic/upper-middle class mothers did in fact engage in infant and toddler interaction, which probably has included playing with the child. The discussion, whether the parents played with their offspring or not is important, since it gives an insight into general parental attitudes towards children in the Classical Attic society. However, this discussion demands better material and iconographic research on parent/child-interactions than that which is available. Moreover, it should be stressed that representations of adults playing with children are sparse and most commonly children are depicted playing alone or with other children (or animals). This may be a result of the art trend of the specific period, where adults and children are often depicted separately (on vases), but it also perhaps shows that children's most common playing partner was not an adult.

## The exploring toddler boy

This section should be seen as a continuing part of child activation and adult/child-interaction in the ancient Greek household. Yet, this section focuses on toddlers aged 1-3, and shows various toddler activities performed in the *oikos*. But why is the human toddler-age the sensori-motor explorative, and spontaneous curiosity period per se? We will answer that question shortly, presenting developmental research about it. This helps us to better understand not only why toddlers in the ancient Greek world are portrayed in a very skilled way crawling, hopping and actively involved with both persons and toys, but also what function such culturally-accepted activity has on their development. In addition, we will also discuss the possible cultural meaning behind portraying the exploring toddler always as a boy and not as a girl.

If we make the 'thought' experiment that a toddler for some reason is not allowed to move around, to crawl, or to walk, what will the result be? We would have a child without the ability to explore the environment on its own and thus have a highly restricted learning milieu; a child without the necessary physical strengths and a delayed sensori-motor development; even a child with inadequate neural and brain development.[305] If, however, toddlers are not greatly restricted in loco-motor and explorative behavior a series of developmental gains will follow. This knowledge is important to carry with us turning to the iconographic evidence of toddlers in Classical Athens. Where do we find them? How are they portrayed?

Toddlers are most often portrayed on choes, vases and steles as active moving beings, caught in the act of 'doing something'. There is rarely any evidence of passivity, stiffness, of fearfulness to be seen here. It is impossible to prove this, but it seems unlikely that the artists could portray toddlers as realistically as they do without having everyday observations as props; or at least when it turns out to be a painting style that could have been inspired and built on living objects. The very way their bodies and limbs are for example caught in the flux of a crawling sequence looks quite realistic to an observer skilled in viewing and decoding the potential meanings of toddler behavior. They are often sitting on the lap of caregivers, crawling on the floor exploring the *oikos* or are interacting with adults, pets, and other children.[306] These scenes are often depicted on choes and should be ascribed a domestic context although the small oinochoes were gifts to children during the Anthesteria festival.[307] Domestic scenes are popular on choes, although sacral child scenes also appear in large numbers.[308] Active toddlers appear on other types of vases like an Attic red-figure pelike from ca. 430-420 BC (fig. 18).[309] Sometimes they are portrayed on their own, sometimes with pets, and other times they are in depicted engaged in social contact with adults.

As mentioned earlier, crawling is a universal and important phase in children's development, as this locomotive activity fulfills various developmental functions. Apparently ancient Greek toddlers were allowed freedom to move around which is witnessed in the substantial material record.[310] Let us take a closer look at the crawling boy on fig. 17: What traces of activity are seen, and what is going on? A rather well-nourished boy can be observed in a 'frozen moment' of locomotion – a picture as it were, cut out of a chain of fine coordinated movements. He is clearly heading forward, leaning and putting weight on his left bending arm and hand, while stretching the right arm in the air with open hand. At the same moment he is leaning on his left leg with the knee firmly on the ground, keeping perfect balance, and with the right leg stretched out. Everybody that has observed a crawling toddler knows that in order to progress he will in the moment to come reverse his body movements, pulling his right arm forward and down, and shifting the position of his legs accordingly.

What is in his mind? Does this boy have a goal, an intention? Or is his crawling just for the pure pleasure of movement? This is impossible to say because we have no direct ancient evidence answering these questions. In addition, even if it was a toddler of today we cannot ask him, because he has not the language capacity to tell us. But, some inferences can be tried out as presented earlier developmental psychologists, skilled in studying 'intentional acts' in the preverbal period, are routinely inferring mind-based intentions and will-power from the observations of infant and toddler behaviors.[311] Without this approach that one can infer from non-verbal behaviors/gestures what is going on in the infant and toddlers minds, the rich and rapidly growing subfield of studies on infant/object permanence, primary/secondary intersubjectivity, preverbal self, cognition and emotion will simply not have existed. Making observation as a basis for mind-reading may also be due here, i.e. what the crawling boy may have in mind, but with one important reservation – that a behavioral sequence as in natural scenes or in film/video is not at hand here. [312] So, with utmost caution, built on the above suggestion that this *chous* depicts a *still-picture of an ongoing locomotive sequence*, a mind-reading will be suggested. Crawling is a locomotively complex, coordinated set of behaviors, and this is not run by a machine or as simple automatic reflexes. Crawling is sometimes just done for the fun of exercising and using the body.[313] At other times and increasingly more when the child grows, crawling becomes a means to get hold of something that the child wants. In other words, the toddler has an intention in his mind, and thereby a motivation to get hold of a wanted object/person either outside or inside the scene. Maybe the boy on fig. 17 is heading for the bird, that is sitting only an arms-length away, ready to grab it with his lifted right hand. On the other hand, his head lifted position and gaze seems to indicate that he is looking further beyond what we can observe on the *chous* scene. Engulfed in his here-and-now joy of movement or in the wish to grab

**Fig. 17.** *A crawling boy (wearing amulets). Attic red-figure chous, Ca. 420 BC.*

**Fig. 18.** *A crawling male toddler with adults. Attic red-figure pelike, Ca. 430-420 BC.*

the bird, this little boy seems to express no fears and worries. Others, however, may worry on his behalf, indicated by his only 'clothing' of protective amulets, worn in a string going around his left shoulder.

What is discernible in the scene in Figure 18? Two adults are shown with a nude male toddler. The female caregiver is making an encouraging gesture towards the child, looking down to him. The child is raised on his arms, looking upwards, and seemingly there is mutual eye-contact. The male standing behind, quite close to the toddler, is leaning forward on a cane seemingly with an enthusiastic expression. This micro-social scene with its three active and engaged figures expresses joy and good feelings at being together. The toddler is clearly placed in the center of the scene with the adults placed on both sides of him. The very presence of an adult male is rather unusual. Most commonly men are not present in depictions of young children exploring or playing.

The scene is of domestic character, which is witnessed by the object hanging on the wall of the 'house'. It is unknown whether the man and the woman are the father and mother or whether it is a pedagogue and a female nurse.[314] However, the fine clothes of the female figure argue for a family scene in an ancient aristocratic household, which makes this pelike a unique object. Scenes, where both mother and father are interacting with their child, are highly unusual. This scene may give a glimpse of family activities and child/parent-interactions in the Classical Greek household, which contradicts the general view of unengaged parents (especially fathers).[315] The scene on the pelike may hint that some parents (and also fathers) did engage in child raising and the daily life of the child.

Earlier we stressed the developmental childhood paradigm about the *active child*. In addition and in line with other studies in childhood archaeology[316], this approach can be an interpretative eye-opener in the study of the material evidence from the Classical period. But even without such a theory at hand it will be quite difficult to see the ancient crawling Greek toddler (boy) as a passive organism after having collected and reviewed the material evidence. This evidence clearly points to a toddler that was not restrained like some infants, but was considered to be an active being. It also indicates that older infants, toddlers and children were allowed to move freely, exploring the household and engaging in relationships with adults. These adult/child interactions are important in the understanding of child conditions in the Greek Classical period. The child seems to have been encouraged to crawl, walk and explore its surroundings, which may indicate that (some) children had enough space, and a relative stable and safe environment to grow up in.[317]

In sum, vase iconography strongly suggests that (some) aristocratic families, were engaged in little boys sensor-motor development i.e. through crawling exercises. Parents also were engaged in activating and amusing their child using various toy objects. Toddlers, especially males, were shown active, explorative moving ahead and/or engaged in things. A gendered norm probably signaled by these portraits on choes.

## Sibling relationships

Research on socialization and caretaking practices until recently in psychology has focused on parents and their care of children (especially maternal care, because of Freudian theories of mother/child bonding). Care taking and socialization done by siblings and other kin members has been left out.[318] But this is far from the case now in child psychology. In this book siblings have until now been mentioned quite a lot, but only 'en passage'. Now it is time to look at that special relationship more in depth. This section will deal with sibling relationships in the Classical Attic household, with a focus on sibling play and caretaking. Sibling relations are examined to show that children were not only taken care of by parents, slaves and nurses but also by older children in the family. Sibling care may once again emphasize the practice of complex alloparenting care in ancient Greece. Considering the many births, and also the high degree of early deaths, a great number of children managed to survive in the long run. A typical family, therefore, most probably consisted of many siblings of both sexes and of various ages, sleeping in the same household, dining together, playing, and perhaps quarreling.[319] Looking after a younger sibling was also expected. Golden tells us about the nature of sibling relationships. He points to the older brothers' responsibility towards their younger siblings: "As for roles related to birth order, older brothers were expected to look out for the younger siblings".[320] The phrase 'expected' implies that parents who told their older son 'to look out for' a younger one (and not vice versa) must have held the view that with age a child's responsibility grows.

Unfortunately, apart from the use of written sources, archaeological studies on relationships between siblings in ancient Greece are very sparse. Few articles have been published, for example about the ties between sisters and brothers, not least concerning young children. No study whatsoever has built on recent sibling research, but are

**Fig. 19.** *Brothers.*
*Attic red-figure chous, Ca. 420 BC.*

all locked into old Freudian one-sided theorizing.[321] According to this thinking there are only negative consequences in having a sibling: Being jealous of the newcomer and rivaling for the favor of the parents all through childhood and adult life. In some instances this happens, but recent research has evidenced several developmental gains as well. This new paradigm in sibling research has revealed somewhat other, more positive consequences of having a sibling. Siblings do things together that they do not do with adults. For example, a child as young as one-and-a-half years old can be drawn into joyful role and fantasy play together with an older sibling, or the two children can share some happy moments just playing with toys (fig. 19 and 20). In fact depictions of siblings together on *choes* are usually very positive, with happy expressions.

As will specifically be discussed in Part 3: 'The functions and meanings of play', there is ample evidence that young children played with their peers in ancient Attica and moreover, that peer-play has important developmental consequences, as seen for example in role play, where older companions/play-mates can function as 'identification objects', from whom the younger child can also acquire knowledge. The same applies for sibling relationships.[322] This is important, because in some instances the age gap between adults and children is so great that learning and understanding may become difficult, especially when the adults are not very child oriented. In such instances the young sibling may learn better from the older one. If the age gap is not too big an older sibling can represent the 'zone of proximal development', meaning just ahead of the child's actual development. Older siblings, then become efficient potential socializing

**Fig. 20.** *Brothers.*
*Attic red-figure chous, Ca.425 BC.*

agents for their younger brothers and sisters growing up in culture and society.[323] As we shall soon see, older siblings were seemingly involved with younger siblings.

Research has shown that especially in rural cultures and in past societies sibling and kin care-giving was practiced in order to help parents with the load of having many children.[324] Sibling care is characterized by being:

1. Activities that include independent care of a child by an older sibling.
2. The performance of specific tasks for another child under the supervision of an adult or older child.[325] This may include verbal or other explicit training and upbringing practice (e.g. correction of a child's behavior) or just keeping an eye on a younger sibling.

In Classical Attic households older siblings have seemingly been used as carers in some way or another.[326] One could argue that aristocratic children were only to a lesser extent used as carers, since the household already employed nurses and slaves. Yet, middle class and poor families may have used older siblings as carers for younger siblings, when parents were doing chores or working (e.g. in the fields, in the markets etc.).[327]

However, it is very reasonable to believe that siblings in all types of households used each other as play companions. Iconographic evidence on vases suggests that siblings were in close contact and played together until older brothers and sisters were placed in another household through marriage.[328] The pictorial evidence on vases shows siblings playing together in the household and it also reveals that siblings played across age groups, as for example evidenced on the previously mentioned *chous* on fig. 16. Besides showing the girl and infant boy playing, the *chous* also shows another boy. Behind the infant boy, another sibling (perhaps an older brother) is seen playing with a toy roller. The scene seems to have been located in the *oikos* (witnessed by the furniture in the 'room') and it is not unlikely that it shows three siblings of different ages and gender engaging in play.

Same gender play, for example among brothers is also portrayed. On a *chous* from ca. 420 BC, an older boy and his little brother are seemingly playing together with a toy roller (fig. 19).[329] On a *chous* from ca. 425 BC, the ball game *passé-boule* may be seen played between two male siblings, an older and a younger brother (fig. 20).[330] Depictions of siblings playing together are also seen on grave steles,[331] which also show important cross-gender relationships in ancient Greece. All in all these scenes help us to make a fair conclusion that siblings obviously played together and that older brothers and sisters played with their younger siblings. It is not evident, however, whether children had actual playmates outside the household or if children were mostly limited to playing within the household. But Plato mentions that *children who meet play together, and that children prefer to play with other children than alone.*[332] This statement might indicate that children from inside and outside the household came together to play.[333] If children were sometimes allowed to go outside in the streets near the *oikos,* it would be highly likely that they met playmates there. Depictions on choes also suggest that play took place both in the *oikos* and outside the household. It may be reasonable to believe however that depictions of children playing in the *oikos* are siblings, since evidence does not specify that children took playmates home to play. Anthropological observations of play indicate that children (if possible) play and drift around together in larger 'packs', with the older children minding them.[334] Children often divide into 'packs' of specific age-groups, and even though cross-age play exists, children prefer to play with children of their own age or within a range of 1-3 years. Interestingly this has also been observed by Plato.[335]

Besides being playmates, siblings may, as mentioned earlier, have taken on the *role as carers*. High child-mortality societies, also with mothers in danger of dying, often have multiple caregivers, and often an older sibling attends to younger siblings when in need of care. Sibling care is practiced in almost all societies and varies from being full-time care to simply looking after a younger sibling.[336] However, it must be noted that the care of siblings only occurs if the organization and structure of the culture and family foster this role.[337] Socialization may happen between the older and younger siblings when engaging in care interactions: The older care-giving children must try to understand the complex social rules and norms created by adults, while they must also correctly interpret the behavior and demands of the child for whom they are responsible of.[338] Research shows that older care-giving siblings do not necessarily copy their parents' upbringing practice, but create their own care-giving styles.[339] This means that younger siblings may not only be socialized by the parents (adults), but also by older children.[340] It also means that the older siblings get an opportunity to learn and practice adult-like functions, and are thereby socialized into a specific role for their future life: The role of parent. Sibling care-giving is more widely practiced in households with five children or more, and care practice changes with the increased number of children i.e. more children means more is expected from older brothers or sisters.[341] These duties besides being of gender specific socialization, may have taught children about social responsibility. It has been suggested that among siblings infant interaction may generalize to interaction with peers and adults for pro-social behaviors, yet the evidence is weak.[342] Yet, some researchers believe that children who become a part of child rearing from an early age develop more social maturity.[343]

It is difficult to conclude whether children, besides playing, took part in the care of other children, since no precise archaeological evidence exists from ancient Athens. However, by looking at anthropological studies of sibling interaction in pre-industrialized and past societies, one may get an insight into the care-giving practices of ancient Greece.[344] It is likely that girls in particular helped with the rearing of younger siblings, and thereby practiced their future role as a mother. Boys may also have helped with child minding until school-age, while the boy was restricted to the *gynaikontitis* (after the age of 7, boys dined in the *andron* with the father and older male siblings).[345] If children engaged in child care from an early age, one could surmise that sibling ties were strong in the Classical Attic household. Siblings are also portrayed together on grave steles, perhaps indicating the bonds between brother and sister (or sister/sister and brother/brother) also after death. However, these close bonds could also result in fights over dowries and inheritance later in life.[346]

Sibling relationships actually last longer in life than the relationship to parents. In general, siblings in ancient Attica may have developed close relationships through childhood and into adult life, since they played together and took care of one another in the early years.[347] In addition, siblings may have engaged in special care relations, which created a 'cross-socialization'. The older child learned about child rearing, future expectations and gained social responsibility, while the younger child was socialized in a multiple alloparenting care system, where older brothers and sisters probably also influenced the behavior of the younger sibling and were involved in his/her upbringing. To what degree were siblings carers? We do not know, but keeping the many potential carers and socializers in the *oikos* in mind, it is unlikely that older siblings were alone with the caring responsibility. Seemingly there was also time for having fun, as proposed by the iconographic evidence of playing siblings.

### The religious world of the child – sacral actions and socialization

In Classical Greece the religious dimension in life penetrated nearly everything – an 'atmosphere' as given as the air you breathe. This fact is so important, and as we shall soon elucidate had such an impact on the next generation that the term *sacral socialization* will now be introduced in order to explain this phenomenon.[348] The research literature about religious and spiritual socialization and development has been quite sparse when it comes to 'our children', i.e. 0-7 year olds living in ancient Attica. But in more general terms there is relevant theorizing and research about 'learning religion', 'religious and spiritual development', 'children as religious resources' and 'magical and religious thinking in children'.[349]

Rites and sacral activities were recurrently scheduled and were highly regarded cultural activities. Religion, by participation in sacred ceremonies in the city, was the main avenue for children into the life of the *polis*.[350] Important to stress, however, is that the sacral universe was not constrained to special sacred places and temples outside the domestic sphere; it was also closely connected to the family and the house. Children were not excluded from this; on the contrary they were involved and had important roles as well. So, religion was so important that the next generation from early in life became involved:

> "That families are so often involved in cult activities of one kind or another is another index of its importance. Some of these revolved around the children themselves" (Golden 1990, 30).

For example, the family could together sacrifice a bull or a ram to the gods. Or, at Athenian wedding ceremonies a boy, crowned with thorns and ahorns, went around among the guests offering small pieces of bread from a basket that resembled a baby's cradle. A symbolic indication, indeed, that marriage is expected to be followed by having children.

The socialization of young children mainly took place in the *oikos*. In this section we will use the concept *sacral socialization,* because religious upbringing was an important part of the next generation's enculturation process. Children were obviously involved in many recurrent activities and were taught how to behave in actual sacral rites, and learn to understand the myths and religious meaning behind these rites. However, keeping in mind the definition of socialization presented in the introduction, the child is not a passive receptor of the sacral environment. As mentioned even young children were active participants in, for example, religious rituals specially made for them. In addition, the material evidence shows that *miniature toy altars were actually in the oikos* and probably in the very hands of children. This opens for discussion that miniature altars could have been used in imaginary play where children enacted various sacral themes and rites. If so, through 'sacral play' the child is enacting its sacral self-socialization. But even before that the child is supposed to have gained important experience of the sacral world because the adults were enacting important rituals on the behalf of the child.

So, perhaps hard to imagine in our relatively secular times, religious and sacral rituals were extremely important in Classical Attica. The sacral world saturated nearly all parts of daily living and gave meaning to it. Even before birth, the child was the center of sacral rituals conducted to ensure the well-being of the unborn child and to protect the mother-to-be during childbirth. Mothers made offerings to the most common goddesses of childbirth, Eileithyiai and Artemis.[351] During birth midwives helped the mother to a quick and safe delivery by physical aid and by chanting spells that would protect woman and child from evil.[352] When the child was born it was influenced by sacral rituals including rites-of-passage acts from the very start. After birth it was included in sacral welcoming rituals after the proclaiming of the gender by the midwife after the physical inspection of the newborn.[353] If the household *Kyrios*, the father, chose to keep the child instead of exposing it, a series of welcoming rituals were carried out. First, the gender of the child was shown by hanging objects on the doorway of the new baby's home: Wreaths of olive branches for a boy and garlands of wool for a girl.[354]

After five or seven days (when the most dangerous and critical days of the infant were over) the so-called *amphidromia* took place. Aristotle gives an insight into this welcoming-ritual, and tells that the family, with the father in front, carried and ran around with the child inside the house and around the hearth of the *oikos*, where the child was officially welcomed to the family.[355] That the father in fact held the baby in his arms, presumingly with body contact, and ran around with it in the rooms of the house is a strong indication that he – as the head of the house – had accepted the child. After finishing the ritual he probably handed the child over to its primary caring person. Besides the father, the baby's siblings were participating in the event as well as the mother and grandparents. So it was what we can call a real family event praising the newcomer. Were others participating in this? This is not clear, but a later source mentions that the particular women, who were involved in the delivery of the child, washed their hands before the-running-around-the-hearth-ritual was conducted.[356] The meaning of this purifying action is unclear; perhaps it was a symbolic statement of starting afresh in welcoming this particular baby? Although the *amphidromia* was a family event it was culturally widely accepted, and was a well-known festive occasion where relatives sent presents. After the 'running around' ritual a sacrifice and a banquet was held, where family members, relatives and midwives participated.[357] In the ancient Greek society with ever threatening infant deaths, short average life-span, and many lost in wars, reproduction, (and thus newborn babies), was very important. It may well be the background behind such celebrations and how they should be understood, involving not only the family but external relatives as well. There seems to be little doubt that after such celebrations the newcomer was an accepted part of the family.

If the family was poor the child was name-given on the same occasion (*amphidromia)*, but rich families had a name-giving ritual on the tenth day called *dekatê.* How the dekatê-ritual was carried out is unknown, yet it is evident that this occasion also was festive.[358] The *amphidromia* and *dekatê* may tend to be reminiscent of the Christian ritual of baptizing, where the child is also name given and introduced as a child of God. However, this ritual included a tour around the house and a welcoming-act around the hearth of the house, which was the sacral heart of the *oikos*.[359] The infant was not brought into the religious world of God, as in the Christian baptizing-ritual, but into the family.[360] Apparently, neither the *amphidromia* nor the dekatê ritual appears in ancient Greek art.[361]

During the first years of a child's life other rituals took place, such as introducing the infant to the goddess that ensured the safe delivery and life of the child.[362] After a successful birth, healthy infants were perhaps brought to Artemis sanctuaries to be presented and to give thanks to the goddess for her aid. This is witnessed on a dedicatory relief from Echinos from the fourth century BC. The marble relief shows a mother presenting a lightly swaddled infant with raised arm to Artemis (fig. 21).[363]

**Fig. 21.** *Mother presents her baby to Artemis.*
*Drawing of votive relief from Echinos, 4th century BC.*

The mother has brought slaves that carry sacrificial gifts to Artemis e.g. fruit, cakes, incense and an ox meant for slaughter. It is likely that mothers, in addition to the pre-birth sacrifice of clothing to Artemis, would come back with her new offspring to offer thanks by performing an animal sacrifice. After the thanking-visit to female sanctuaries, the infant was introduced to another rite-of-passage ritual: Within the first year of birth, the infant (both sexes) was included and registered into its fathers *phratry* during the three-day festival of *Apatouria*, which was a public festival held annually in October/November by the Athenians. An animal sacrifice was made by the father to either Zeus Phratrios or Athena Phratria, where the father also swore the legitimacy of the child.[364] Later there was a feasting and this ritual was also a festive event.[365] No specific depictions of this ritual exist perhaps with the exception of an archaic relief found on the Athenian Acropolis.[366]

At the *age of three* children joined the religious and public sphere through the festival of *Anthesteria*. The Anthesteria was a Dionysian festival held in early spring (February), and the second day was the so-called *choes*-day, the day of children.[367] Children from the age of three participated in this religious event, which included play and games for children, cart racing, and the chance to drink wine for the first time.[368] The festival also included a drinking contest, where the winner won a cake.[369] Children were given small *choes* with wine, which they were allowed to take home. These *choes* are apparently found often in child graves, which indicates that they were held dear to the child.[370] The iconography on *choes* is the best source of information regarding children's activities during play and in daily life, it is also showing specific ages in ancient Athens, from crawling babies and toddlers to adolescent boys playing with balls or knucklebones. Younger children are most often seen on small *choes*, while older adolescent children are

**Fig. 22.** *Father swings his son while brothers are watching. Attic red-figure chous, Ca. 425 BC.*

seen on larger *choes or oinochoes*, and boys are more frequently represented than girls. Various scene types exist on *choes*, both sacral and domestic, both in connection to the Anthesteria-festival and without any link to the Dionysian theme. Most *choes* date from the last half of the fifth century BC and the early-fourth century BC.[371] Another type of ritual that may be connected to the Anthesteria-festival is the swinging-ritual *Aiora*, where children are pushed on a swing by their father.[372] This scene is depicted on a choes painted by the Eretria painter from around 435-420 BC (fig. 22).[373]

This rare scene shows a father about to place his son on a swing, or perhaps he has already started to push the swing, holding the son with both hands. The scene is also a social scene, with two older brothers to the left watching and, to the right, perhaps the grandmother.

Perhaps this ritual was a part of the introduction to the religious public sphere or perhaps it was a private religious event happening in the *oikos*. It may however, have been connected to the ritual of *Aiora* (means swinging), which was associated with the myth of the young girl Erigone's suicide.[374] Apparently the girl committed suicide after her father was wrongly accused and killed in an unfair dispute. The swinging ritual was perhaps a purification ritual carried out to appease the ghost of Erigone, and this myth and ritual has been closely connected to the Dionysiac festival of Anthesteria.[375] When children joined festivals, they may have also joined the city's rites as adulescent equals and as

**Fig. 23.** *An extended family.*
*Votive marble stele from Brauron, Ca. 450-400 BC.*

the representatives of a specific family.[376] Cult activities may have brought children into community life, preparing them for their future roles. This may have been the case with both boys and girls, yet, girls could have held stronger positions in the sacral world.

The ritual life of ancient Greek girls might well have been richer than that of boys.[377] Girls could serve many different roles and were not restricted to serving only one goddess.[378] The various sacral roles differed according to the traditions of worship of specific goddesses. [379] Girls would carry out different religious roles and titles, often starting from the age of seven, which is mentioned in Aristophanes' play 'Lysistrata'.[380] It tells that a girl served as Arrephoroi at the age of seven, and at the age of ten as a religious servant for Athena (grinding corn as Aletris), before serving as Bear for Artemis in the festival of Brauronia. Girls may have served as Arktoi during the Artemis Brauronia festival from the age of three, but there is no iconographic evidence to support this idea. However, the function of the 'she-bear' only happened during the festival, and perhaps younger girls before the age of seven served other functions than that of the dancing she-bear in the sanctuary.[381]

During excavations of the Artemis Brauronia sanctuary several statues of infants and young children were found, including toys, which may have been offered as votives before the day of marriage.[382] The sanctuary may have functioned mainly as a female cult, where young adolescent girls were engaged in rites-of-passage. These girls had probably donated their toys when coming of age and moving into adulthood. Furthermore, maybe the cult was also used as part of sacral birth-acts, where both

**Fig. 24.** *A family joined in a sacrifice ritual. Votive relief, Ca 350 BC.*

pre-natal and post-natal rituals may have been carried out.[383] The numerous family votive reliefs found at the sanctuary are very interesting, however, indicating that the Artemis Brauronia cult may also have been a family cult centered on children. These reliefs date mainly from the second half of the fourth century, and show families sacrificing to Artemis. The reliefs are dedicatory votives and some of them still bear the inscriptions of the dedicator(s).

A fragmented marble votive relief is seen dating from around 450-400 BC (fig. 23).[384] The scene shows a family of seven adults and one child (more people may have appeared on the relief, but are not preserved on the fragments) approaching Artemis standing with her deer. There are four adult women, one adult man, two adolescent boys and what appears to be one female child. The adults are making a gesture towards the goddess, while the girl holds out a ball or a piece of fruit. The round object may very well be a ball since balls are found among toys sacrificed to the goddess, and statues of children holding a ball have also been found.[385] This relief perhaps shows a rites-of-passage scene, where a girl disclaims her favorite toy (in this instance a ball) to move into adulthood. However, the girl seems to be too young to be in the marrying-age. So perhaps families and children are sacrifying toys to ensure a healthy childhood for children in the family? This protective-sacrificial-ritual is perhaps also seen on other votive reliefs from the Artemis Brauronia sanctuary. Another example is seen on a marble votive relief from 350 BC (fig. 24).[386]

**Fig. 25.** *A family joined in a sacrifice ritual. Votive relief, Ca. 340 BC.*

**Fig. 26.** *Three generations. A family with children and grand-children. Votive relief, Ca. 350-330 BC.*

The scene shows a family of worshippers, which has just reached the sanctuary to sacrifice a goat to Artemis. The goddess with her favorite deer is seated on a rock, while a young man (probably a slave) leads a goat for sacrifice. He is followed by the members of the family and one servant bearing a box on her head. Three children are seen on this relief: Two small boys and an adolescent girl. One of the small boys is in front of the family, while gazing respectfully at the goddess. This may once again show a family-sacrificial scene, where the family makes an animal sacrifice to ensure the well-being of their offspring.[387]

Another marble relief is seen dating to 340 BC (fig. 25).[388] The scene depicts the family of Lycoleon advancing towards an altar in front of the Apollonian Triad to sacrifice a bull. At the right of the altar stands Artemis holding a torch, who is accompanied with her mother Leto and her brother Apollo. A young man (a slave) leads the bull for sacrifice. Lycoleon, his wife Peisis and their four children follow along with a nurse and a servant who carries a box on her head covered with cloth. The group of children consists of two boys and two girls. The girls are the oldest and seem to be in early adolescence, while the boys are smaller perhaps between the age of eight and five. All the children are turned towards the goddess showing her proper respect. Most commonly families are seen with children of their own, but an exception is the unique votive relief of Antiphates that dates between 350-330 BC (fig. 26).[389] This scene depicts the family of Antiphates moving towards Artemis to sacrifice a bull. On the left Artemis is seen with her deer and she is depicted in front of the altar wearing the characteristic attic peplos, while holding a phiale and a bow. A young man (a slave) leads the bull for sacrifice. Antiphates, his wife Aristonike, the rest of the family with children *and* grand-children follow with a slave carrying a box on her head.

It is quite unusual to see three generations on dedicatory votives and the Antiphates-relief is one of a kind.[390] This scene may once again show that the ancient Greek family consisted of several family members and cross-generational carers. These dedicatory votive reliefs indicate that not only young girls and mothers-to-be made sacrifices in the Artemis Brauronia, but that the whole family participated in rituals together. Perhaps the rituals had apotropaic values and were carried out to ensure health and security of the smallest members of the family, children.[391]

Family visits to sanctuaries may have had socializing values and sacral visits may have been a way to show children appropriate behavior. As mentioned earlier in this section, the term *sacral socialization* was suggested and implemented on the specific type of child, socialization happening through sacral acts, for example sacrifices, visits to sanctuaries, and festival-participations. It is likely that sacral events in children's lives in the Classical period have been of a socializing character. Besides family visits to sanctuaries to sacrifice animals or items to the deities, as witnessed on reliefs, dedicatory child statues may also have been part of the sacral socialization of children. Marble statues of children were placed in several sanctuaries in Attica in the Classical period, and they were dedicatory statues commemorated by rich parents.[392] Many of the preserved statues are from the late Classical/early Hellenistic period, and all age-groups are represented including both sexes.[393] The statues are almost always made of marble, and are what can be called 'life-size'.[394] Girls are always dressed, boys are often naked or semi-naked, and children above the toddler-age are most often standing. As mentioned in the introduction, the statues are anatomically-correct, and show increased

**Fig. 27.** *A crawling infant.*
*Dedicatory marble statuette, early 4th century BC.*

awareness and general understanding of human anatomy. Infants are frequently seen sitting or crawling, and typically have plump bodies. A marble statue of an infant/ toddler boy from early 4$^{th}$ century BC found in Brauron is an example of a votive statue of the youngest group of children (fig. 27).[395]

This baby boy is clearly smiling, and if we observe the positions of the remaining legs and arms and 'add' the missing limbs this vigorous boy is obviously portrayed crawling forward, exploring his surroundings. Supporting this impression is that his head is held in a lifted position with open eyes that makes him focus ahead. Although not totally naturalistic, his strong crawling style, happy expression, intent on making headway with coordinated movements, reminds one of a present-day toddler engaged in his environment. Toddlers are not just sculptured 'real toddlers' by an ancient sculptor, they bear a more or less underlying cultural message as well. Beyond its obvious sacral connotations, what meaning does such a portrait convey? One answer may adhere to the strictly gendered Classical Greek culture and society. Male and female roles in adult life (and before that) were very different in ancient Greece. Males were expected to be involved not only in social life outside the family, but also in gymnastics, sports and, not least, war. In sum a readiness to 'act, compete and concur' was an essential and necessary part of male identity. This interpretation is supported by the fact that the crawling toddler always is a boy, as scarce evidence exists of crawling toddler girls.

Small children are often not seen 'as they actually are', but rather in the perspective of the adult. Adult's perceptions of children vary considerably in time and place, but the tendency to see children from 'in the eye of the beholder' is, and has been, profound.[396] The relationship between polarized gender values and the different treatment, socialization and systematic education of older girls and boys in Classical Greece has been determined.[397] But the sharp division of the nature of the two sexes probably influenced the perceptions as early as the toddlerage. Thus, seeing some basic qualities of the 'future

**Fig. 28.** *A sitting infant.*
*Dedicatory votive statue, early 4th century BC.*

man in the toddler' may likely have influenced the adult construction of the activity-driven Classical Greek male toddler: Even before he can walk he is the eager and happy explorer. Realistically or not, probably being an idealized portrait, this may reflect a cultural child-norm that free movement and the will to act is appreciated in boys.

The boy looks a bit like a miniature adult, which is normal in this period of time. Infant statues look *more naturalistic* by the second half of the 4th century BC.[398] Another votive statue, which dates from the same time, shows a sitting, chubby infant (or toddler) (fig. 28).[399] These statues of infants may once again indicate that the youngest children were also brought to sanctuaries with their families.

Older children until the age of nine are still shown as being chubby and soft, while children beyond the age of nine have bodies that look adolescent.[400] Numerous and various types of child statues have been found at the Artemis Brauronia sanctuary, which once again may underline the importance of children in the cult.[401] An example is a marble statue, which shows a semi-nude boy from the last part of the 4th century BC (fig. 29).[402] The boy is holding a ball and a dove, which are typical child-objects, while his himation is slung over his left forearm. He has a chubby little tummy, which may indicate that he is under the age of nine. Statues of girls are also found; a head of a marble statue of a girl dating to the end of the 4th century shows this (fig. 30).[403] The girl's hair is styled according to the fashion of the specific period and she is smiling in a cute childish way. This type of smile is evident on almost all round-statues of children in

**Fig. 29.** *A boy with ball and himation. Dedicatory votive statue, late 4th century.*

**Fig. 30.** *A smiling girl. Marble head, late 4th century.*

this sanctuary, and may indicate that smiling children were treasured. Dedicatory votive child statues are also found outside the sanctuary of Artemis Brauronia, and perhaps they were a common feature in the sculptural program in so-called family-sanctuaries.

There is also an example of a statue found outside of Brauron, which shows a seated girl dating from 340-330 BC (see fig. 64).[404] The girl wears a short-sleeved chiton with straps that are crossing her breast with a medallion in the middle. She holds a dove in her right hand (the left arm is missing), which is resting on her knee. The bird is once again seen in connection with a child, and is a typical pet (and child object) in the Classical period. These statues may have been part of sacral socialization. Based on the recording of find locations of child statues in the sanctuary of Artemis Brauronia, it is evident that child statues were tending to be placed in areas with great visibility.[405] In addition, all statues show children that are attractive in appearance and behavior, with smiling faces, perfect hairstyles and beautifully arranged clothing. Children are often engaged in typical child activities such as playing with balls or pets, which is also seen on grave steles and on vases.[406] Dedicatory statues were placed in sanctuaries for various reasons, but these reasons are not always evident in the epigraphical record.[407] Perhaps, they were dedicated to pray for the health of children-to-come or perhaps in gratitude for a successful childbirth, or they may have been sacral 'requests' for the continuing health and safeguarding of children already in the family. Statues could also have been commemorated during a specific festival. Plato states in *Laws* that children from the age of three, and until they reach the age of six, should congregate in village temples.[408] At the same time they should be kept in order and retrained from bad behavior by their nurses, who themselves also should be supervised. In Plato's ideal state, children should visit temples, probably as part of a socializing process (which he also believes play is), to get acquainted with sacral costums.

It is very likely that real children came across these child statues that showed model child behavior, since they were often placed in areas of great visibility. Child statues may indirectly convey the message of how to behave to children near and around temples and sacral places, i.e. with great respect, and happy smiling faces.[409] Child statues in sanctuaries may have demonstrated the expectations of adults when it came to their offspring and other children in the Classical Attic community, and children visiting sanctuaries with parents during sacrifices were expected to behave in the manner the statues exemplified. Statues may therefore in this regard have played a great part in implementing the correct and appropriate behavior on children. Child statues were perhaps active elements in sacral socialization by teaching children (indirectly) the ideal and proper behavior tolerated for their age.[410] Whether or not this ideal-child-behavior plan actually succeeded is unknown, yet the iconographic evidence on, for example, vases suggests that childish and 'uncontrolled' behavior was also a known side of children.[411]

To sum up, it can be concluded that children were both influenced by and actively engaged in sacral rituals from an early age:

1. Expectant mothers seemingly performed pre-natal sacrifices to specific female deities e.g. Artemis, Eileithyiai and Demeter to ensure a successful birth.
2. After the birth of the child, the gender was announced by the midwife, and gender specific decorations were hung over the doorway to the *oikos*.
3. If the child was accepted by the *Kyrios*, then the so-called '*amphidromia* welcoming ritual' was held on the fifth or seventh day and performed by the household family. This ritual included running around the house with the baby, followed by the delivering of gifts from relatives and a feast. The baby was now a part of the family.
4. If the family was from the upper class, a name-giving ritual was held on the thenth day, the so-called '*dekatê*', which was also a festive occasion.
5. Next, the child was annexed and introduced to its father's phratry in the autumn of the same year the child was born. It then became part of a brotherhood/ specific family tree.
6. At the age of three, the child was first introduced to festivals during the Dionysian festival Anthesteria. On the second day, children were given presents in the form of miniature oinochoes called *choes*, and different children's games were played. The child was now allowed to drink wine, and it was now part of the public and sacral community.
7. After the age of three, girls were probably annexed into different sacral roles in various sanctuaries, e.g. as she-bear at Artemis Brauronia. Boys were re-introduced to the phratry at the age of 14-16.

Besides these well-known rituals, children may have been brought to sanctuaries on a weekly basis with the mother and female nurses.[412] These rituals/religious traditions of the family may have been an important part of socializing ancient Greek children. It was recommended by Plato that children were brought to temples from the age of three, but iconographic evidence suggests that even infants were brought to sanctuaries to thank a goddess for a successful childbirth.[413] The sacral world of the child was probably rich and manifold, and in close connection to the family.[414] It included several rituals and traditions during childhood ranging from visits to different temples for thanksgiving and protective sacrifices, to participating in festivals and performing rites-of-passage rituals when coming of age. The annexation of small children into the sacral sphere of Attic society may have ensured the family and society correct religious socialization. The younger the children were, the easier it would have been to teach them accepted behavior and *sacral responsibilities*. Sacral obligations became familiar to children at an early age, and ensured the continuation and reproduction of ancient Greek polytheistic religion, rituals and festivals. Sacral socialization may not only have been a socialization process connected to the family. It was probably also connected to a societal socialization, where Attic society ensured the correct religious education of children through family visits to sanctuaries and participations in rituals. This may have been an advantage and a necessity for the Classical Attic society in ensuring the continuity in and fulfilment of sacral responsibilities by the next generation: The children.

# PART 3

# YOUNG CHILDREN'S PLAY AND TOYS

## The functions and meanings of play – a brief history

How does children's play become a legitimate archaeological subject? Well, first archaeology has to consider children as an important object of study – and although sparse in comparison to archaeology for adults this subject has grown in the last few decades. Thus, special worlds for children and their special activities have to be conceptualized. For example, Lillehammer (2000), dealing with the theoretical perspectives of how to study children in archaeology, introduces interesting ways of grasping what the world of children is. Although related to the world of adults, i.e. adults secure the survival of infants and small children, the two worlds are clearly separated. Children are occupied in 'doing' things that adults do not usually engage in. More generally this has consequences for how to deal with the material culture. Lillehammer: "A (…) radical approach is to develop the contrast between the world of adult and the world of children as a method for exploring the archaeological record".[415] Children sometimes use objects as adults do, for example eating soup with a spoon. But other times objects are handled in a specifically 'childish' manner that would not be expected of adults. In addition, young children are spontaneously engaged in play, even without using objects as props. Play also demands 'space' (both culturally and physically) in order to exist. As a consequence the archaeological study of (young) children's play becomes a legitimate matter of study in itself.

Play seems to be universal among mammals, and homo-sapiens are no exception.[416] Play in humans is extended and dominates our impression of the juvenile period, because children have so much to try out and learn.[417] So, the urge to play is a fundamental drive in humans with important developmental functions, although it is the cultural and historical conditions of a child's life that regulate whether there is a room for play or not. Harsh environments, for example hard child labor in a culture struggling for basic survival can suppress play, whereas more affluent cultures could allow and even appreciate children's play, as in ancient Attica for example, where various toys were produced and parents purchasing toys made specifically for children.

Even if play is widespread, or perhaps because it is, play has challenged scholars for centuries. Is 'just having fun' an idle and useless activity? Or is play highly important for not only the individual child but for cultural reproduction or even species survival? Is the purpose of play immediate, for example enhancing social competence, or has it long-term consequences, such as preparing the child for its coming adult roles? There have been affirmative answers to all the questions indicating that each has its supporters. Interestingly – perhaps coined with other words – such a polarization seems to be evident also today.[418] The role and importance of child's play have also been treated by ancient writers, for example (as we shall see later) Plato and Aristotle, and various theories exist.

In the puritan tradition of northern Europe, child's play was believed to be connected to the animal expression of instincts, and was therefore restricted or channeled into civilized activities, like chores.[419] A later oppositional approach to play appeared with the ideas of *Rousseau* (the age of enlightenment: 1712-1778), who believed children to be 'pure souls', and were therefore in no need of purifying activities. *Herbert Spencer*, the English philosopher (1820-1903) postulates in *Principles of Psychology* his influential 'superfluous energy' theory. Built-up energy is the basic explanation why play happens. His approach led to the conclusion that all energy not used for species survival and maintenance of life has to be channeled and released in another activity. So, in essence play was just spill-over without importance. This idea is not uncommon behind beliefs that it is 'childish' and redundant and as such should not be part of serious learning and developmental education. Interestingly, his energy-model, probably an analogy to the damp-engine, crept into the later highly influential Freudian catharsis theory of play.[420] In recent evolutionary childhood theory this view has been discarded: "Play is costly and risky. Few now accept the hypotheses that play is a mere discharge of excess energy. (…) It has long been noticed that the smartest mammals are the most playful."[421] In other words, it seems that play is not an idle and useless activity, it has important functions, otherwise it would be difficult to explain its costliness in time and energy.

This perspective was introduced earlier by the American psychologist *Karl Groos* (1861-1946). He has been an important figure since early 1900 coining an approach that still today is part of the thinking about the evolutionary functions of play.[422] Gross, who was highly influenced by Darwin, saw play as the immature organism's necessary practice for behaviors that are essential for later survival. In principle, Gross equated the function of plays as the same for both animals and humans. In mammals, play was highly functional as practice to adult life. For example, kittens play 'hunt' and 'chase' in order to become efficient hunters when grown-up.[423] So, the function of play is in principle explained by being a necessary preparation for the future. Interestingly, although coined in other words, this idea of play as 'preparation-for-the-future' was stated much earlier as it was inherent in the thinking of Plato. For example, in the future a boy may become a Greek warrior and ride a real horse equipped with sword and garments. Preparing for the challenges of coming manhood will be enhanced by imaginative and playful role-taking in a relatively non-dangerous and restrictive environment. Similarly, in order for a girl to become a future culturally 'normal' woman, enacting various role-playing scenes, for example using the grown up, adult-like terracotta dolls, could be a developmental path to adulthood. Interestingly, when girls in Classical Attica reached their early maturity period on the brink of adulthood, in a cultural transition ritual they had to leave their adult dolls behind as offerings to the goddess.[424] This also indicates a cultural message that the doll-playing period was now over and had performed its function in female socialization.

So, in order to prepare to become competent adults, children create and rehearse functionally important play scenes, which seem to be 'natural simulators' for the development of future skills. This 'preparation-for-the-future-idea' is an important principle still held by evolutionists.[425] But this does not exclude the more immediate gains and short term ontogenetic importance of play. For example, a ball game can have both immediate socializing and cooperative functions for the participants as well as preparing for future necessary spatial and locomotive competences to be used in athletics and war.

An opposite perspective, however, is seen in the theory of the English psychologist *Sully* (1842-1923). He was especially keen on defining how play was distinct from other activities. In *Essay of Humor* Sully compared play to pleasurable feelings connected with laughing, and he saw play as pure pleasure. So, play is not identified by the action itself but the concomitant 'atmosphere'. Just observing the child's expression – does he look happily engaged? – one can see if he is playing or not.

As a pleasurable activity in itself, play is not having an external purpose or goal and thus becomes the opposite to work. In Sully's perspective the child is creating and enacting its own constructed here-and-now play world. Interestingly, this approach is in line with recent childhood sociological ideas about childhood as a unique and valuable life period in itself, in opposition to the idea of a 'becoming'.[426] In the 19th century three play theories dominated. Firstly, in *Freudian theory* play was identified as a defense-mechanism and a 'self-therapeutic' activity for 'releasing' and 'relating' traumatizing experiences from infancy/childhood.[427] Thus doll play in this perspective had not many future purposes; instead it was revealing the child's experience of the negative sides of the intimate adult-child relationship in the family. Secondly, in *Piaget's theory* play was an 'assimilative' activity, not directly developmental in itself.[428] 'Chewing on experiences' by constantly repeating and rehearsing already-learnt skills will solidify competences. This has two important developmental functions: Establishing a foundation to build new competences on, and making the organism ready for the next steps in learning. Playing with a ball for example by throwing it against a wall and trying to catch it, repeating the same action over and over, is not an infrequent activity for children. Obviously, as the coordinative skills behind successful catching and throwing are not achieved quickly, play as assimilative activity ensures that this and other relevant competences are learnt in childhood. Thirdly, in the so-called *activity theory* the child must learn about its culture through practical participation in relationships with other people.[429] Here play is seen as an activity where the child's purpose and motivation lies in the process itself.

Thus, a playing child is absorbed solely for the sake of playing. The themes of play are primarily based on the child's everyday life experiences. So, for example some answers to the question "what did a small child in Classical Athens play?" could be: Themes taken from the domestic family sphere; the immediate physical neighborhood where he lives; the experiences from having participated in sacral activities. Quite similar to the 'preparation-for-the-future' idea, activity theory – with its point of departure in the child's wish to be like the adults – means that in play the child often simulates adult-like scenes. For example, in playing war a prop becomes the 'real thing'. Thus a stick is not a stick but a spear, because it is used like a spear. Finally, in the pre-school period the dominant and most developmentally important activity is play. So, if play and playtime are allowed in a culture, children cannot help being engaged in spontaneous play. It seems that ancient Attica – as will be seen later in this section, with the mass production of various toys for children – was indeed a culture that allowed (middle- and upper class) children the opportunity to play.

There have been warnings that 'play objects' or children shown 'playing' on choes were primarily for ritual and sacral purposes and should not be seen as play.[430] Cautiousness is called for here, so in a later section this important issue will be discussed. But using existing theories of play, for example evolutionary perspectives on the development of homo-sapiens, it would be very unlikely that small children in Classical Attica did not play. By giving them the various play objects the adults simply trigged play behavior. So, tentatively it is assumed that – despite or together with some important sacral functions of toys – children in ancient Attica played and thus gained the possible developmental and socializing effects of that. Importantly, activity theory has classified play into various types connected to developmental periods:

*Infancy period (0-2 years)*: Practice- and functional play (sensor-motor).
*Toddler period (2-3 years):* Construction play (props and toys).
*Preschool period (3-6 years):* Role, imaginative, symbolic play.

This type of classification will be useful later in this section. As we will see, both the written material and the iconographic evidence of children's play and the many types of play objects indicates that practice, construction, and role-play, (imaginative/symbolic) has probably been used by children in ancient Attica with the concomitant developmental and socializing consequences.

What characterizes human beings is a profound absence of reflexes and the enormous capacity for learning. According to new research on cultural development, humans seem to be ready for culture integration from birth, being equipped with the necessary basic capacity to cooperate with other fellow beings in various systems of meaning and a spontaneous eagerness to learn and decode meaning.[431] In essence, there does not seem to be a non-social being that needs to be made social through a cultural socialization process. But a lot must be learned by a novice entering the world, especially when the culture is highly complex. Play is one important activity that enhances this process in the juvenile period. Play in humans is extended because children have so much to learn that they not only require a long time to do so, but also safe environments in which to master their eventual adult role. To behave in accordance with cultural rules and customs is not grasped quickly and easily. The ancient Greek society was, indeed, highly complex which demanded sophisticated experience and knowledge to a degree that long term preparative training and learning was necessary. Play could have been an important 'practice arena' for doing that in the juvenile period.

Recent research on play and theory has suggested that play is a socializing and enculturation mechanism, where children can safely experiment and learn how to act and live in a specific culture – play is seen as a practice for real life situations (as seen in anthropological and psychological theories on socialization and problem-solving).[432] In any culture at any time there is a need for healthy brain development for the next generation. Play is not only important for the development of the child (for instance sensori-motor play), but for brain development as well. Children, for example, who are not engaged in play or played with may even be in risk of brain-damage.[433] It seems, for example, that loco-motor play accelerates cell growth in the cerebellum, by developing connections between axons. Therefore, it appears that play keeps children mentally healthy, and that the brain develops through play, which means that children in play are, so to speak, directing their own brain assembly. The practical consequences of that are enormous as together with other developmental agents, play, seems to be beneficial to the healthy development of the next generation and thus cultural and societal reproduction. But what if the material record – especially *images* of children with play objects – cannot be used to show that children in ancient Attica really played? Then we are on shallow ground and it becomes irrelevant in this context to discuss the developmental importance of play. This issue will be dealt with in the next section.

### Did young children really play in ancient Attica? – the iconographic ambiguity

It has to be carefully considered whether these children were *really* playing or merely painted on the vases for reasons unknown. Some archaeologists take the iconic evidence as documentation of the fact that children depicted in play are in fact playing.[434] Conversely, Beaumont (2012), amongst others, cautions against taking a naive stance in this regard. In a section on play, she briefly states that children played and that certain types of dolls for example, were used to play with. On the other hand, the following is given much more space and attention:

> "When we turn to the *representation* of child's play in Athenian art we must also approach the images with a degree of caution. All too often they are treated by modern commentators, as simple illustrations of ancient children at play in the context of everyday life. We must, however, keep in mind that these images were not created as a photographic, true-to-life record but are, rather, artistic constructs that, while reflecting Athenian society, are likely to present idealized and socially acceptable versions of child's play that may, in some instances, be overlaid with deeper symbolic and ritual resonances" (Beaumont 2012, 129).

Is it playing when two boys are actively seen engaged with their spinning tops accompanied by Hermes the divine protector of youth? Obviously not, argues Beaumont: Instead it shows a transitional stage where the boy(s) are under the protection of Hermes in the coming shift to manhood. The spinning tops symbolize the play objects of childhood that the boy must leave behind in order to be a man. The same goes for balls and knucklebones. So, in this principal case and in similar cases, *real play is not evident, but a serious cultural transition ritual.* This is highly crucial when it comes to the interpretation of the many depictions of children's 'play' with various objects as presented in the iconographic material. For example, according to Beaumont (2012) images of children on a swing and boys with the 'wheeled stick' or 'with a pet' can be connected to distinct ritual meaning obviously not play.[435]

Despite that Beaumont, interestingly, does not call the objects mentioned 'transitional', 'symbolic', 'ritual' or 'sacral' objects, but 'play objects'. This seems to indicate that she allows room for play also. So, interpretations of *images* do not necessarily have to involve choosing between: 'is-it-a-play scene' or 'is-it-a-ritual scene'? But in order to gain a fuller picture other evidence besides images on *choes* has to be considered: For example, findings of dolls seem to show, that although dolls ritually are delivered by girls to the gods in a transition ritual, most findings do not have religious associations:

> "Some 253 Greco-Roman contexts have produced evidence of dolls, and none of them have religious associations. About 203 contexts are generally domestic (houses, streets and storerooms), and 35 are tombs whose occupants are now unknown. 15 more are tombs containing the bodies of children" (Wileman, 2000, 38-39).

Thus, before the transition rite dolls were in the possession of young girls who were free to use them as they preferred: For example as play objects used in imaginary play.

Arguments will now be put forward here that children in ancient Attica really must have played. This stance, however, does not deny that when children are portrayed with playing objects on choes the underlying cultural intention could have been both ritual and idealized. The following eight points argue that play was *not only* idealized or enmeshed with sacral and symbolic meanings, but that play was also an essential part of young children's lives in ancient Attica:

1. If, as in this book, holding the basic evolutionary idea that play is intrinsic to the human species, especially in the juvenile period, then it is hard to imagine that toys were not played with 'outside' the idealized and ritualized connotations of iconography.
2. It seems hard to imagine that every 'play scene' portrayed on choes are totally made up fiction without any props or observations as basic material.
3. Did parents buy a spinning top, a doll, or a ball only for ritual use, or to be placed out of the reach of their children? Probably not. Other evidence besides

iconographic motifs indicates that toys were directly handed to children for fun, play and practice (Plato).

4. Several play objects that are not portrayed on choes/vases are found in child graves or on grave steles e.g. dolls (fig. 32-34, 36-38); horses on wheels (fig. 48-49), and spin tops (fig. 51).[436] They had been in the possession of young and older children and thus it would be unlikely if they had not been played with.
5. The powerful cultural pressure in ancient Attica towards excellence in sports and gymnastics (and war) in adolescence, probably allowed for the 'pre-learning' of skills in play.
6. When leaving childhood and entering manhood play objects (spinning tops, balls, knucklebones) were left behind and given to the gods (as votive offerings) by the boys.[437] Girls gave Artemis their dolls and other female artifacts. This indicates that before their abandonment, these objects, were used as toys by children before their transition into manhood/womanhood.
7. Concerning the 'dual function' of some toys, Kamp (2001a) in her research of ancient Greek children supports the interpretation that animal figurines, for example, have functioned as both toys and votives, depending on context. Some of these objects were even made by the children themselves.
8. As we soon shall see, the written sources adhere to children's play in various ways outside its ritual and sacral meanings. In addition, linguistic Classical philological evidence confirms that the ancient Greek word for 'child' has its roots in words like 'play', 'games' and 'sport'.[438] This indicates that, for example, early childhood for the Greeks was probably synonymous with play, which was later followed by games and sport.

The above considerations give us reasonable arguments for believing that young children in fact played and were allowed to play, by actively using culturally skilled manufactured objects as props for play. Let us move a step further now and turn to the written sources that reveal an awareness of the importance of play and even show socializing aspirations on behalf of play.

## Children's play in Classical Attica

If a phenomenon exists and is considered meaningful in a culture and is part of human consciousness, it will be given a name that characterizes and defines it. Thus, there will be one or more words in the language about the particular phenomenon. Here, Classical philological sources are of great help in gaining insight into how children's play was viewed and understood in ancient Greece. Linguistic evidence suggests that the idea of childhood was closely related to the world of play: The word παις (child) shares roots with words like παιζό (I play), παιγμα (play and sport) η παιγπια (sports and game), and το παιγνιον (toys).[439] The Greeks also had specific words related to play: παιδιά (refers to children's games); δυρμα (refers to silliness and futile play); ἀγών (is used for competitions and games).[440] It is hard not to conclude that the very concept of 'play' was interspersed with the semantic identification of a child. This locates play and playing, with all its distinct mental and behavioral qualities, in the childhood period in human ontogeny. This understanding is not far from recent understandings that the 'play age' follows an inverted U-curve. Raising rapidly in toddlerhood, having its peak in young childhood, after which play declines in middle childhood and for example is taken over by rule-games.

Moreover, many Greek philosophers have commented on children's play, for example, Plato mentions that children from age 3-6 love to play and invent games when coming together.[441] Children were supervised by nurses and undisciplined 'lawless' play was punished which means that it therefore existed. It was believed that unruly children were unlikely to mature into law-abiding citizens.[442] Probably this has sometimes been what we today call noisy rough-and-tumble play, which most often is seen in male peer-play.[443] Plato also emphasizes the societal importance of play, and he notes that it should be channeled into 'productive results'. He states that play could be used to identify the intelligence of the child, and that toys should help the child in practicing for its future role in life. Plato gives a 'house constructor' example: Future house builders (probably boys) should play with and construct toy houses using the same types of tools.[444] This 'one-one' idea that play is a miniature-copy and practice arena for a coming adult world, seems simplistic in light of recent understandings of play. But as mentioned earlier Plato coined a historically very early idea of 'play-as-preparation' that to some extent is still today held in evolutionary thinking about the reproductive functions of play.

Practicing for future roles in adult life, children have seemingly learned about *expected gender behavior and roles* through play with toys. By giving a doll to a girl and hoops to a boy, and not the other way round, adults thus characterize gender norms of the next generation. The cultural function of gender-role socialization has to do with preparing girls and boys for their different future roles. A child will rehearse over and over again potential future adult roles, when playing roles as mother/father, worker, shopper, farmer, sportsman, lawyer, warrior, priest, etc. Being imaginative does not have to be a true imitation of behavior, but realistic enough to count, for example, when playing mother and child, or an Olympic game athletic. *Role play* is a kind of pretend play with (or without) imaginary items, but can also include real play objects of various characters (like dolls, miniature figures of animals, miniature tools etc.). Role play is dominant among 3-6 year olds.[445] It is vital to realize that although gender differences were seen as culturally important in ancient Attica, in order to make toys 'work' in play the child actively has to construct play scenes of its own. In other words, gender socialization is not only imposed on children, but also becomes a process of self-socialization and in role play (i.e. imaginative) girls and boys identify with their coming adult roles. Although role play can turn gender specific when the child is given gender specific toys, there have been arguments that latent biological preferences to masculine/feminine toys exist in boys and girls, which cannot be connected to socializing or cultural expectations.[446] On the other hand, differences between the sexes at birth are quite small, and the characteristics of boys and girls overlap greatly. According to Bjorklund & Pellegrini:

> "The two sexes may have evolved nearly identical brains, biologies and aptitudes, but different biases (…) that orient them *slightly* towards different aspects and interpretations of the world. When these different orientations *receive support from the environment* boys and girls have different experiences and develop different expertise" (Bjorklund & Pellegrini 2011, 320).

Interestingly, recent evolutionary thinking on gender differences has left the position favoring the one-dimensional approach that evolution evolves either 'masculine' or 'feminine' characteristics. Instead, there seems to be more human commonalities than differences, and the differences are quite small from the start and mostly contingent on socialization practices. This is supported by recent developmental research on gender differences in ontogeny.[447]

In addition, it is doubtful that the small differences at birth in boys and girls can 'trigger' and thus create gender-selective behaviors in adults.[448] More likely it is the initial identification of the newborn child's sex (is it a boy or a girl?) that will determine gender specific treatment. When spontaneous behavior is repeated (as it often is in gender-specific behavior towards children) some underlying norms are at work. For example, in ancient Attica, a gender script about the different roles and functions of women and men may influence the ways parents behave towards their male and female children. In relation to gender-socialization, giving different toys to girls and boys thus serves as a vehicle for acquiring and mastering important sex-specific behaviors. Sex differences both emerge and widen in gendered play (for example girls playing with dolls and boys with swords) and may serve as a proximal mechanism for adult differences in behavior.[449] Thus children's play combined with the cultural acceptance of play becomes important in cultural reproduction – not least concerning the sharply divided gender roles in ancient Attica.

According to Pellegrini & Bjorklund (2004) fantasy play is observed universally during the human juvenile period, although forms and frequencies vary across social and historical ecologies. Free-play can be make-believe and fantasy, but even then it is not a total escape from reality. For instance, in role play there is a hidden set of rules that are decisive for how roles are enacted. Using specific props in play, for example dolls, has an inbuilt affordance character. Dolls in Classical Athens were, as mentioned earlier, clearly made as female adults and not as baby-like dolls. Although this will not determine play, it will frame it. Although we cannot know for certain, using a 'mother-baby' play with a female doll with breasts and other visible indications of being an adult will not be likely (see figures 31-38). Instead, enacting a role play in which the girl identifies herself with her adult female doll, making it behave and move like her mother for example, or perhaps a female dancer (fig. 41) seems more likely. Non-findings can sometimes also be 'findings': Boys in Classical Attic iconography are never portrayed with a doll, indicating that this object is only meant for and used by girls. Thus, gender roleplay and -identification, practicing a future role to come, may have been an important cultural idea behind giving dolls only to girls (even in today's Western societies with profound changes in gender roles with the equal right of women to education and employment, this different gender socialization practice seems prevalent: It is still rather unlikely that boys are given a doll as a present).

As presented earlier, activity theory points to the child's fundamental wish to be like an adult. In the eye of the child adults are powerful, in charge and doing interesting things. They are persons to observe, learn from and identify with. *Identification* ('to be like') is a much more powerful gender role internalizer than imitation ('to do like'). Instead of just copying an adult role model by imitating its external behavior, identification builds on the motivation 'to be like' and thus 'behave like' the other person. Thus role play experiments with, and builds up, a future identity through the identification process. In addition the process of identification in play seems to develop the socio-cognitive competence of 'taking the perspective of the other', thus understanding what is going on in other peoples minds.[450] This competence is developed in early childhood in homo-sapiens and has during the history of mankind from ancient times until today been fundamental for face-to-face group and social living.[451] Obviously social life in ancient Attica was complex and governed by strict rules of duty, for example for adolescents and adults. We do not know what rules children were explicitly taught, and which expectations of behavior were implicit but expected. But growing up with a 'social handicap', not learning to know the explicit norms and sensing the untold basic rules of social life could have devastating consequences later in life.

An interesting correspondence exists between the ancient and modern view of child's play. Plato is clearly normative, suggesting that play *ought to be of* learning importance, preparing the child for their future role in society. Modern research suggests that play *can* (also) be beneficial for cultural integration, especially through the process of self-socialization. In his view on child's play, Plato, compared to modern research, is setting a future goal for what has to be expected of the child. As children obviously did not read Plato, the encouraging of socializing during role-play was clearly educationally directed towards adults. Were Plato's socializing ideas about play based on observations of role-playing children? Or perhaps he wrote about what he believed the function of play should be in his ideal state?[452] Anyway, according to Plato between 3-6 years of age there is a phase where children are engaged in games with other children. Interestingly, though, he also recommended mild forms of discipline but this is probably an unintended connection between discipline and play. Evidently, harsh discipline and curtailing young children are counterproductive to play.[453] Plato even encouraged adults to spur children into role-play in the proper manner. According to Plato, role-play *should be the correct type*, preparing the child for its specific future role and work in adult life (e.g. future carpenters should in role-play use miniature carpenter tools etc.).[454] Interestingly, Plato was a true 'functionalist' concerning this – play is not seen as an idle outburst of superfluous energy, instead it fulfills important learning purposes. In addition, Plato's basic paradigm here seems to be teleological with a definite end-goal: Childhood is a preparation phase towards the state of adulthood – children are thus seen as 'beings in passage' and less as 'small beings' living in their own right.

## Toys in Classical Attica – the evidence

The theoretical scene is now set about the role and functions of play and play objects, these have been connected to the ancient Greek period as well. This was done in order to facilitate an understanding of the importance of objects and toys for the developing child, also in that historical period. In addition, such knowledge can influence the way one 'looks' at the material record. This section is devoted to a rather detailed archaeological record and interpretation of specific toy objects from ancient Attica. First, a section dealing with dolls and the next section will be about rollers, push- and go carts. After that various other types of play objects will be presented. Miniature toys are specifically dealt with, and then, last but not least, living animals as children's pets.

### *Dolls*

Dolls are not only played with, held and carried, they also fulfill important socializing and gender identity functions, having been integrated into the everyday life of young girls in the Classical period, and even long before that. This section will deal with Greek dolls, which are abundant in ancient Greek history. The dolls will be classified chronologically and typologically to give a wider perspective on the development of ancient Greek dolls from the earliest Geometric type until the Hellenistic period.[455] In addition, the question: 'Why have a doll?' will be answered by discussing the role and function of dolls in relation to theories on role play and coming-of-age-rituals.

Ancient Greek dolls existed over a large span of time, and had different names corresponding to specific types of dolls.[456] Toy-dolls were called *plangónes*, *nymphs* or *kóres*, but string dolls were called *neuróspasta,* when associated with cults.[457] With regards to dolls, the identification as toys can be difficult, because dolls existed across the domestic (secular) and sacral spheres: They were probably used as toys before they were sacrificed to the goddesses.[458] As stated earlier, this means that a toy object by the same token could have fulfilled 'dual functions', both as a toy and as a transitional sacral object. Doll makers were known as *coroplasts*, which meant 'moulder of maidens' (*kóre* means maiden but is also a synonym for dolls).[459] *Coroplasts* made other types of figurines like votives, statuettes and other types of toys, and workshops were often situated outside the city. In addition, they may have had stores/stands in the city.

Several larger production centers have been identified inside and outside of Attica, and toy making may have been a larger industry.[460] Wileman (2005) points to the cultural significance of the whole industry, which was dedicated not only to the production of the necessary materials/equipment for making e.g. feeding bottles, but also of in principle for making luxury objects such as toys. Of course, if a society was struggling for basic survival, artifacts such as toys hardly have been made. This principle of 'fulfilling basic needs first' means that having sufficient food, clothing, protection against bad weather, etc. will be of primary importance. However, this was not the case – at least for the wealthy in ancient Greece. Not just making toys for non-productive non-adults, but putting this in an organized system, shows a culture with a lot of surplus energy, producing 'useless' things with no obvious practical purpose. In addition, much of this was even made for society's juveniles. Obviously this investment in doll production for

**Fig. 31.** *Corinthian terracotta doll with painted clothes and hat. Early 5th century BC.*

example, demanded a whole infrastructure with special building structures placed in special locations. Moreover, there were numerous workshops, storage facilities, fireplaces, as well as ways of organizing sales. In addition, not just anyone, but skilled craftsmen were needed. We do not know, but in order to qualify as a *coroplaster* some apprenticeship must have been necessary. For example, skills in how to make and burn clay, make dolls or figurines, and turn them into terracotta objects that were of acceptable quality to sell to customers. Making dolls must have been so culturally accepted that the profession had an official title, indicating that the ancient Attic culture really valued and therefore invested in this production.

The earliest dolls can be traced back to the Geometric period and were mostly found in graves.[461] They are primitive and bell shaped, but develop into more elaborate figures with geometric decoration.[462] The bell shaped dolls are often found in Attica and Boeotia, but there are indications of the existence of more *production centers*.[463] Should this prove to be a fact, it could mean that already in the archaic period dolls were sought-after objects that could have been widely distributed. The dolls change appearance during the prehistoric period and they gradually lose the shape of a bell and began to look more human-like.

*The archaic doll* is either naked or comes with painted clothes.[464] It wears a hat (*plume/polo)* (fig. 31) pulled over the characteristic daidalic hair and the face shows the enigmatic archaic smile. It is most often of the jointed type with arms and legs attached by strings.[465] The arms are jointed at the shoulder, which is the case with all types of dolls. The legs are often attached anatomically incorrect to the middle of

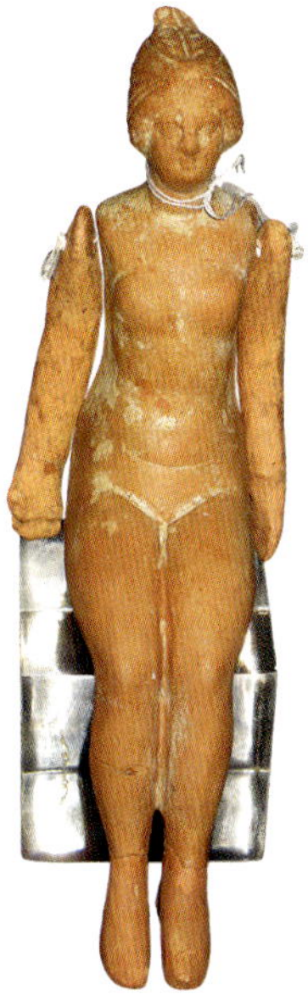

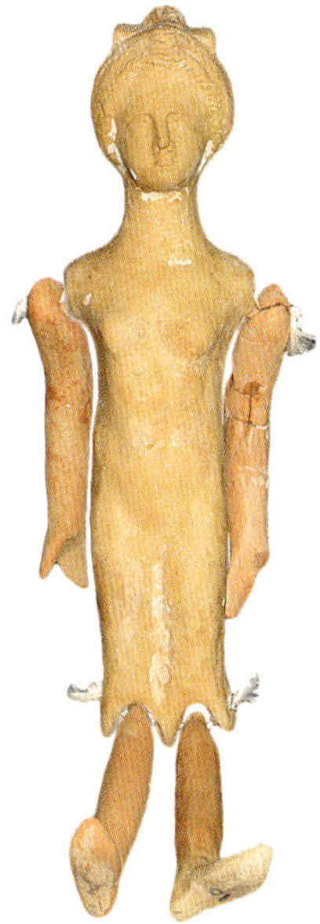

**Fig. 32.** *Attic seated doll. Mid-5th century BC.* **Fig. 33.** *Attic jointed doll. Early 4th century BC.*

the thighs, perhaps caused by the remnant of the bell shape, which disappears during the middle Archaic period. Archaic dolls are almost always from Corinth, which may indicate a central production center (based on the numerous findings of dolls). The dolls were often painted, as remains of paint are traceable: Black, dusty red, dusty yellow and white. From the late 6th century, female dolls are painted white according to the new art-trend and fashion style of the painter Eumaros, and the painted clothing disappears.[466]

The anatomy of the *Classical period dolls* evolves into looking much more natural. Two types of dolls exist, a seated[467] and a jointed type. The seated has static legs but moveable arms (fig. 32), and the jointed has both moveable arms and legs (fig. 33).[468] The legs are now jointed at or near the knees. Seated dolls are found with miniature stools and benches, and in an Athenian child grave several types of accessories were found accompanying a doll (fig. 34): A beautiful stool with human-head decoration, miniature vessels and utensils, a pair of shoes, an epinetron and a nuptial lebetas. All things were made of terracotta, and these accessories may have been standard equipment for dolls (as with the Barbie-doll). [469]

*Classical dolls* are always naked with no painted clothes (although some have remains of white painting on the body) and the hair is molded and engraved according to the fashion style of the period. Sometimes they had shoes modeled on their feet. They sometimes have small holes in the ears or on top of the head indicating accessorizing jewelry such as earrings and diadems. Sometimes they are holding a *kroatala* (castanet-like instrument), which places them in a dancing context (fig. 35).[470] The kroatala is

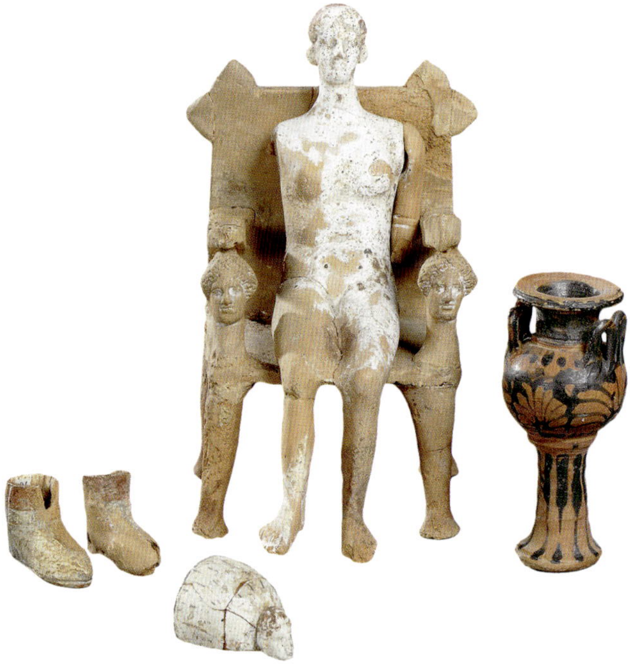

**Fig. 34.** *Attic seated terracotta doll with accessories. The Classical period, Ca. 420 BC.*

**Fig. 35.** *Attic doll with kroatala in hand. Mid-4th -century BC.*

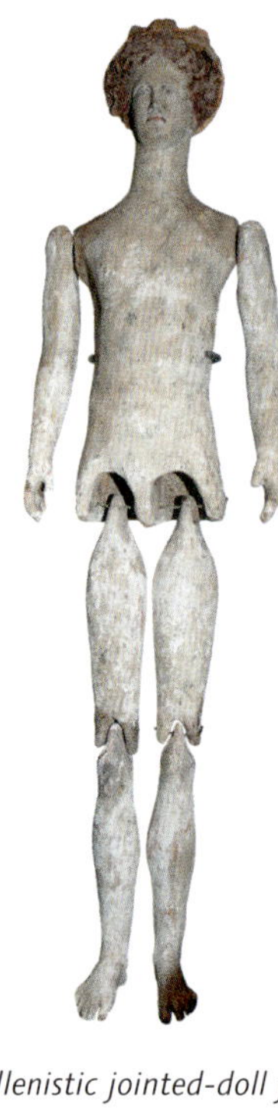

**Fig. 36.** *Hellenistic jointed-doll from Tanagra. Last part of 4th-century BC.*

**Fig. 37.** *Attic jointed doll. Late 5th century BC.*

**Fig. 38.** *Attic jointed doll. Ca. mid- 4th century BC.*

seen on red-figure vases, as on a pelike from 460 BC, which shows a girl dancing to the sound of a flute, while clapping the castanet-like instrument.[471] Wileman allows herself to speculate that, making the female doll dance may have tickled the girl's imagination: "Perhaps the dreams of little girls extended beyond the household roles their society usually planned for them, and were explored with these exciting figures" (Wileman 2005, 37).

In the Classical period dolls are most often found either in graves or in sanctuaries, for instance the Artemis at Brauron, and the Demeter and Kore at Corinth. Most Classical dolls are found in Attica and Corinth and may indicate *production centers*. At least the wealth of dolls indicates that a professional and skilled production system was in place.

During the Archaic and Classical period standard measurements are traceable: Archaic dolls are often smaller (around H. 10-12 cm.) than the Classical ones, which often measure H. 15-18 cm., but variations occur.[472] Dolls found in Attica are made of terracotta, and perhaps from standard terracotta forms like the miniature figurines and statuettes.[473] In the Hellenistic period dolls become larger (up to H. 50 cm.) and now have three joints; at the shoulders, the hips and the knees, which indicates the increased awareness of human anatomy.[474]

Classical Attic dolls have various designs and change appearance during the Classical period, but exact dating is hard to establish, and so are typologies.[475] However, dolls

**Fig. 39.** *A girl with her doll and dog. The Melisto-stele (close-up). Attic marble stele, Ca. 340 BC.*

may be dated according to the method of leg attachment; earlier dolls often had legs attached by strings, and later dolls from the mid-5th century BC often had their legs attached by projecting spurs (fig. 37 & 38).[476] Yet, exceptions exist and it is perhaps not a satifiying dating criterium.

The contexts of Classical Attic dolls are both sacral and domestic. Dolls are found in sanctuaries, which are connected to 'rites-of-passage' rituals like the Artemis Brauronia cult, where young girls, among other rituals, sacrificed their doll(s) the day before their wedding day. The dolls may have symbolized the past years of childhood and play, which married girls left behind. The disclaiming of their dolls was perhaps a farewell to childhood, and the beginning of a new life as an adult, wife and mother. If this is true, the ritual may indicate a distinct awareness of life stages dividing childhood from adulthood.[477] The indication of dolls being used as toys mainly comes from iconographic evidence as well as the finding context – usually child graves. They may also have had several functions, for instance as play things, as apotropaic figures to ward-off evil spirits, as votive offerings to goddesses or perhaps also as decorations on shelves in the house.

Children with dolls are depicted on Classical Attic grave steles. Girls are often from the age of 5 and older when shown playing with dolls, but, younger girls may have also played with them.

**Fig. 40.** *A girl with her baby doll?*
*Attic Pentelic marble stele, Ca. 360 BC.*

The Melisto-stele is an example of an Attic grave stele depicting a girl with her doll (fig. 39).[478] The girl is engaged in play with a doll, a dove and a dog. The dog at her feet is jumping and trying to catch the dove she holds in her right hand. The stele is late Classical from around 340 BC. The doll does not appear to be of the jointed type but seems more static – perhaps indicating another type of doll, commonly interpreted as a votive type.[479] Another stele depicts a girl with a doll in her hands (see fig. 40).[480]

As documented, dolls were almost always made as adult females and not as babies. However, perhaps the stele on fig. 40 is an exception. This young girl, maybe around the age of 13, looks at her doll as if it was a baby. She bends her head towards the doll smiling at it, creating an intimate situation. The scene resembles the mother/female-and-childcaring-scenes also depicted on grave steles in the Classical period, like the Ampharete-stele (see fig. 4).[481] This sentimentalized depiction may tell about the societal role of toys and gender-specific role-play encouraged by adults in ancient Greek times. As mentioned by Plato, child play was encouraged to have societal and socializing meaning so the child could practice its future role in life.[482] For young girls in ancient Athenian society the most important role in adult life, besides being a wife, was to be a mother, and perhaps, miniature dolls were given to young girls to practice their skills as mothers.

One could think that this type of gender role-play is forced upon children by adults who steered children to play with gender-specific items. However, children were probably not 'victims' in this regard.[483] Remembering that play is defined as being free, spontaneous and without external goals, so adults cannot command children to prepare their gendered future. Instead it is primarily during the child's self-socialization process that adults can indirectly influence the procedure by 'organizing the play environment',

**Fig. 41.** *Doll held in string. Attic Pentelic marble stele, early 4th century.*

**Fig. 42.** *A hole for the string in doll's head. Early 4th-century.*

for instance introducing dolls as play objects. Recent research shows that children from ages 3-6 often engage in role-play by themselves, and this can also be referred to as the role-playing-age.[484] Should gender-specific toys not be available to a child in the role-playing age, then it probably would create its own preferred toy. For example, a wrapped blanket could function as a rag-doll. Girls with dolls do not appear on choes and vases in general. Yet, on a white-ground lekythos from 440 BC a young girl (perhaps aged 13) is depicted bringing a doll to a tomb.[485] This image corresponds well with the finds of dolls in graves. Perhaps some dolls were placed on the tomb and not in the grave, which was the case with some types of funerary pottery.

The fact that Classical dolls do not wear painted clothes has led to the hypothesis that these dolls must have worn clothing made of fabric, but the fabric had of course decomposed. A stele from early 4th century, however, shows a slave girl with a doll in her right hand passing it to her maiden (only some part of the left hand is preserved) (fig. 41).[486]

It is clearly observable that the doll is held on a string, which matches the hole often found on the top of the head of dolls (fig. 42).[487] This string may be connected to the 'dancing' aspect of the dolls, making them move and 'dance', when the string was activated (like a jumping jack or a marionette, as suggested by Argyriadi [1991]). However, on this stele the doll is not wearing clothes, but looks nude (fig. 41), and dolls on other steles also appear to be naked (fig. 39 and 40). This nudity is strange since earlier dolls often wore painted clothes, and wore a hat.[488] The naked dolls on the steles may indicate that dolls wore no clothing from the 4th century onwards.[489] The dolls are slim, portrayed with the hair fashion of the specific period, which perhaps made them modern and fashionable in past society. Dolls may represent the ideal picture of an adult woman; an ideal which young girls could emulate.

Dolls were likely used as toys for younger girls until they married. They may have had several functions, and perhaps symbolized young childhood as 'play time'. Dolls

**Fig. 43a.** *A boy with his toy roller.* **Fig. 43b.** *Close-up of toy roller.*
*Attic Pentelic marble stele, Ca. 400-350 BC.*

seen on grave steles may have symbolized the untimely death of an unmarried girl.[490] They could be placed in both domestic and sacral contexts, and were possibly connected also to several female cults and rites-of-passage rituals. They are found in female child graves, and just like today, perhaps dolls were a favored toy of young girls in ancient Greece.

### *Rollers, push- and go carts*

In this section, various types of play carts will be described: Push carts, go carts and wheeled horses, and reflections on the use of carts are presented. Following that, selected types of toys, which exist in the material record of Classical Attica are outlined. The intention is to give an insight into the impressive material record of ancient Greek toys, and to document the objects children were buried with after an untimely death.

When studying ancient Greek toys the archaeological record is not always sufficient. Some types of toys have only sparsely been found in the archaeological record, but are instead witnessed in the iconographic evidence. This is the case for *toy rollers* and *push carts*, which have rarely been found in the material record. An exception is a bronze toy roller found in a child's grave outside of Attica (Michalitsi in northwestern Greece).[491] However, evidence of toy rollers and push carts are mainly coming from depictions on choes and grave steles like the Mnesikles-stele from around 400-350 BC (fig. 43).[492]

*Rollers and carts used by boys and girl(s).*

**Fig. 44.** *Chous from Ca. 430 BC.*

**Fig. 45.** *Chous from Ca. 425-420 BC.*

**Fig. 46** *Chous from end of 5th century.*

**Fig. 47.** *A boy in a cart pulled by a goat.* Chous *from early 5th century.*

The stele depicts an older boy with a toy roller; he is holding the handle of the roller and the wheel is visible behind his left foot. The stele tells that also older boys used this type of toy, which was therefore not only suitable for the youngest children. In addition, based on iconographic knowledge, the design of toy rollers can be described: They consisted of a long pole connected to two wheels, and were most often made of wood.[493] The roller could be transformed into a go cart or push cart by adding a basket or a platform above the wheels. The rollers/carts could either be pulled or pushed around. It has been

**Fig. 48.** *Wheeled horse Black-glazed. Ca. 950-900 BC.*

**Fig. 49.** *Wheeled horse. Geometric, Ca. 800-750 BC.*

proposed that the push cart was originally a piece of stabilizing equipment, a walking frame, to help children learn how to walk. Perhaps later the supportive roller could have been transformed into a go cart for the older child to play with.[494] The rollercarts may have had several functions and were probably also used by adults for transporting various items such as vases and groceries, as well as smaller children.[495] Perhaps these carts were the first type of a baby pram?

Depictions of rollers and carts on choes also show that both boys and girls played with them and also youths, but it is boys that are most frequently depicted with toy rollers or carts (fig. 44, 45, 46).[496] Rollers were even more sophisticated when made and used as small carts to sit in, with animals in front pulling children around.

The depictions of children pulled by animals may be Dionysian, because of the Anthesteria-festival context. Yet, 'child chariot races' may have been held during the festival, the carts were often pulled by goat(s) (fig. 47).[497] Rollers are depicted on 4$^{th}$ century choes and vases, but are not seen before the Classical period. In addition, the roller appears on Roman sarcophagi indicating a continuous production.[498] The rollers and carts do not seem to have been gender-specific toys, as they were used both by boys and girls of almost all ages.

Another type of rolling toy is *the wheeled horse*. Different from the before-mentioned rollers and carts, this toy is not seen depicted in iconography, but is found solely in the material record. Wheeled horses are dated back to the Geometric period, and some horses are not toys but votives.[499]

However, some wheeled horses are interpreted as toys and the earliest example from Attica is dated to 950-900 BC found in a child's grave (fig. 48).[500] Due to the finding context, the horse is interpreted as a toy. The horse has black glazing and geometric ornamentation on the head and back. The horse has modeled ears, mane and tale. The hole on its nose indicates that it has been pulled by a string. The horse on wheels (fig. 49) from the middle Geometric period ca. 800-750 BC is another example of a geometric horse from Attica.[501] It is decorated with typical geometric patterns, but has no ears or tail. The horse resembles those found on pyxis lids but is somewhat larger. No wheeled horses from the Classical period have been found, either in iconography or in the material record. However, wheeled horses from the Hellenistic and Roman periods exist in Attica, which may indicate continuing production since the Geometric times.[502]

### *Other types of children's toys*

The following section is about other types of toys, and the importance of these toys in the socialization process of children. Socialization of children in ancient Greek may have been based on specific play types with the use of special toys, which are suggested in this section. Several types of toys have been found in Attica, and most often in graves. Sometimes the toys are found in sanctuaries and are therefore connected to the 'rites-of-passage' rituals.

One of the oldest toys may be *the ball*. We know that children in ancient Attica had balls and played with them. But as balls (and other toys) are made of non-durable materials none have been found. Instead we have to look at the iconographic evidence. This gives some interpretative challenges because this evidence always has important sacral connotations also and therefore is not real-life evidence of play. This was discussed earlier in a separate section with the conclusion that although balls can be seen on grave steles, it is difficult to see if the round object is a ball or something else like a piece of fruit.[503] Nonetheless, an infant boy or toddler is seen playing with a dove and a ball on a grave stele from second half of 4th century (fig. 50).[504]

The boy is resting his left hand on the ball, while holding a pet dove in his right hand as if showing an invisible person his favorite toys. The ball on this stele has been identified as a play-object and not a piece of fruit. The stele is located in the National Archaeological Museum of Athens, and the provenance is unknown, yet it was found in Attica. Ball games played by older children and youths are depicted on red-figure vases, and a number of different ball games have been identified, i.e. the *passé-boule* (fig. 20).[505] Yet the ball may have been used in several ways and in different games: For example is the juggling of balls depicted in iconography.[506]

Besides balls, *the spin top* was a popular pastime for children in Classical Attica. Various types of tops exist within the archaeological record around the world, but one specific type, the whip top, seems to be the kind used in Classical Attica.[507] The whip top does not have a stem as the twirler has, and it was lashed with a whip, which made it twirl.[508]

Observe the fine parallel rings around the upper part of the spin top (fig. 51). Getting the tip of the lash into one of these could result in a faster spin that could make the top rotate for a longer time. We do not know, but perhaps in the highly competitive ancient Greek culture people were challenging each other in a playful contest about who could make the top spin longest before tilting?

This nicely made spin top is exhibited in the National Archaeological Museum in Athens, and is black-glazed with a clay-colored stripe in the middle (fig. 51).[509] The top

**Fig. 50.** *A little boy with his ball and dove. Marble grave stele, second half of 4th century BC.*

is around H. 7 cm. with a diameter of ca. 6 cm. where it is widest. Depictions on vases most frequently illustrate adults playing with whip-tops and not children.[510] Yet, some tops are found in child graves as if belonging to the dead child, which indicates that the top was probably a children's toy as well.

*The yoyo* is not a recent invention; in fact it is supposedly the world's oldest more advanced toy and originates from China. Yet, yoyos also existed in ancient Greece, and

**Fig. 51.** *Attic spin top. The Classical period.*

**Fig. 52.** *Attic yoyo. The Classical period.*

**Fig. 53.** *A boy playing with his yoyo. Red-figure cup, Ca. 420 BC.*

**Fig. 54.** *Astragaloi (knucklebones) made of bone and metal.*

are found in graves and depicted on vases. An Attic black-glazed yoyo from the Benaki Toys Department measures dia. 5.3 cm (fig. 52).[511] It has a furrow and a penetrating hole in the middle, where the string probably was attached. A similar yoyo is seen being played with by a youth on an Attic red-figure cup from ca. 420 BC (fig. 53).[512] Most likely it was older children with better motor skills that played with yoyos. Learning to handle a yoyo is not easy and is a skill that demands fine-tuned, hand-eye coordination and movements.

The very popular game with the use of the so-called *astragalos,* also known as *knucklebones,* was played by older children, youths and adults. Astragaloi were mostly made of bone (fig. 54)[513], yet they have also been found in bronze and glass.[514]

Most often it would be a group of five people playing, both girls and boys. A knucklebone consists of four sides, each side representing a value point: One, three, four and six. Each throw of the knucklebones would make up the scores and the one with the highest points would win. Various types of knucklebone-games existed and specific throws were given names such as the lucky Venus throw or the Chian throw.[515] Sometimes the

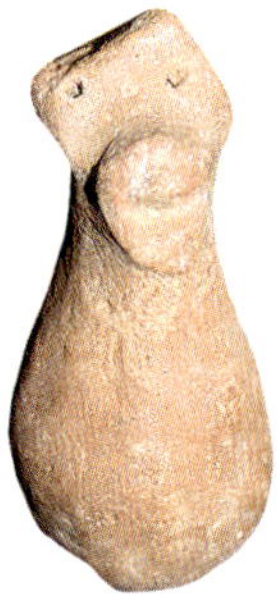

**Fig. 55a.** *Attic whistle. The Classical period (front).*

**Fig. 55b.** *The whistle seen from behind (mouthpiece).*

knucklebones had initials written on them, which have been ascribed rites-of-passage, where children would consecrate their play objects to a deity when coming of age.[516] Knucklebones were a favored toy and existed from prehistory to Roman times, they are also found outside of Greece, for instance in the Near East and Anatolia. Copious numbers have been found in different contexts: In graves, domestic quarters, sanctuaries and caves, which indicates multiple functions and values.[517] It is uncertain if younger children played with knucklebones, since pictorial representations on vases only show older children and youths playing. Also small terracotta statues of girls playing indicate that they were older than 7 year.[518] Yet, younger children are portrayed with a sack of knucklebones. This sack was either of net or leather, with a flap.[519] These sacks were called *phormiskos*, and ceramic counterparts also existed and were used as knucklebone-containers too. Since younger children are portrayed with *phormiskos* it is possible that they also played knucklebone-games.

Another type of item that may have been used as a toy is *the whistle*. The Attic whistle (fig. 55a & b)[520] from the Classical period is perhaps formed as a rooster, but this is not precisely identified.[521] The whistle was discovered in a child-grave and may therefore be interpreted as a toy to the deceased child.

The whistle measures H. 4 cm and W. 3.4. and has a mouthpiece by the tail, and two blowing holes situated above the spout. The whistle is fragmented, but is still functional today. Flute-playing youths are shown relatively often on vases; perhaps the whistle was used by smaller children before learning to play the flute.

*Hoops* may also have been used as toys since they are witnessed in the iconographic record most frequently on vases.[522] In addition, it is for the most part often older (adolescent) boys, who are seen playing with hoops. The hoop has also been connected to the courting of a young boy (lover) by an older male (which is also the case with roosters and hares, which symbolized the gifts of male lovers). However, the hoop has been an identified toy since ancient times and was especially favored by boys in the middle

**Fig. 56.** *Attic miniature toy altar. Marble. The Classical period.*

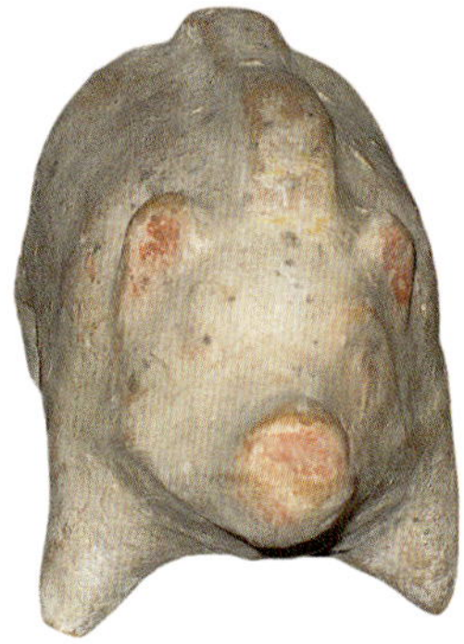

**Fig. 57.** *Miniature terracotta pig with paint. The Classical period.*

ages, and is still used today (for instance the hula hoop).[523] It was also probably used by younger children in Classical Attica.

### *Miniature toys*

A *toy altar* was found in a child-grave from the Classical period in Athens (fig. 56).[524] The altar measures H. 10.2 cm and W. 5.5-6 cm and is made of white marble. It has decoration on each side, and one side may show a child with a Hermes stick.

Assuming that the miniature altar was not only put on a shelf as decoration, and knowing that young children like to enact what they experience in daily life, this altar may have been an accessory for child-play, for instance to accompany play with dolls. If handled by the child the toy altar may have been used in pretend-play, i.e. the child taking the role of priest giving presents to the gods, or being a specific family member who enacted the ritual family sacrifices to the house spirits. Then this toy may have been an important artifact that children were actively using in playful (but serious) 'sacral self-socialization', but not as Plato thought, always being a preparation towards a specific adult role in society. Imagining and playing a priest that deliver 'gifts' to the supernatural will not for most children result in becoming a real priest. But this early self-socialization, actively 'playing in' this important societal role as part of individual and cultural identity, may constitute early ontogenetic acceptance of 'the realities' of a sacral world. Moreover, the time and energy invested by adults in organizing the production of toy altars, plus giving them to children, indicates underlying cultural beliefs that early involvement in sacral rituals may be have been seen as important.

In addition, ancient written sources witness that children used tools and toys resembling real life items.[525] This was encouraged since it prepared the child for adult life, and would also teach them about hierocracy and their future position and role in society. Plato's statements about play may have been a general view on child's play, as being a

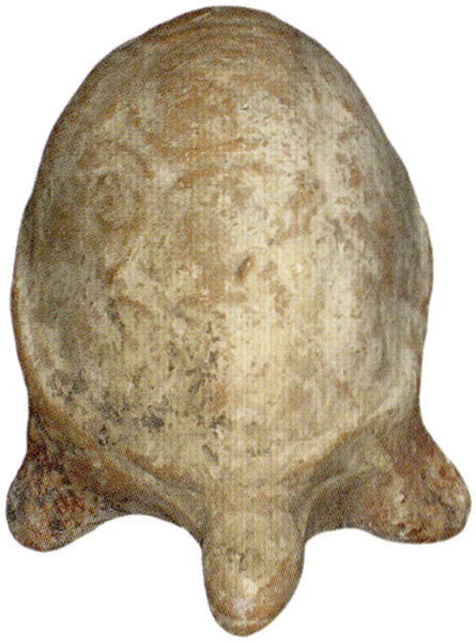

**Fig. 58.** *Toy turtle in terracotta. The Classical period.*

**Fig. 59.** *Miniature dove in terracotta. The Classical period.*

socializing and enculturation practice.[526] Aristophanes' play, *Clouds*, also tells that *children made toys and toy accessories themselves* e.g. baby houses and boats.[527] The miniature altar in fig. 55 is too sophisticated to have been made by a child, but as argued it may well have been used as a toy by a child. However, it can by the same token have functioned as an apotropaic item, to protect the child in the afterlife and therefore belong to a sacral context. If so, the mini-alter can also be one of more examples of adult sentiments in ancient Attica, i.e. that children were worshipped even in afterlife.

Miniature *animal figurines* may also have been used in pretend-play, for instance as farm animals on a child's imaginary farm. The clay animals are often of domestic breed, and the horse and pig are most common.

Clay *pigs* (fig. 57)[528] are often of standard size: H. 5-7 cm. L. 8-10 cm. W. 3-4 cm. and standard sizes exist within each miniature animal group, like turtles which are: H. 3-4 cm. L. 6-7 cm. W. 3-4 cm. and doves: H. 8-9 cm. L. 11-13 cm. and W. 3-4 cm. However, other types of animals also appear in the material record e.g. *turtles*, *doves*, and *dolphins*, which are not connected to the domestic sphere (fig. 58 and 59).[529]

In addition, no *mythical animals* exist within this toy group, and all animals are 'natural' and were probably known to ancient Greek children. Plato mentions that "… to make a good farmer he must play at tilling land", which once again underlines that children were encouraged to play out their future roles in pretend play.[530] The child may have had various types of animals on his imaginary farm, both domesticated (pigs, horses) and natural animals (turtles, dolphins). Some of the animals may be of apotropaic value and should not be interpreted as toys, thus the latest research indicates that most of them are found in child graves.[531] Dove figurines outside graves are not identified as toys but are connected to Aphrodite cults.[532]

### Children with pets

Children's use of pets in the Classical Attic society will be presented in this section, and various iconographic representations of children and pets will be described and discussed.

**Fig. 60.** *'Living dove'. The Mnesagora-Nikochares stele. Attic marble stele, Ca. 420 BC.*

**Fig. 61.** *'Living bird'. The Theokles stele. Attic marble stele, the mid-4th century BC.*

This is done in order to give insight into the range of child-play that took place without the use of toys. Ancient Greek children also used other types of play-objects (companions) like living animals, which is suggested in this section. As discussed earlier in the section 'Did young children really play in ancient Attica? – the iconographic ambiguity', animals portrayed with children could have and very often had sacral connotations. It is very important to realize that any iconographic representation of a child with a pet had sacral purposes and meanings. It also infers that animals had probably been household pets for children in everyday life. So, domesticated animals were a natural part of most children's everyday life and experience. Considering juvenile human beings in their play-mode, it is very likely that young and older children interacted in many ways with pet animals. Even used for sacral purposes the iconographic evidence is sometimes quite realistic, indicating that there has been some kind of 'real events' serving as props for the artists. For example: 'girl chasing bird' (fig. 63), an 'up-and-get-it' scene with a boy holding food up high for the dog to get (see fig. 69), or girl throwing stick for the dog to fetch (see fig. 67). These are quite common phenomenons in everyday interaction between children and a pet. In this section this approach will be followed, not denying the important sacral connotations as well.[533]

It appears that *live animals* were used by ancient Greek children as play companions. Iconographic evidence on steles and vases indicates that live animals were cherished by children. Pets represented in the iconographic record are of various types and breeds, the dog and dove being most common. Yet roosters, geese, hares, deer, goats and horses,

**Fig. 62.** *A toddler with bird.*
*Attic red-figure* chous, *Ca. 425-420 BC.*

**Fig. 63.** *A girl chasing a bird.*
*Attic red-figure* chous, *Ca. 420 BC.*

etc. are pictured accompanying children in Classical Greek iconography.[534] Having a relationship with a pet has significant positive effects for a child. Having a live animal as a companion is very different from having an inanimate toy animal, and although we do not know in what ways children at that time played together with their pets, some inferences can be made. Practical and socio-emotional skills will probably be developed if given the responsibility to nurse and sustain an animal.

In the pet group of *birds* various types have been identified on vases, steles and in graves: Doves, geese, swans, ducks, cocks and smaller birds, e.g. starlings are represented.[535] On the previously mentioned Melisto-stele (see fig. 39), the girl seems to be playing with a little dog and a dove.[536] The dove is held tightly around the wings, upside down, while the dog tries to catch it. Doves on steles may be interpreted as clay pigeons. However, some scenes portray birds in 'active poses', which perhaps indicates that they should be interpreted as *living birds*. This is the case with the Melisto-stele, where the bird is seen spreading its tail feathers.[537] Doves are also shown being held by the wings, like the ones seen on two Classical Attic grave steles (figs. 60 & 61), which is not possible to do with clay pigeons that mostly have folded wings.[538] Fig. 60 shows the scene of the two siblings Mnesagora and Nikochares playing with a 'living' bird. The boy is eager to get his big sister's dove to play with. On fig. 61, the boy Theokles is playing with his dog and a bird of some kind. The boy teases the dog with the bird

**Fig. 64.** *A girl holding a dove.*
*Attic marble statuette, Ca. 340-330 BC.*

in his hand, and the bird looks like it is flapping it wings to get away. Doves are the most frequently represented bird on steles and in round-sculpture, and may have had a symbolic value, e.g. of peace, love and innocence, and were also connected to the cults of Aphrodite.[539]

Other types of birds are shown in the company of children, for instance on a red-figure *chous* from 420 BC, which shows a toddler holding on to a table, while tempting a bird with a *streptos* cake (fig. 62).[540]

Behind him a toy roller is leaning against a 'wall', another favorite toy of the toddler in Classical Attica. The species of the bird is not identified, but may be of the starling family, which is a talkative bird that can mimic human language (like the Indian Hill Myna and the Tui-bird). Birds of the starling family are easy to tame and may have been used as pets in ancient Greece. Another *chous* from 420 BC (fig. 63) shows a girl chasing a frightened bird.[541] The girl is holding a toy roller and is trying to hit the bird with it. The scene shows a less idyllic version of children with pets and probably not all animals were treated well by children in the Classical period (which is also the case today). Perhaps the artist of the *chous* intended to show another part of child-pet-relationships, or perhaps show the more temperamental and aggressive side of child behavior. A marble statuette from 340-330 BC also shows a girl with a pet bird in her right hand (fig. 64).[542] The bird may be a dove or a sparrow of some kind, and the statuette shows that children also were portrayed with pet animals in ancient Greek sculpture.[543] Observe the way she holds her animal, quite loosely in order not to squeeze it, but firm enough so it cannot escape.

In the 4th century BC, round-sculptured statues of children would often hold some kind of animal: Birds of various types, hares or dogs, and these sculptures are found throughout the Classical Greek world and are not only an Attic trend.[544] Larger birds, like geese and swans, were probably also pets or companions to children, as seen on an Attic grave stele where an older girl with a doll is accompanied by a goose that is looking at her (see fig. 40). Likewise, bones of birds have been found in children's graves, underlining the pet interpretation.

As with many children today, another favorite pet was *the dog*.[545] The dog is often seen in active play with children, both male and female, which is the case with the Melisto-stele (fig. 39).[546] The dog is a pure-bred Maltese, which is an ancient breed.[547] On other child-grave steles, dogs are seen in the same position as on the Melisto-stele, on the previously mentioned Attic grave stele of the boy Theokles, where the dog is also on its hind legs reaching for a pet bird (fig. 61). The boy is holding the bird (probably a dove) by the wings, which once again indicates that the bird should perhaps be seen as a living creature, otherwise why should the dog chase a clay figurine? The dog is of unknown breed and seems to be smaller than that which is normally portrayed on steles, however, the scene is typical for a child grave stele from the 4th century BC.[548] Another stele shows an older boy with a bird in his right hand and a dog jumping up to reach it (fig. 65).[549]

The dog on fig. 65 seems to be identical to the dog on the Melisto-stele, and stands in the same posture on its hind legs. In his other hand the boy seems to be holding either a ball or a piece of fruit, perhaps a pomegranate. On a stele found in Piraeus and dated to the middle of the 4th century, an older girl is holding what may be an exotic type of bird, while her dog is leaping for it (fig. 66).[550] In her other hand she is holding a fan, which may indicate that she was an older girl, but not yet of the marrying age before dying. In general, age variation is traceable on Attic grave steles from the 4th century BC; however, the scenes are often standardized showing children with pets and/or favored toys.[551]

Dogs are frequently seen on vases, especially on a *chous* from the end of the 5th century, where a girl is shown playing with her dog; she may be playing fetch with the stick in her hand (perhaps she is balancing the stick on her finger, which was a popular balancing game), while running next to her pet (fig. 67).[552] Here, the particular animal seems to be of the sledge-dog type, which is one of the earliest breeds originating from the wolf.

Children can do many things with a dog: Hug it, sleep with it, run with it, and tease it. A dog also invites and encourages certain interactive games, such as the well-known (also present-day) activity of 'go-and-get-it', where the child throws something that the dog will run after. Playing *fetch* with a dog was also typical in Classical Attica, where a person threw an object and the dog retrieved it. And perhaps this *fetching* game, in practicing cooperative man-animal hunting, would have a functional future: The dog bringing the prey back to the hunter. But from a here-and-now practicing perspective this game demands rather advanced cooperative 'give-and-take' skills from both parties. In addition, training a dog from scratch to be able to play fetch is not a given thing:

**Fig. 65.** *A boy with dog. Attic marble stele. Second half of 4th century BC.*

**Fig. 66.** *A boy with dog and bird. Marble stele. Piraeus, mid-4th century.*

**Fig. 67.** *'Throwing a stick' A girl with dog. Attic red-figure chous, end of 5th century.*

**Fig. 68.** *Dog threatening a toddler boy? Attic red-figure chous, Ca. 420-410 BC.*

**Fig. 69.** *'Up-and-get-it'. A boy with dog. Attic red-figure vase, Ca. 420 BC.*

**Fig. 70.** *Boys with dogs and sticks. Attic red-figure chous, 4th century.*

What if the dog begins to tear the object apart or even eat it? What if the dog is not interested in finding the object and even less in coming back with it? What if the dog takes the object and runs away from the thrower? How does a child (perhaps accompanied by an adult) – without scoulding the dog or treating it too harshly – make such a creature learn that it should not run away? Presumably dogs from ancient times just like present-day dogs function after the 'pleasure-principle', avoiding punishment and coming back when rewarded. We do not know the answers. However, without spending a considerable amount of time and experience in training both parties the necessary *fetch* skills seen on *choes* would not have been possible.

Another type of sledge dog (or perhaps a Maltese) is seen on another *chous* from ca. 420-410 BC showing an eager or angry dog jumping towards (what seems to be) a scared or surprised toddler (fig. 68).[553] The toddler is wearing an amulet to protect him from 'evil' forces, yet he is not protected against an attacking dog. Perhaps the artist of the *chous* wanted to show a comical scene of an overly eager and playful dog jumping at a child, yet the scene may also be more serious, showing an angry dog attacking a male toddler. It is hard to tell since the face of the child is partly erased by time, but the dog looks angry, so the scene may be of a negative character. On a *chous* from 420 BC a boy is shown training his dog in 'up-and-get-it', holding a piece of meat or grapes in his hand (fig. 69).[554] The dog is rising up on its hind legs, ready to jump to reach for the food in the boy's hand.

On another *chous* two older boys are depicted with two dogs (fig. 70).[555] The boys are holding sticks that seem to have food attached to the end, perhaps indicating the same type of training as mentioned before. However, the scene could also be interpreted less jovial and may perhaps show two boys beating the dogs.

**Fig. 71.** *A boy fetching a jumping hare. Attic red-figure* chous, *Ca. 425-420 BC.*

Other types of pet animals: As seen on a *chous* from 425-420 BC a boy is playing with a *hare* (fig. 71).[556] The boy is reaching for the hare while it is leaping into his arms. This charming scene may indicate that children in Classical Attica used hares as pets, like rabbits are used today.[557] In addition, the hare is a symbol of love between an older male and his young lover. We have earlier discussed that, on the one hand, play objects shown on choes (most) often had symbolic connotations. But on the other hand, supported by other types of evidence, could also function as real play objects, and in this context as real pet companions in the everyday life of ancient Greek children.

Also, perhaps deer were used as pets, as shown on a *chous* for example, where a young boy is riding a fawn.[558] Depictions of fawns pulling carts also exist, similar to the goat-cart depictions.[559] The riding of fawns may be inspired by earlier depictions of young Silens riding wild deer, and may therefore not have happened in reality.[560]

Charming child/pet scenes witnessed on various choes may indicate that children were brought up with pet animals, and may show that they often had sentiments towards their pets. These sentiments are for instance seen on a *chous* from 425-420 BC, where a boy kisses his pet duck although this scene, based on interpretation, may also have homo-erotic references (fig. 72).[561]

Pet types may have been even more various than the animals depicted in the Classical Attic iconography. Although evidence is lacking we can cautiously assume that children from different parts of society may have played with different types of animals. Some children may not have had pets at all. Animals such as deer, pure-bred dogs and horses, and the more extravagant animals e.g. cheetahs and exotic birds were perhaps

**Fig. 72.** *A boy kisses a duck.*
*Attic red-figure* chous, *Ca. 425-420 BC.*

only pets of aristocratic children.[562] However, within the pet range several domestic and farm animals such as pigs, goats, mix-breed dogs and natural birds, having been around every day, may have been companions to children from lower classes. Children living in rural houses may have had many types of domestic pets which were separated from the animals meant for slaughter. Playing with and taking care of animals in childhood may have given practical experience for the responsibilities of raising infants in adulthood and in addition could foster early responsibility. (Parents today use this type of explanation for giving their young child a pet).

We appreciate that children and pets shown on choes clearly had sacral and other symbolic meanings. But once again, in everyday life playing with and keeping pets may have functioned as an early socialization of the child into future responsibilities and duties in a relaxed, motivated and playful matter. A young child living in its 'here-and-now mode' does not have the perspective of the future that adults can have. So this 'serious' preparative function does not exclude the child from having experienced a pet as very enjoyable.

## Toys – objects to be used in many ways

With the exception of Plato's idea that child's play had a societal role, the ancient understanding and views on children's play in the Classical world are not well known. We do not know if the ancient Greeks knew about the mental and physical benefits of play, because no written sources exist on that subject.[563] However, by looking at the material record as well as the iconographic evidence on grave steles and various types of vases, it is reasonable to believe that not only did children actually play, but that they also were encouraged by adults to play. Considering the abundant material record, one is forced to conclude that: Ancient Greek society was indeed 'a culture of toys'. Toys found in ancient Greece were often of the finest craftwork, made by adults for children – and not by the children themselves.[564] So, adults actively structured and enriched children's environment by bringing toys early into their life:

> "Once a baby could crawl or walk he or she might receive a toy on wheels to push or pull" (Niels & Oakley 2003, 266).

Doing this without any sense or purpose is rather unlikely. Instead, some underlying cultural beliefs, appreciating the (unknown) positive functions of toys, are more likely in Classical Athens. Maybe toys were made just to amuse children? Maybe the adults sensed that it was healthy and beneficial for children to play? Perhaps it was a way to keep an energetic child occupied while the adults were busy doing their chores? Anyway, children could acquire what the environment had to offer, in this case play objects.

Children aged 3-7 are very often portrayed playing with different types of toys or animals on either grave steles, vases, but most frequently on choes. In sum, there is a rich collection of evidence laying the foundation for making inferences and interpretations. Taking into consideration the huge amounts of utensils and play objects that have been found, it is highly unlikely that there has not been some sort of organized production and skilled employment behind all this. The term 'cultural message' would indicate that investing time, skill and economic resources in an artifact signals that it has some sort of latent cultural function that is valued – perhaps as a socializing tool. In principle any culture is free to 'invest' in almost anything when it comes to artifacts that are not directly produced in order to secure survival. Investing in artifacts made only for small children may appear extravagant, but it can have important functions as well. The same can be said about children's use of time and energy in play.[565]

Several types of toys exist in the material record from the Classical period. This indicates various types of play, not only role-playing, but also pretend play, physical play, mental and social play. Children are not only portrayed as playing with toys but also with other children and pets, and imaginary play is witnessed in all cultures and seemingly goes back to the earliest time in the history of homo sapiens.[566] In addition, from the anthropological record it is well known that role play and imaginary play has widespread appeal among young children.[567] So it is reasonable to infer that ancient Greek children also practiced imaginary play with and without the use of items. Early in ontogeny objects are necessary as props for imaginative play, because mental representation and symbolic thinking is rather weak and thus demands "scaffolding". But in young childhood the symbolic function runs by itself, making possible pure imaginative play. Imaginative play has an 'as if' attitude, for example using a stick to represent a spear, or to play at being Zeus ruling the world. One should remember that the realm of the gods was a 'real' and intimate part of everyday life for the Greeks. In ancient Attic culture there is evidence that children were introduced early in life to the complex imaginative sacral world of the gods. Religious actions, rituals and the 'presence' of the gods were all a given part of life (see Part 2, section: 'The religious world of the child – sacral actions and socialization'). According to activity theory presented earlier, the 'stuff' that play themes are built of derives from the child's everyday experience. Participating in sacral rituals, seeing statues of gods, perhaps overhearing adults talking about the sacral world, having an altar in the home, and, as the material record shows, even having toy-altars (see fig. 55) – all may have had an impact on the imagination of the young child. In addition, the sacral world invented by the adults was an imaginary one, but highly important. So, socialization into this realm followed by later more formalized sacral education, demanded an 'as if' and imaginative stance. Although there is no evidence to confirm this, and therefore it will be a hypothesis, imaginative play (with and without play objects) during young childhood could have been an informal, but important and even necessary, early sacral socializer.

As argued previously, there is reason to believe that young children in ancient Attica played, and were probably also engaged in pretend play and if so, this will have important implications for understanding their development. As mentioned earlier, research on imaginative play shows that it has important developmental functions. The identification with adults seen in role play is beneficial for the understanding of others, thus contributing to social competence. This is highly relevant for a new generation gradually growing into a complex social world consisting of plural roles and positions, norms and expectations. Early in life the ancient Attic child was involved in many social relationships and more people were actually around than in a contemporary nuclear family. As shown in Part 2, the Classical Attic family and household was a much more complex social entity than the modern nuclear family and consisted not only of mother and father, but of grandparents, wet nurses, slaves, servants, pedagogues, and others coming and going – all having different relationships with the child. Outside the *oikos* was the immediate neighborhood with its shops, houses and multitude of social activities. This social reality reminds us that the ancient Attic child was from early in life surrounded by a 'community of minds', and from the age of 3 she/he became involved in 'mind exchanges' determined by the activities of their particular community.[568]

In relation to roleplay and imaginary play, this context enhances the necessary development of the social cognition of the next generation so as to become a competent participant in culture and society. Recent empirical research, although not Freudian theory of 'play as self-therapy', shows that pretend play can help and is used by young children to cope with distress.[569] In the ancient world, the ultimately death of close family members: Father, mother and siblings, was much more common than today. How seriously the deaths of close relatives (for example, older siblings) were taken can be seen on several grave steles from the period, with adults mourning and their sadness clearly expressed when it was a *wanted* child.[570] (See also the same conclusion in Part 2, 'Beyond sentiment? High Child Mortality and Infanticide'). Thus, the young child was more frequently confronted with loss than is the case today. Perhaps the 3-6 year olds (but we do not know) would in imaginative play repeat the event over and over again, and in this way gradually come to terms with the loss?

Gender specific toys are customary: For instance, only girls are seen with dolls, and boys with hoops, but many toys are also unisex.[571] There are types of play that do not seem to be gender divided, e.g. playing with animals, and various games like playing with knuckle bones and balls. *Gender specific* play is observed across time and culture, and is also evident today.[572] Gender specific play is usually supported by and even reinforced with gender specific toys. Take a trip to the local toy store and it clearly becomes evident that gender specific toys are as common today as in the 5th and 4th century BC, and some toys are even similar to ancient types: Dolls with accessories for girls and 'cars' and push carts for boys.[573] 'Board' games, dice games and balls are more unisex (with the exception of footballs, which are mostly used by boys). The hoop, which is also evident in the ancient Greek records, is used both by girls and boys today and known as the hula hoop. The same can be said about the yoyo. Wheeled horses, miniature animals and miniature furniture are also produced today, yet the material now is either plastic or wood.

As mentioned previously, play seems to be universal among children and exists across time and space, but play is, to an extent, highly influential within types of culture.[574] Toys are also universal and have in fact existed for at least 9,000 years (Anatolian), but found all over the world.[575] Toys are one of the oldest artifacts created by man[576] and the oldest types of toys are miniature stone animals, dolls and rattles.[577] They are interpreted as toys because they are found in child graves. The similarities between ancient and modern toys are striking, and may indicate that adults in ancient Greece also had an idea and understanding of child's play. As mentioned in Part 2, rattles are hugely important to sensorimotor and brain development of infants and it is therefore somewhat intriguing that it is one of the oldest types of toys in the history of mankind. Adults and parents in Classical Attica probably did not know the specific developmental gains of child's play, but perhaps they learned from observation that a playing child was a happy and healthy child.[578] Adults may also have learned that children's mental and physical health depended on/improved with different types of play (with different types of toys), and perhaps not only socializing role-play were encouraged by parents.[579] One thing is certain however, children were encouraged to play in Classical Attic society, and play types and toys were numerous, and not only of sacral importance.

In the world of a young child today, it is a given thing that there are lots of toys. The production, distribution and purchase of toys for children is not a fringe economy, but a global, multi-billion business. On a more modest scale ancient Attic children also had toys, but probably not all children had toys that were bought. We do not know the cost of a doll or a wheeled horse, for example, or the cost of producing them. Obviously toys had a price and were a part of the economic system in ancient Attica. Supposedly, toy objects were purchased in special shops and produced by skilled craftsmen, who used materials, time, and skills to make a living. So, in the budget of an ancient household, perhaps a surplus economic reserve had been set aside for the purpose of buying these objects. Not surprisingly, therefore, the material records of various play objects and toys stem mostly from relatively well-off families. A child living in poverty would probably have had less access to play objects that had to be purchased but such children may have produced self-made toys, for example binding two feathers onto a stick and running around making the 'bird' fly, by holding it up in the air. Or a child could have made a miniature fence out of wood sticks, a collection of small stones inside, representing the herd. However, slave children in Ancient Greece had working duties from an early age, which constrained the time and energy available for play.

Several toys – either made by the child or manufactured – that were made of fragile material, for example, cloth or wood – were too delicate to preserve to the present day. But it would be unwise to claim, that they have not existed. 'Not found' does not always mean 'non-existent'. It is presumed that there were plenty of toy horses made of wood, but none have been found.[580] Instead the only ones that have survived are the clay horses. However, 'fragile' toys or part of toys can be seen in the material evidence. For example, the stick attached to the roller seems to be made of wood. The ball is another example – never found – but seen on both *choes*, steles and child statues. That a ball was made of a light and probably soft material is seen on fig. 20: The attic red-figure *chous* from ca. 425 BC where two boys are playing the so-called '*passé-boule*' (a game where a ball has to be thrown through a hole in an upright board placed on the ground). [581] The string that was used to go through the hole on the top of the head of dolls decayed long ago. But it did exist and can be seen on an Attic marble stele from the early 4$^{th}$ century (see fig. 41). Here a girl is seen lifting her doll by holding the string with a fine pinching grip. And, although it is a 'frozen' moment in time, the young girl has probably been playing with the doll, making it hop and dance – perhaps even imagining herself to be the dancer. If not doing that mechanically it is likely that a young girl making her doll dance may be imaginary involved and perhaps taking the role as the female dancer herself.

## Objects and toys – developmental perspectives

Most objects are simply 'what they are'. Some are useful and others are not. Some are natural objects and others are deliberately made, easing various practical functions. For example, the skilled Stone Age toolmaker produced arrows and spears for hunting and stone scrapers for treating fur to be used as clothing. But there are also objects that are not only what they seem to be, because they are used in a special way to represent something else – for example, a sacral symbol – or even a toy. An object is transformed into a toy when a child uses it in a manner not expected in the 'how-to-use affordances' lying in the object. When playing 'a farmer' the child might use various small stones/clay animals to represent domestic animals, and small sticks too, as fences, so the animals cannot run away. Observing young children today involved in their imaginative play reveals a creative and extended use of objects, either self-invented objects that are at hand or objects intentionally made for them by adults. But before that age, the toddler also engages in object play, although the items have to be more realistically made showing iconic resemblance to the real thing. For example, the miniature horse will be played with as if it was a real horse, and as mentioned, the production of toy objects was a highly skilled cultural activity.

With specific examples of toys from ancient Attica, this section will point out some important developmental functions for young children in having and using toy objects. Their significance and function for the human child will be presented using recent research from both evolutionary and developmental psychology. In the evolution of homo sapiens, artifacts like tools, utensils and other objects have been an inevitable and necessary part of life.[582] Toys seem to have been surprisingly evident quite early. It is likely that Stone Age kids played with 'novice made' stone products arranged in a game-like design which could be attributed to young children.[583] Infants and older children's environments are not only social – they are physical as well. Humans are not born into a chaotic world that has to be structured and pieced together as previously thought in developmental theory.[584] This points to a very early ontogenetic cognition, i.e. some basic knowledge about physical laws in the ways objects are perceived and handled very early in ontogenesis. Empirical studies of human knowledge about basic physical properties, seems to indicate that 'solidity' for example is inborn as 'core knowledge', or at least very quickly learnt after birth.[585] A leading developmental researcher even claims that cognitive development and learning starts in the womb.[586] This demonstrates – just in this domain of physical objects – a recent paradigm that acknowledges some much earlier ontogenetic competences of humans than thought in previous developmental psychology. In conclusion, humans are both prepared for and very interested in objects from the beginning of life. Young children experience that 'live' and 'dead' objects 'behave' very differently, and infants show in their behavior that they are aware of the differences.[587] Objects, especially play objects and toys, are 'attractors' that have important developmental functions. Highly interesting in this perspective, there is ample evidence that ancient Attic infants and young children grew up in a world not only filled with people but with various toys as well: Rattles for infants and dolls and rollers for young children. The developmental functions of play objects are not explained, however, by a mere archaeological presentation of these objects taken from the material record, with detailed information about size, shape, type of material and so on. Toys would not have continued to be made in abundance by skilled professionals and distributed widely in the Mediterranean area if they had not had some direct or indirect functions.

Solo-play with an object is developmentally important, but qualitatively different from playing with companions, practicing the rules of social reciprocity. Let us take an example of an ancient Greek toddler with its solo experiences of what to do with a ball. The ball, lying 'dead' on the ground, demands that the child itself initiates and continues various actions with his toy object. For example: The child takes it up, looks at it, turns it around and squeezes it. If the child is very young, it will perhaps suckle on it as infants do. As a toddler the child may try to sit on it, with the risk of tumbling over. With time, having explored and learned much more about the ball's properties everything works much better: When the ball is rolled, pushed, bounced, thrown, kicked, gripped either by the child itself or in coordinated social play with a peer. During human infancy and toddlerhood the intricacies of hand-eye coordination are fine-tuned, and grasping an object for example is learnt between 3-7 months. But the whole arm coordination and perceptual precision that makes it possible to roll or throw a ball at something, into something and to someone usually develops gradually between the age of 18 months and 3 years. Later in life practices with various objects, both alone and with others develop necessary skills. It seems clear from the various material evidence that the juvenile period in Classical Attica was devoted to such important practices.

Children's object play is greatly influenced by the objects that are available to them – various play objects have their 'usability affordance qualities'. As previously concluded, the material evidence clearly shows that toy objects were handed to, and played with, by children. From this, it follows that parents and other 'cultural agents' deliberately enriched the child's environment in decisive ways by giving them toys. The rich material evidence shows young children surrounded by and using various play objects evidently brought into their life by adult 'childhood architects' – representatives of ancient Greek child socializers. This seems to indicate a sense of cultural value that 'toys are good for children'. As we saw earlier Plato appreciated the future benefits of children's play as a kind of 'preparation' for adult life. We do not know if this idea was representative at all, but this makes it easier to understand why many toys were mini replicas of living persons and animals and, most interesting, not miniature copies of gods and other things taken from the supernatural world. This fact is a further argument that the specific toys actually produced in the ancient Attic culture served more purposes than just being sacral.

According to Wileman (2005) physical education and competition in sports was regarded as very important, particularly by ancient Greek society, for example various ball sports. For a male adult who was unable to throw and catch a ball while running and jumping – which would demand rather complex hand-eye and spatial coordination, there may have been negative social consequences because he did not live up to traditional and cultural expectations. Both this actual and normative competitive context was a reality in which boys would later have to participate. Not surprisingly, balls as evidenced earlier, were a common play object for young and older boys (and occasionally also girls). Balls and spinning tops could – outside their sacral function shown on images – have had important preparation functions by playing with them for fun and getting experienced in good time before it becomes serious business. If a child is not skilled in throwing and catching it is not likely that he will be allowed to participate in games where these skills are needed. So, therefore, to give a youngster his first ball was both an important cultural message of 'learn to handle it', as well as an option for the practicing future, more elaborate game skills, which were greatly valued. Games for older children in ancient Greece for instance the three 'tug-of-war' games *dielkystina, helkystina* and *ephelkystina*, tested strength and endurance and were very common.[588] Moreover these games added a social and cooperative dimension to competition because it was team against team contesting who was the strongest. Non-object play, such as chasing games, is another example of testing and strengthening both endurance and evasive running skills. Juggling balls and balancing a stick on the end of a finger or on the palm of the hand was also allowed.[589]

Toddlers and young children are the explorers per se of their environment. Objects are used both exploratively and in play. An important distinction between *object exploration* and *object play*, however, is made by Bjorklund & Gardiner. In exploration children gather important information and learn about an object:

> "Through exploration, children are essentially asking "What can *it* do?" – investigating the properties of the object, material, shape, color, weight, solidity. Such an orientation is different from the more person-centered orientation that guides play, as traditionally defined, where children essentially ask "What can *I* do with it?" (Bjorklund & Gardiner 2011, 154)

In object play children are trying out the affordances of the object in relation to the environment. For example, a ball is 'demanding' to be thrown and rolled. Whereas a doll is 'demanding' to be held, put in bed, or placed on a chair, or taken for a walk with support from the child. In imaginative play, using an object as prop for fantasy, there are few rules and the affordances of the toy object are loosened. So specific toys are environmental props that do not determine, but 'suggest' play themes, in addition the child draws on its experience from everyday life in order to construct the specific play theme. This is important because cultures use for example 'the horse' in different ways. In a contemporary Western society where cars have taken over, the horse is used in a more 'leisurely' way than in an ancient Attic culture where horses were, among other things, used in war and sport. So, toys and other play objects evidently had important cultural and ontogenetic developmental functions. Some of these functions were perhaps sensed by people living in ancient Attica, but we do not know. However, that being said, we know from very convincing recent research that this is so, irrespective of whether or not it was known by cultural agents.[590]

# PART 4

# CONCLUSIONS AND PERSPECTIVES

How are infants and young children to be understood in ancient Attica when it comes to family living, care, socialization and play? In this book on Developmental Childhood Archaeology this question was answered by describing and interpreting important parts of children's lives based on the use of a multitude of artifacts, iconographic evidence and written sources. We have for example seen how socio-historical events had impact on the general view of children in ancient Greece, from the late Archaic period to early Hellenistic times. Such changes in views and attitudes are reflected in the material records and in the iconographic representations of children, i.e. on steles. The main conclusions will now be drawn from each of the major parts of the book. A discussion about interpretative validity will also be taken up, because the various ways that childhood archaeologists interpret the material and iconographic evidence varies considerably. On the one hand, there seems to be a relatively 'realist wing' considering artifacts as reasonable (albeit often idealized) 'evidence' of some sort of underlying reality. On the other hand, there is a relatively 'ideal wing'; when it comes to the interpretation of iconography this is in essence not about reality per se, but serves solely idealized, spiritual and religious purposes. In that discussion we will make clear the standpoint of Developmental Childhood Archaeology. Finally, some future perspectives will be dealt with concerning the importance of interdisciplinarity.

## Conclusions

In Part 1, it was concluded that the growing discipline of childhood archaeology has from its very beginning been interdisciplinary. But also that the use of recent developmental and evolutionary theory has been very modest. To remedy this, Part 1 presented a new professional interdisciplinary perspective called 'Developmental Childhood Archaeology', which combines child-archaeological evidence and approaches with new developmental and evolutionary childhood psychology. The specific definition and understanding of the book's main conceptualizations: *Care, socialization* and *play,* were also introduced. These approaches have been used throughout the book as interpretative tools. Did the ancient Greeks have specific child perceptions? If they did, what were they? The conclusion, based on literary sources and material culture, is that they definitely did have specific child perception, although not like the strict 'ageism' of our times, but they (loosely) distinguished between age groups. The purpose behind this can be manifold, but the Greeks obviously knew about childhood and its stages long before modern academics.[591]

Based on Part 2, it is reasonable to conclude that ancient Greek upperclass mothers did nurse and care for their children, for instance through breastfeeding and other types of child-mother interactions (like potty training). However, since wet nurses and housemaids were used to some extent in elite households it is not clear whether aristocratic and upper class mothers engaged in primary nursing themselves. If they did employ wet nurses it was probably due to reproduction issues or because of aesthetic reasons. Infant nursing and caring does not seem to have been gender divided and the gender of the child did not perhaps become important until the toddler age. Besides newborns and the youngest infants that were restrained by swaddling, it seems reasonable to draw the conclusion that children in general, were from a very young age, engaged with by adults (for example with the use of rattles). Toddlers were encouraged to explore activities such as crawling and were also included in child-adult interaction on a daily basis.

It is also reasonable to conclude that a child's role in the ancient Greek household was numerous. Children were not seen merely as offspring, but were also carers, playmates, siblings, and some were slaves, and not least the focus of several religious rituals. In addition, they were regarded as future citizens of Athenian society. Children had multiple relationships in the *oikos*. Iconographic evidence shows sentimentalized depictions, where attachments between *mothers and children* seem evident. It is more difficult to come to conclusions, however about the relationship between *fathers and children* since father/child depictions are less common. On grave steles fathers often look stern and serious, exuding the ideal picture of the *Kyrios* (the father of the household). Primary written sources create a kaleidoscopic picture of fatherly behavior, ranging from ruling children like a king (Aristotle), to denouncing bad behavior (Euripides). A male-dominant society such as the Classical Attic society may indirectly have restricted depictions showing softer sides of fatherly behavior, which are only evident on very few vases and steles. However, from moralist philosopher's examples of over-doing fatherly sentiments towards offspring (probably warning males not to be too sentimental) there are some indications that such tender behavior occurred occasionally. Why else warning against it?

Despite maternal love for the wanted children, unwanted children were exposed of (often females) before the age of 5-10 days, to accommodate and ensure the needs of other children in the specific household (siblings) or to uphold the ideal picture of an elite family. Infanticide was practiced to some extent, especially in the upper classes, to either deselect a specific gender, handicapped infants or to ensure the wealth and position of elite families. *Infanticide* could co-exist with high child mortality because children that were exposed were 'dehumanized' – not yet viewed as human beings and members of the family. The rituals used for transferring the infant from 'not-belonging' into a 'member of the family', and the possible psychological mechanisms dealing with that, were described in detail in order to explain why some children became the loved ones, while other children were killed – probably without much remorse. Yet, slave-, poor- and exposed-children are hard to find in the material record and in written sources.

*Alloparenting* and *cooperative breeding* was probably normal in the *oikos* and consisted of various adults. Among them *grandparents* were engaged in close child-relations and both grandmothers and fathers were a part of grandchildren's lives, which is evident from steles and epitaphs. Adult slaves and slave children were most likely also a part of the ancient Greek household, but evidence is indistinct and further research is necessary. *Siblings* had special relationships and most probably played together. Perhaps older siblings took care of smaller brothers/sisters, which taught them about nursing, care and responsibilities. The Classical Attic household consisted of several co-inhabitants ranging from parents, siblings and grandparents to nurses, pedagogues and slaves. This complex family probably did include alloparenting, which resulted in the multiple-caring of children. This seemed to ensure the best survival and living conditions for children, and secured their daily care. According to new research, *multiple attachments* ensures the best mental and physical development of children since they are protected, activated and nursed by various adults. However, it must be stressed that not all children had a pleasant upbringing, for instance slave-children and poor children, or even those who were mentally and physically abused.

It can also be concluded that the *sacral world* was part of daily living – a highly integrated part of children's lives in relation to their family and society. From an early age children were in focus or part of several religious rituals and events. Children were brought for example to temples to bring sacrifices; they were themselves the very focus of several rites-of-passage rituals such as the Amphidromia, the Dekatê and the Apatouria. They were included in festivals such as the Anthesteria where they engaged in competitions and were given gifts (choes). They were also annexed into various sanctuaries (like the Artemis Brauronia), and cultural systems such as the phratry. Our suggestion has been that children's active participation in these ritual acts did result in and ensured a *sacral socialization* often processed by *self-socialization*. This educated children on their sacral responsibilities and also gave them skills for sacral practise, thereby securing and upholding this important dimension of Greek culture for hundreds of years – a complex polytheistic system.

From Part 3 it can be concluded that *play* seems to be a universal activity in the human juvenile period. Toys have been found to exist very early in ancient history, being at least 9,000 years old (Anatolian), and found all over the world. Toys are one of the oldest artifacts created by man and the oldest types of toys are miniature animals, dolls, yoyos and rattles. They are interpreted as toys because they are found in child graves. It is likely that Stone Age Kids played with 'novice made' stone products arranged in a display of game-like designs. So, it is not surprising that young children in ancient Attica also played, which there is ample evidence to conclude. In Part 3 a brief history of theories about the functions and meanings of play showed that play has been understood in contradictory ways – as an outlet for excessive energy, as preparation for future adult roles with no particular purpose or goal; as a defense mechanism and self-therapy; as an assimilative activity, 'chewing on experiences'; as important for mental and brain development; as culturally integrative. Discussing the *iconographic ambiguity* concerning the representations of children in play it was concluded that young children really played in ancient Attica. It was concluded by using Classical philological sources that 3-6 year olds loved to play and invented games when being together. Based on Plato and modern socialization research, it seems evident that children were given toys that would encourage and engage them in specific types of play like role play and pretend play, which both developed important 'life skills' and prepared them for future roles, for instance as mothers or laborers. Also gender-specific play occurred.

Based on the actual material evidence of toys it can be concluded that young children in ancient Attica had *many different toys* at hand. The toys were made by skilled craftsmen and probably made in rather big production centers and perhaps (although the evidence is thin here) distributed in the Mediterranean area. Toys were plenty, serving a multitude of developmental, socializing and cultural functions, for example, dolls, rollers, push- and go carts, wheeled horses, balls, spin tops, yoyos, knucklebones, whistles, and miniature altars. Also animals made in terracotta were at hand for children to play with, for example pigs and turtles. Pets – for example living birds, hares, dogs and, for some children, domestic animals were also a part of the Classical Attic household, dogs and birds being the most common types. Children being responsible for pets gained experience in nursing, care and responsibility. It can be concluded also that playing with toy objects has many developmental and socializing functions, both when it comes to sensorimotor play, imaginative and pretend play. The latter not only as gender specific role-taking but probably, in some instances, the young child was also as an early sacral self-socializer.

## Interpretative validity? – discussion and conclusion

Especially when it comes to iconography there is no shared agreement on how to interpret this. Earlier in this book, in the section 'Did children really play in ancient Attica – the iconographic ambiguity', we have touched this matter to some extent. But, before closing this book, it is very important to point out some key elements in childhood archaeology in order to reach a conclusion on how to interpret the many objects that constitute the actual raw material, for the subject of childhood archaeology.

On the one hand, there seems to be a 'realist wing' considering artifacts as reasonable (albeit often idealized) 'evidence' of some sort of underlying reality. On the other hand, there is an 'ideal wing': When it comes to the interpretation of iconography this is in essence not about reality but serves solely idealized, spiritual and religious purposes.

A realist approach, for example, clearly takes emotions shown on grave steles as evidence of real emotions felt by parents in mourning their dead child. In her introduction to *Constructions of Childhood in Ancient Greece and Italy*, Cohen (2007) in her discussion of funerary art is setting the interpretative course in this way:

> "Funerary art of the type discussed above and in several chapters below suggests that artists devised strategies for showing emotional moments of physical connection that must have been keenly felt. (...). Although representations like this are frankly factious idealizations, they allude convincingly to less elegant moments

of despair, experiences in private. Reading states of mind is not all that difficult in such cases, and it is hard to miss the affection, the nostalgia, or the intimacy that body language communicates" (21).

In essence this is mainly in line with the approach of Developmental Childhood Archaeology, but there is another important side of the coin to consider. It is well known that public portraits of parents and children carry important cultural messages, for example, they have sacral meanings or are intended to idealize motherhood. In some instances we can see this as an early kind of 'propaganda'. For such purposes, realism is obviously not the agenda, and the iconographic 'evidence' shows portraits of idealized and desired ways to live or the right way to express feelings as the 'mourning parent' for example. Another example would be a vase with clear erotic content found in sexually immature children's, and even in infant graves.[592] This is not realism, among other things, because adults and not small children are portrayed involved in sex scenes. In addition many of the scenes are taken from Greek mythology. The vases with their motives have probably been selected by the parents to indicate an important message on gender control and customs. It seems to allude to, for example, what a girl would miss in her adult life because of her premature death. So, this custom probably promotes popular social ideologies and ideals about the expected roles of women (and men) in both sex and marriage.[593] The only 'realism' here is the fact that the scenes depicted in the various hetero- and homosexual erotic portrayals on the vases were obviously a normal and appraised practice in society.

An important warning about reading 'realism' into the iconographic record comes from Beaumont (2012) who adheres to the 'ideal wing':

> "...we must resist the inclination to interpret Athenian iconography as presenting us with simple vignettes of childhood. We must always remember that it was not the artists' intention to present us with a pictorial record of child life. (...). In utilizing the iconographical evidence to attempt to reconstruct childhood experience we must therefore be very cautious, as the ideal and the reality were almost certainly not always congruent".[594]

If holding this position, the same can be said about iconography showing parents relationships to children. They were also constructed with specific intentions not necessarily showing realism. On the other hand, mourning mothers, fathers and grandmothers are used as evidence of real sentiments.[595] So, a schism is clearly evident here in childhood archaeology. How should it be decided in what ways the so-called 'iconographic evidence' gets its status as evidence? We will follow this important path turning to – and given as an exemplary example – the discussion of 'is it play, or not play, we see on vases?'

First it is important to say that iconography should not be the sole object of evidence, for instance play scenes on vases that lead to interpretative conclusions. Rather, it is the complex joining of the different sources of ancient information that lead to that. Let us take an example: Besides the rich iconographic representations of children' play scenes, there is the massive evidence of real play objects which are exactly like those children 'play' with on vases. Moreover, the ancient written sources do not only appreciate play but also confirm that play really took place.[596] We also have the information that adults gave play-objects to their children to play with. Having this information from separate sources turns the interpreter back to the iconographic evidence once more, perhaps with a 'new look'. For example, the well-known scene of the girl 'throwing a stick for the dog to get' has its own idealized adult-construed meaning, created for special sacral purposes. But such adult 'symbolic coloring' is seemingly built on a highly probable event; throwing sticks for a dog to retrieve is what is likely to happen when a playful child and a dog are together. So, what is seen on a vase is also a prototype-event of everyday child-dog play that *does not carry the adult-made connotations for the parties involved.* Said in other words, securing interpretative validity is dependent on two different intentions: 1) Are we trying to understand the ancient adult Athenians' (and artists') inducement of meaning in the particular scene? or 2) Are we trying to take a child's perspective – viewing this with the child's own eyes as a 'prototype real' scene?[597] The conclusion consequently, is that the two very different interpretations of the 'same scene', on the same vase, can (although not in all cases) both be valid and do not necessarily exclude each other.

This guiding principle of *interpretative perspectivism* – a 'both/and' stance – can be used on other material than vase iconography, for example grave steles: On the one hand, we 'read' grave steles as culturally idealized images. On the other hand, steles also can be seen as representing parents' 'true' grief and sorrow on the loss of a child. Despite her important warnings against reading realism in iconography cited above, Beaumont (2012) also uses, among various sources, iconography to show how Athenian boys and girls were dressed in reality:

> "Furthermore, when we (…) turn to examine the iconographic indicators of the various phases of childhood, we also find that it is in the early childhood stage that boys and girls regularly adopt gender-specific ways of displaying or clothing the body" (20).

This obvious realism interpretation does not undermine the notion that these differently clad boys and girls are also to be understood in a context that has sacral meanings and purposes. So, interpretative perspectivism – allowing more than one reading – has been the guiding principle in this book's Developmental Childhood Archaeology approach.

## A repeated call for interdisciplinarity

Research on children and childhood in ancient Greece is a field in its infancy. Further research is necessary to enhance our knowledge about the lives and conditions of children, from 0-7 years, in Classical Attica. More extensive collecting of empirical data, for instance of toys, nursing objects and iconographic representations of children will be crucial in future childhood archaeological research. Particularly, there is a great need for chronological and typological categorizing to develop a fundamental evidence base and an understanding of children's artifacts. This field is however, growing, and new research is created every year, which will contribute to a broader and more complex picture of children in ancient Greece.

In Part 1 of this book we drew attention to the important fact that childhood archaeologists from the very beginning were attuned to interdisciplinarity. In this work we have responded to Kamp's (2001) and Beaumont's (2012) call for interdisciplinarity. We believe that knowledge of children and their childhoods taken from different research fields can be especially fruitful in the further understanding of ancient societies, including Greece, and that childhood archaeology will benefit from an interdisciplinary research approach. The application of the developmental as well as evolutionary childhood psychology paradigm is new in this context. However, theory in this book has been rather bottom-up, based on solid and rich evidence stemming from the material record. But this is only one approach among many, and future studies of children's roles, lives, conditions, relationships, religious life and human interactions are greatly needed. Research on children's relationships with their co-inhabitants and co-citizens will especially contribute to our knowledge about the ancient Greek society in general.

The interdisciplinarity calls and recommendations from childhood archaeologists have been very promising to witness, but up till now especially the integration of recent developmental and evolutionary psychology has been very limited. This is probably because this wealth of new knowledge is not well-known outside psychology. Instead we have witnessed that archaeologists – in order to understand childhood – have applied other types of recent theory (see types in Part 1, the section 'Childhood archaeology: Interdisciplinary from the beginning'). For example, when archaeologists have been dealing with the childhood part, we have witnessed not just a few turning to contemporary childhood sociology. Although this has proven useful for gaining an understanding of what a child is, as well as an understanding of its childhood in culture and society, there are major problems with this approach on other explanatory levels. For example, when it comes to the understanding of the socio-emotional functions for humans of early care in extended family relationships.[598] This is because sociology primarily reduces the child to a 'societal being'; in this regard, developmental psychology, in combination with an evolutionary-childhood stance, has been used in this book as it will be able to explain this in depth. For example, the evolutionary, cultural and ontogenetic functions and importance (or the lack) of 'relationship intimacy' in the early breast and bottle-feeding of ancient infants; the socializing importance of 'multiple care' and 'alloparenting' in the *oikos*; the specific functions of fantasy-, object-, loco-motor- and other activity with play objects. This has been addressed to a minor degree within childhood archaeology, and there is clearly a place for understanding that in child psychology.

The route to interdisciplinarity work within childhood archaeology has until now mainly been through 'importation'. This means that the archaeologist (or historian) herself is using a non-archaeology approach. With some notable exceptions in mind this has led to the impression that the outlines seem introductory and sketchy. The 'outsider theory' functions mostly as theory-scaffolding, but not much in actual interpretative use when it comes to archaeological material evidence. Interdisciplinary work can be done in many ways, but we suggest that in the future more collaborative childhood archaeological projects should be undertaken with academics from various disciplines who work together for prolonged times.[599] Interdisciplinarity that makes science breakthrough will probably not arise from mixing various disciplines together in one big melting pot, hoping that a complete understanding will appear. If interdisciplinarity is to become really beneficial, it is vital that individuals, highly skilled and rooted in each of their profession, join together and work on the same archaeological projects. Despite the many requests from childhood archaeologists for the use of interdisciplinarity, real collaboration efforts so far have not been overwhelming. The more researchers from various disciplines join together – embracing a perspective that recognizes the prominence of the childhood traces in ancient times seen in the material record – the more the study of childhood archaeology will prosper.

# BIBLIOGRAPHY

All abbreviations in the book (both ancient and modern) are based on *The Oxford Classical Dictionary*.


Alexander, G.M. & Heines, H. 2002. "Sex Differences in Response to Children's toys in Nonhuman Primates (Cercopithecus Aethiops Sabaeus)". *Evolution and Human Behavior*, 23, 467-479.

Alexandrakis, D.S. 1988. *The Education of Children from Birth to Age Fourteen in Classical Athens (500-300 BC)*. Dissertation. Michigan: Ann Arbor University Press

Ammerman, R.M. 2007. "Children at Risk: Votive Terracottas and the Welfare of Infants at Paestum". *Constructions of Childhood in Ancient Greece and Italy*. A. Cohen & J.B. Rutter (eds.). American School of Classical Studies in Athens: *Hesperia* suppl. 41, 131-153.

Argyriadi, M. 1991. *Dolls in Greek Life and Art from Antiquity to the Present Day*. Athens: Lucy Braggiotti Publications.

Ariès, P. 1962. *Centuries of Childhood*. New York: Alfred A. Knopf.

Baillargeon, R. 1994. "How Do Infants Learn about the Physical World?" *Current Directions in Psychological Science*. No. 3, 133-40.

Bartsocas, C.S. 1978. *Ancient Greek Feeding-Bottles*. Transactions and studies of The College of Physicians of Philadelphia. Fourth series, 45, no. 6, 297-298.

Baxter, J.E. 2005. *The Archaeology of Childhood – Children, Gender, and Material Culture*. California: Walnut Greek: Altamira Press.

Beaumont, L. 1998. "Born Old or Never Young? Femininity, Childhood and the Goddesses of Ancient Greece". *The Sacred and the Feminine in Ancient Greece*. S. Blundell & M. Williamson (eds.). London and New York: Routledge, 71-95.

Beaumont, L. 2000. "The Social Status and Artistic Representation of 'Adolescence' in Fifth Century Athens". *Children and Material Culture*. Ed. J.S. Deverensky. London: Routledge, 39-51.

Beaumont, L. 2003. "The Changing Face of Childhood". *Coming of Age in Ancient Greece*. Eds. J. Neils & J.H. Oakley. New Haven: Yale University Press in association with the Hood Museum of Art, Dartmouth College, Hanover, New Hampshire, 59-84.

Beaumont, L. 2012. *Childhood in Ancient Athens*. London and New York: Routledge.

Beazley, J. 1968. *Attic Red-Figure Vase Painters*. Oxford: Clarendon Press.

Berk, L. 2009. *Child Development*. 8th Edition. Boston: Pearson.

Berk, L. 2013. *Child Development*. 9th Edition. Boston: Pearson.

Berliner, D. & Sarré, R. (eds.) 2007. *Learning Religion: Anthropological Approaches*. Methodology and History in Anthropology, no. 17. New York & Oxford: Berghahn Books.

Bjorklund, D.F., & Gardner, A. 2011. "Object Play and Tool Use: Developmental and Evolutionary Perspectives". *The Oxford Handbook of The Development of Play*. A.D. Pellegrini (ed.). Oxford: University Press. Chapter 13.

Bjorklund, D. F. & Pellegrini, A. D. 2002. "All in the Family: Parents and Other Relations". *The Origin of Human Nature. Evolutionary Developmental Psychology*. D. F. Bjorklund & A. D. Pellegrini (eds.). Washington, DC: APA. Chapter 8.

Bjorklund, D. F. & Pellegrini, A. D. 2002. "Homo Ludens: The Importance of Play". *The Origin of Human Nature. Evolutionary Developmental Psychology*. D. F. Bjorklund & A. D. Pellegrini (eds.). Washington, DC: APA. Chapter 10.

Bjorklund, D. F. & Pellegrini, A. D. 2002. "Epilogue: Evolution and Development". *The Origin of Human Nature. Evolutionary Developmental Psychology*. D. F. Bjorklund & A. D. Pellegrini (eds.). Washington, DC: APA. Chapter 11.

Bjorklund, D. F. & Pellegrini, A. D. (eds.) 2002. *The Origin of Human Nature. Evolutionary Developmental Psychology*. Washington, DC. APA.

Boardman, J. 1989. *Athenian Red-Figure Vases: The Classical Period*. London: Thames & Hudson.

Boardman, J. 1995. *Greek Sculpture: The Late Classical Period and Sculptures in Colonies and Overseas*. London: Thames and Hudson.

Bobou, O. 2010. "No Playing Allowed? Depictions of Children in Ancient Greek Sculpture". *Socialisation – Recent Research on Childhood and Children in the Past*. G. Lillehammer (ed.). Stavanger: G. AmS-Skrifter 23, 33-44.

Bonfante, L. 1997. "Nursing Mothers in Classical Art". *Naked Truths – Women, Sexuality and Gender in Classical Art and Archaeology"*. A.O. Koloski-Ostrow & C.L. Lyons (eds.). London: Routledge, 174-196.

Bornstein, M.H. (ed.) 2002. *Handbook of Parenting*. 2nd. ed. Mahwah, N.J.: Lawrence Erlbaum.

Bornstein, M.H. (ed.) 2010. *Handbook of Cultural Developmental Science*. New York: Psychology Press.

Boyatiz, C. J. 2005. "Religious and Spiritual Development in Childhood". *Handbook of the Psychology of Religion and Spirituality*. R.F. Paloutzian & C.L. Park (eds.). New York & London: The Guildford Press.

Bretherton, I. & Munholland, K.A. 2008. "Internal Working Models in Attachment Relationships". *Handbook of Attachment*. 2nd ed. J. Cassidy & P.R. Shaver (eds.). New York and London: The Guildford Press. Chapter 5.

Breitenstein, N. 1941. *Catalogue of Terracottas – Cypriote, Greek, Etrusco-Italian and Roman in the Danish National Museum* I & II. Copenhagen: Munksgaard.

Brulé, P. 1987. *La Fille D'Athènes – La religion des filles à Athénes à l'époque classique. Mythes, cultes et société*. Paris: Annales Littéraires de l'Université de Besancon, 363.

Bruner J.S., Jolly, A. & Sylva K. (eds.) 1976. *Play – its Role in Development and Evolution*. Harmondsworth: Penguin Books.

Burman, E. 2008. *Deconstructing Developmental Psychology*. 2nd. ed. London: Routledge.

Cahill, N. 2002. *Household and city organization at Olynthos*. USA: Yale University Press.

Cameron, A. & Kuhrt, A. (eds.) 1983. *Images of Women in Antiquity*. London: Croom Helm.

Cassidy, J. & Shaver, P.R. (eds.) 2008. *Handbook of Attachment, Theory, Research, and Clinical Applications*. New York: Guildford Press.

Charlier, M.T. & G. Raepsaet. 1971. "Étude d'un Comportement Social: Les Relations entre Parents et Enfants dans la Société Athénienne à l'Èpoque Classique". *L'Antiquité Classique*, 40, 589-606.

Cicirelli, V.G. 1994. "Sibling Relationships in Cross-Cultural Perspective". *Journal of Marriage and Family* 56, no. 1, 7-20.

Cohen, A. 2007. "Gendering the Age Gap: Boys, Girls and Abduction in Ancient Greek Art". *Constructions of Childhood in Ancient Greece and Italy*. A. Cohen, & Rutter, J.B. (eds.). The American School of Classical Studies at Athens: *Hesperia* suppl. 41, 257-278.

Cole, M. 1996. *Cultural Psychology*. Cambridge, MA: Harvard University Press.

Cole, M. & Cagigas, X.E. 2010. "Cognition". *Handbook of Developmental Science*. M.H. Bornstein (ed.), New York: Psychology Press.

Cooper, R. & Sutton, K. 1999. "The Effects of Child Abuse on Preschool Children's Play". *Australian Journal of Early Childhood* 24. Electronic source:
www.findarticles.com/p/articles/mi_hb6418/is_2_24/ai_n31675441 (31-05-2011)

*Corpus Vasorum Antiquorum*. CVA-Deutschland (Vol. 3). München: C.H. Beck.

Cox C.H. 1988. "Sibling Relationships in Classical Athens: Brother-Sister Ties". *Journal of Family History*, 13, 377-395.

Cox, C.H. 1997. "Sibling Relationships". *Household Interests: Property, Marriage Strategies and Family Dynamics in Ancient Athens*. Princeton: University Press, 105-129.

Crelier, M.C. 2008. *Kinder in Athen im Gesellschaftlichen Wandel des 5. Jahrhunderts v. Chr*. Remshalden: Greiner.

Crouwel, H. 1992. *Chariots and Other Wheeled Vehicles from Ancient Greece*. Amsterdam: Allard Pierson.

Cunningham, H. 1995. *Children and Childhood in Western Society Since 1500*. 2nd Ed. London and New York: Longman.

Dasen, V. 2008. "All Children are Dwarfs. Medical Discourse and Iconography of Children's Bodies". *Oxford Journal of Archaeology*, 27, no. 1, 49-62.

Dasen, V. 2011. "Childbirth and Infancy in Greek and Roman Antiquity". *A Companion to Families in the Greek and Roman Worlds*. B. Rawson (ed.). Chichester, West Sussex, U.K.; Malden, MA: Wiley-Blackwell, 291-314.

Demand, N.H. 1994. "Birth, Death and Motherhood in Classical Greece". *Ancient Society and History*. Baltimore & London: John Hopkins University Press.

DeMause, L. 1974. *The History of Childhood*. New York: Peter Bedrick Books.

Dencik, L. 1999. "Fremtidens børn: Om postmodernisering og socialisering" ["Children of the Future: About Postmodernization and Socialization"]. *Børn og familie i det postmoderne samfund* [*Children and Family in Postmodern Society*]. L. Dencik & P. Schultz Jørgensen (eds.). Copenhagen: Hans Reitzels Forlag.

Dillon, M. 2002. *Girls and Women in Classical Greek Religion*. London: Routledge.

Diner, H. 1965. *Mothers and Amazons: The first Feminine History of Culture*. J. P. Lundin (ed.). New York: Julian Press.

Dipla, A. & Paleothodoros, D. (2012). "Selected for the Dead. Erotic Themes on Grave Vases from Attic Cemeteries". www.academia.edu.

Doumanis, M. 1983. *Mothering Greece: From Collectivism to Individualism*. London: Academic Press.

Dunn, J. 2004. "Sibling Relationships". *Blackwell Handbook of Childhood Social Development*. P. K. Smith & C. H. Hart (eds.). Oxford: Blackwell, 223-237.

Elderkin, K.M. 1930. "Jointed Dolls in Antiquity." *American Journal of Archaeology*, 455-79.

Fahlander, F. 2011. "Bilder av barn och barndom" [Images of Child and Childhood]. *Spåren av de Små.[The Traces From the Little Ones]*. F. Fahlander (ed.), *Stockholm Studies in Archaeology*, no. 54. Stockholm: University Service.

Field, T. 1990. *Infancy.* Massachusetts: Harvard University Press.

Fildes, V. 1986. *Breasts, Bottles and Babies – A History of Infant Feeding*. Edinburgh University Press, Scotland.

Fildes, V. 1988. *Wet Nursing – A History from Antiquity to the Present*. Oxford: Basil Blackwell.

Fischer, K. et al. 2011. "Playing Around in School: Implications for Learning and Educational Policy". *The Oxford Handbook of the Development of Play.* A. Pellegrini (ed.). Oxford University Press, Chapter 25.

Fogel, A. 2004. "The History (and Future) of Infancy". *Blackwell Handbook of Infant Development*. G. Bremner & A. Fogel (eds.). Oxford: Blackwell.

Foley, H. 2003. "Mothers and Daughters". *Coming of Age in Ancient Greece*. J. Neils & J.H. Oakley (eds.). New Haven: Yale University Press in association with the Hood Museum of Art, Dartmouth College, Hanover, New Hampshire, 113-137.

Franco, P. et al. 2005. "Influence of Swaddling on Sleep and Arousal Characteristics of Healthy Infants". *Pediatrics* 115, no. 5, 1307-1311.

French, V. 1991. "Children in Antiquity". *Children in Historical and Comparative Perspective*. J.A. Hawes & N.R Hiner (eds.). England: Greenwood, 13-29.

Freud, S. 1981. *On Sexuality: Three Essays on the Theory of Sexuality and Other Works*. Harmondsworth: Penguin Books.

Gallagher, S.K. 2007. "Children as Religious resources: The Role of Children in the Social Re-formation of Class, Culture, and Religious Identity". *Journal of the Scientific Study of Religion*,46, no. 2, 169-83.

Garland, R. 1985. *The Greek Way of Death*. London: G. Duckworth.

Garland, R. 1990. *The Greek Way of Life*. New York: Cornell University Press.

Ghosh, A. (ed.) 1990. *An Encyclopedia of Indian Archaeology*, II. New Delhi: Munshiram Manoharlal Publishers.

Gettler, L.T. "Direct Male Care and Hominin Evolution: Why Male-Child Interaction is More Than a Nice Social Idea". *American Anthropologist*, Vol. 112(1), 7-21.

Golden, M. 1981. "Demography and the Exposure of Girls in Athens". *Phoenix*, 35, no. 4, Classical Association Canada, 316-331.

Golden, M. 1985. "Pais, 'Child' and 'Slave'" *L'Antiquité Classique*. Bruxelles, 91-114.

Golden, M. 1988. "Did the Ancients Care When Their Children Died?" *Greece and Rome*, Second Series 35, no. 2, 152-163.

Golden, M. 1990. *Children and Childhood in Classical Athens*. Balitomore & London: The John Hopkins University Press.

Golden, M. 1997. "Change or Continuity? Children and Childhood in Hellenistic Historiography". *Reconstructing the past: Historicism, Periodization and the Ancient world*. M. Golden & P. Toohey (eds.). London: Routledge, 176-191.

Golden, M. 2003. "Childhood in Ancient Greece". *Coming of Age in Ancient Greece*. J. Neils & J.H. Oakley (eds.). New Haven: Yale University Press in association with the Hood Museum of Art, Dartmouth College, Hanover, New Hampshire, 13-29.

Gopnik, A., Meltzoff, A.N. & Kuhl, P.K. 1999. *The Scientist in the Crib.*New York: William Morrow and Company.

Gottlieb, G. 2007. "Probabilistic Epigenesis". *Developmental Science* 10, 1-11.

Grimm, L. 2000. "Apprentice Flintnapping: Relating Material Culture and Social Practice in the Upper Palaeolithic". *Children and Material Culture.* J.S. Derevenski (ed.). London: Routledge, 53-71.

Grossman, B. 2001. *Greek Funerary Sculpture: Catalogue of the Collection at the Getty Villa.* Los Angeles: J. Paul Getty Museum.

Grossman Burnett, J. 2007. "Forever Young: An Investigation of the Depiction of Children on Classical Attic Funerary Monuments". *Constructions of Childhood in Ancient Greece and Italy.* A. Cohen & J.B. Rutter (eds.). American School of Classical Studies in Athens *Hesperia* suppl. 41, 309-323.

Grubbs, J.E. & Parkin, T. (eds.)(2013). *The Oxford Handbook of Childhood and Education in the Classical World.* Oxford: Oxford University Press.

Harcourt-Smith, C. 1929. "Whip-tops", *JHS,* 49, part. 2, 217-219.

Harris, P.L. 2000. *The Work of the Imagination.* Oxford: Blackwell.

Hassett, J.M. et al. 2008. "Sex Differences in Rhesus Monkey Toy Preferences Parallel those of Children". *Hormones and Behavior* 54, 3, 359-364.

Herbert, K. 1964. *Ancient Art in Bowdoin College.* Cambridge: Harvard University Press.

Hewlett, B.L. 2000. "Vulnerable Lives. The Experience of Death and Loss Among Aka and Ngandu Adolescents of the Central African Republic". *Hunter-Gather Childhoods.* B.L. Hewitt & M. Lamb (eds.). New Brunswick & London: Aldine Transactions, 322-342.

Heywood, C. 2001. *A History of Childhood.* New York: Wiley & Sons.

Higgins, R.A. 1954. *Catalogue of the Terracottas in the Department of Greek and Roman Antiquities.* London: British Museum, Greek 730-330 BC, I (text & plates).

Hindman, S. 1981. "Pieter Bruegel's Children's Games, Folly and Chance". *The Art Bulletin,* 63, no. 3, 447-475.

Hirsh-Pasek, K. & Golnikoff, R.M. 2008. "Why Play = Learning". *Encyclopedia on Early Childhood Development.* Centre of Excellence for Early Childhood Development.

Hoffmann, H. 1997. *Sotades – Symbols of Immortality on Greek Vases.* Oxford: Clarendon Press.

Houby-Nielsen, S. 2000. "Child Burials in Ancient Athens" *Children and Material Culture.* J.S. Derevenski (ed.). London: Routledge, 151-166.

Howes, C. & Speiker, S. 2008. "Attachment Relationships in the Context of Multiple Caregivers" *Handbook of Attachment, Theory, Research, and Clinical Applications.* J. Cassidy & P.R. Shaver (eds.). New York: Guildford Press, 317-332.

Hrdy, S.B. 2009. *Mothers and Others – the Evolutionary Origins of Mutual Understanding.* Cambridge: Harvard University Press.

Huizinga, J. 1963. *Homo Ludens – Om Kulturens Oprindelse i Leg.* Copenhagen: Gyldendal.

James, A. 2009. "Agency" . *The Palgrave Handbook of Childhood Studies.* J. Qvortrup, G. Valentine, W. Corsaro & M. Honig (eds.). Basingstoke: Palgrave, 34-45.

Johansson, S.R. 1984. "Deferred Infanticide: Excess Female Mortality During Childhood". *Infanticide: Comparative and Evolutionary Perspectives.* G. Hausfater & S.B. Hrdy (eds.). New York: Aldine Publishing Co., 487-502.

Johnston, S.I. 1995. "Defining the Dreadful: Remarks on the Greek Child-Killing Demon". *Ancient Magic and Ritual Power.* M. Meyer & P. Mirecki (eds.). Leiden; New York: E.J Brill.

Kaltsas, N. 2002. *Sculptures in the National Archaeological Museum, Athens.* Transl. Dr. Hardy, D. Los Angeles: J. Paul Getty Museum.

Karmiloff-Smith, A. 1995. "Annotation: The Extraordinary Cognitive Journey from Foetus through Infancy". *Journal of Child Psychology and Psychiatry,* 36(8), 1293-313.

Kamp, K.A. 2001a. "Prehistoric Children Working and Playing: A Southwestern Case Study in learning Ceramics". *Journal of Anthropological Research.* Vol. 57, 427-449.

Kamp, K.A. 2001b. "Where have all the Children Gone?: The Archaeology of Childhood". *Journal of Archaeological Method and Theory.* 8(1).

Kavanaugh, R. D. 2011. "Origins and Consequences of Social Pretend Play". *The Oxford Handbook of The Development of Play.* A.D. Pellegrini (ed.). Oxford: University Press. Chapter 22.

Kern, J.H.C. 1957. "Feeding Bottle" of the 4th Century B.C. in Leyden". *Mnemosyne,* Fourth Series 10, Fasc. 1, 16-21.

Kimball, A.S. 2007. *The Infanticidal Logic of Evolution and Culture.* Newark: University of Delaware Press.

Klein, A.E. 1932. *Child Life in Greek Art.* New York: Columbia University Press.

Konner, M. 1975. "Relationships Among Infants and Juveniles in Comparative Perspective". *Friendship and Peer Relations.* M. Lewis & L.A. Rosenblum (eds.). New York: Wiley.

Konner, M. 2010. *The Evolution of Childhood. Relationship, Emotion, Mind.* Cambridge, Mass.: The Belknap Press of Harvard University Press.

Kozloff, A.P. 1981. *Animals in Ancient Art From the Leo Mildenberg Collection.* Cleveland: Cleveland Museum of Art; Bloomington: Indiana Univ. Press; [then] Mainz: P. von Zabern, Cop.

Kullman, W. & S. Föllinger (1997): *Aristotelische Biologie: Akten des Symposions über Aristoteles' Biologie vom 24.-28. Juli 1995 in der Werner-Reimers-Stiftung in Bad Homburg.* Stuttgart, 287-323.

Kübler, K. 1954. *Kerameikos – die Nekropole des 10. Bis 8. Jahrhunderts.* Berlin: Walter de Gruyter.

LaCaille, A.D. 1950. *Infant Feeding-Bottles in Prehistoric Times.* Section of the History of Medicine, Proceedings of the Royal Society of Medicine, XLIII, 565-568.

Lagia, A. 2007. "Notions of Childhood in the Classical Polis: Evidence from the Bioarchaeological Record". *Constructions of Childhood in Ancient Greece and Italy.* A. Cohen & J.B. Rutter (eds.). American School of Classical Studies in Athens: *Hesperia* suppl. 41, 293-308.

Lamb, M. (ed.) 2004. *The Role of the Father in Child Development.* 4th. ed. New York: John Wiley & Sons.

Lawton, C.L. 2007. "Children in Classical Attic Votive Reliefs". *Constructions of Childhood in Ancient Greece and Italy.* A. Cohen & J.B. Rutter (eds.). American School of Classical Studies in Athens: *Hesperia* suppl. 41, 40-60.

Layne, J.M. 2008. "The Enculturative Function of Toys and Games in Ancient Greece and Italy". Masters of Arts thesis, University of Maryland, www.fairplayforchildren.com (11-04-2011).

LeVine, R.A. 1977. "Child Rearing as Cultural Adaption". *Culture and Infancy: Variations in the Human Experience.* P.H. Leiderman, S.R. Tulkin & A. Rosenfeld (eds.). New York: Academic Press, 15-27.

Levitt, M.J. (2005). "Social Relation in Childhood and Adolescence: The Convoy Model Perspective". *Human Development* 48, 28-47.

*Lexicon Iconographicum Graecae Classicae* II,2, 1984, München.

Lillehammer, G. (1989). "A Child is Born. The Child's Worls in an Archaeological Perspective". *Norwegian Archaeological Review.* Vol. 22, Issue 2, 89-105.

Lillehammer, G. (2000) "The World of Children". *Children and Material Culture.* J.S. Derevensky (ed.). London: Routledge. Chapter 2.

Lynch, K.M. & Papadopoulos, J.K. 2006. "A Study of the Potty in Archaic and Classical Athens". *Hesperia,* 75. The American School of Classical Studies at Athens, 1-32.

Manson, M. 1975. "Le Droit de Jouer Pour Les Enfants Grecs et Romains". *L'enfant.* Vol. 1, Recueils de la Société Jean Bodin 39, Brussels, 117-150.

Masten, A. 2001. "Ordinary Magic: Resilience Processes in Development. *American Psychologist,* 56, 227-238.

Matwiejczuk-Yardley, K.M. 1997. *Role Play – Theory and Practice.* London: Thousand Oaks.

McNiven, T.J. 2007. "Behaving Like a Child: Immature Gestures in Athenian Vase Painting". *Constructions of Childhood in Ancient Greece and Italy.* A. Cohen & J.B. Rutter (eds.). The American School of Classical Studies at Athens: *Hesperia* suppl. 41, 85-99.

Monrad, S. 1936. *Moderens dagbog – det sunde barns pleje. [The Mother's Diary – the Healthy Child's Care.* 7th Edition. Copenhagen: Gyldendal Nordisk.

Morgan, J.E. 2011. "Families and Religion in Classical Greece". *A Companion to Families in the Greek and Roman Worlds.* B. Rawson (ed.). Chichester, West Sussex, U.K.; Malden, MA: Wiley-Blackwell, 447-464.

Morris, I. 1987. *Burial and Ancient Society – The Rise of the Greek City-State.* Cambridge: Cambridge University Press.

Moseley D.T. et al. 1981. "Psychological Factors that Predict Reaction to Abortion". *Journal of Clinical Psychology* 37, 376-379.

Moss, J. & Solomon, H. C. 1979. "Swaddling Then, There and Now: Historical, Anthropological and Current Practices". *Matern. Child Nurs J.* (fall) 8, no 3, 137-51.

Murray, S.P. 1985. *Collecting the Past: Antiquities from the Joseph Veach Noble Collection.* Tampa: Tampa Museum.

Neils, J. 2003. "Children and Religion". *Coming of Age in Ancient Greece.* J. Neils & J.H. Oakley (eds.). New Haven: Yale University Press in association with the Hood Museum of Art, Dartmouth College, Hanover, New Hampshire, 139-161.

Neils, J. & J. H. Oakley. 2003. "Catalogue". *Coming of Age in Ancient Greece.* J. Neils & J.H. Oakley (eds.). New Haven: Yale University Press in association with the Hood Museum of Art, Dartmouth College, Hanover, New Hampshire, 198-312.

Neils, J. & J. H. Oakley. 2004. *Striving for Excellence: Ancient Greek Childhood and the Olympic Games.* Suppl. to Coming of Age in Ancient Greece. New York: Onassis Cultural Center.

Oakley, J.H. 2003. "Death and the Child". *Coming of Age in Ancient Greece*. J. Neils & J.H. Oakley (eds.). New Haven: Yale University Press in association with the Hood Museum of Art, Dartmouth College, Hanover, New Hampshire, 163-194.

Oakley, J.H. 2009. "Children in Athenian Funerary Art During the Peloponnesian War". *Art in Athens During the Peloponnesian War*. O. Palagia (ed.). Cambridge: Cambridge University Press, 207-235.

Oliver, V. 2003. *History of the Top*. Spintastics skill toys at www.spintastics.com (11-04-2011)

Opie, I. & Opie, P. 1969. *Children's Games in Street and Playground*. Oxford: Oxford University Press.

Patterson, C. 1985. "Not Worth the Rearing: The Causes of Infant Exposure in Ancient Greece". *Translations of the American Philological Association*. 115, American Philological Association, 103-123.

Pellegrini, A. D. & Bjorklund, D. F. 2004. "The Ontogeny and Phylogenety of Children's Object and Fantasy Play". *Human Nature*. Vol. 15, No. 1, 23.43.

Pellegrini, A.D. Dupuis, D., & Smith, P. K. 2007. "Play in Evolution and Development". *Developmental Review*, 261-276.

Pellegrini, A.D. (ed.) 2011. *The Oxford Handbook of The Development of Play*. Oxford: University Press.

Pellegrini, A.D. 2011. "The Development and Function of Locomotor Play". *The Oxford Handbook of The Development of Play*. A.D. Pellegrini (ed.). Oxford: University Press. Chapter 14.

Pellis, S. M. & Pellis, V. C. 2011. "Rough and Tumble Play: Training and Using the Social Brain". *The Oxford Handbook of the Development of Play*. A. D. Pellegrini (ed.). Oxford: Oxford University Press, 245-259.

Petersen, A.F. 1988. "Why Children and Young Animals Play – A New Theory of Play and its Role in Problem Solving". *Historisk-filosofisk Meddelelser no. 54*, Viborg.

Piaget, J. 1965. *Play, Dreams and Imitation in Childhood*. London: Routledge & Kegan Paul.

Poehlmann, J. 2003. "An Attachment Perspective on Grandparents Raising their Very Young Grandchildren: Implications for Intervention and Research. *Infant Mental Health Journal*, 24, 149-173.

Pollock, L.A. 1983. *Forgotten Children*. Cambridge: University Press.

Pomeroy, S.B. 1975. *Goddesses, Whores, Wives and Slaves: Women in Classical Antiquity*. New York: Schocken Books.

Price, T.H. 1978. "Kourotrophos – Cults and Representations of the Greek Nursing Deities". *Studies of the Dutch Archaeological and Historical Society*, III. J.P.G. Best, A.B. Breebart & M.F. Jongkees-Vos (eds.). Netherlands.

Qvortrup, J., Corsaro, W.A. & Honig, M.S. (eds.) 2009. *The Palgrave Handbook of Childhood Studies*. Basingstoke & New York: Palgrave & MacMillan.

Rawson, B. 2011. *A Companionship to Families in the Greek and Roman Worlds*. London: Blackwell Companions to the Ancient World, 503-520.

Reilly, J. 1997. "Naked and Limbless – Learning about Feminine Body in Ancient Athens". *Naked Truths – Women, Sexuality and Gender in Classical Art and Archaeology"*. A.O. Ostrow & C.L. Lyons (eds.). London: Routledge, 154-173.

Riemann, H. 1940. *Kerameikos – Die Skulpturen vom 5. Jahrhundert bis in Römische Zeit*. Berlin: W. de Gruyter.

Rogoff, B. 1990. *Apprenticeship in Thinking*. New York and Oxford: Oxford University Press.

Rosengren, K.S., Johson, C.N. & Harris, P.L. (eds.) 2000. *Imagining the Impossible: Magical, Scientific,and Religious Thinking in Children*.Cambridge: University Press.

Rotbaum, F. et al. 2000. "The Development of Close Relationships in Japan and in the United States: Paths of Symbiotic Harmony and Generative Tension". *Child Development*, 71(5), 1121-1143.

Rühfel, H. 1984. *Kinderleben im Klassischen Athen – Bilder auf Klassischen Vasen*. Kultur-geschichte der Antiken Welt, band 19, Mainz am Rhein: Von Zabern.

Rutter, M. 2008. "Implications of Attachment Theory and Research for Child Care Policies". *Handbook of Attachment: Theory, Research, and Clinical Applications*. J. Cassidy & P. R. Shaver (eds.). New York Guildford Press, Chapter 25.

Scheper-Hughes, N. 1987a. "Basic Strangeness: Maternal Estrangement and Infant Death – A Crititique of Bonding Theory". *The Role of Culture in Developmental Disorder*. C.M. Super (ed.). San Diego: Academic Press, 131-151.

Scheper-Hughes, N. 1987b. "The Cultural Politics of Child Survival". Child Survival: Anthropological Perspectives on the Treatment and Maltreatment of Children. N. Scheper-Hughes (ed.). Dordrecht: Kluwer Academic Publishers.

Scheper-Huges, N. 1992. *Death Without Weeping*. Berkeley, CA: University of California Press.

Schnapp, A. 1997. "Images of Young People in the Greek City-State". *A History of Young People in the West*. Vol. 1:

Ancient and Medieval Rites of Passage. G. Levi & J.-C. Schmitt (eds.). Transl. C. Naish. Harvard: The Belknap Press of Harvard University Press, 12-51.

Shapiro, H.A. 2003. "Fathers, Sons, Men and Boys". *Coming of Age in Ancient Greece*. J. Neils & J.H. Oakley (eds.). New Haven: Yale University Press in Association with the Hood Museum of Art, Dartmouth College, Hanover, New Hampshire, 85-111.

Sheridan, M. 2001. *Play in Early Childhood – From Birth to Six Years*. New York: Routledge.

Shorter, E. 1975. *The Making of the Modern Family*. New York: Basic Books.

Smith, P.K. 2010. *Children and Play*. Series: Understanding Children's Worlds. London: Wiley-Blackwell.

Sommer, M. 2011. "Toys, Play and Swaddling – Indication of Early Childhood in Ancient Greece". *Spåren av de Små. Arkeologiska perspektiv på barn och barndom*. F. Fahlander (ed.). Stockholm Studies in Archaeology, no. 54. Stockholm: University service.

Sommer, D., Pramling Samuelsson, I. & Hundeide, K. 2010. *Child Perspectives and Children's Perspectives in Theory and Practice*. London & New York: Springer Science.

Sommer, D. 2012. *A Childhood Psychology – Young Children in Changing Times*. Basingstoke & New York: Palgrave MacMillan.

Sommer, D. & Bak, H. 1981. *Leg og udvikling – tre teorier [Play and Development – Three Theories]*. Copenhagen: Dansk Psykologisk Forlag.

Spelke, E.S. & Kinzler, K.D. 2007. "Core Knowledge". *Developmental Science*. 10(1), 89-96.

Stern, D. 1985. *The Interpersonal World of the Infant*. Basic Books.

Sutton, R. 2004. "Family Portraits: Recognizing the "*oikos*" on Attic Red-figure Pottery". ΧΑΡΙΣ*: Essays in Honor of Sara A. Immerwahr. Hesperia* suppl. 33, 327-350.

Sutton-Smith, B. 1986. *Toys as Culture*. New York: Gardner Press.

Sylva, K., Bruner, J.S. & P. Genova. "The Role of Play in the Problem-solving of Children 3-5 years old". *Play – Its Role in Development and Evolution*. New York, 244-261.

Tanner, J. 2001. "Nature, Culture and the Body of Classical Greek Religious Art". *World Archaeology* 33, no. 2. World and aesthetics, 257-276

Thomas, B. 1984. "Early Toy Preferences in Four-Year-Old Readers and Non-readers". *Child Development* 55, no. 2, 424-430.

Thompson, B. 1966. "The Origin of Tanagras", *AJA*, 70, no. 1, 51-63.

Tomasello, M. 2009. *Why We Cooperate*. Cambridge, Mass., The MIT Press.

Triandis, H.C. 2001. "Individualism and Collectivism: Past. Present and Future". *The Handbook of Culture and Psychology*. D. Matsumoto (ed.). New York: Oxford University Press.

Trümper, M. 2011. "Space and Social Relationships in the Greek *oikos* of the Classical and Hellenistic Periods". *A Companion to Families in the Greek and Roman Worlds*. B. Rawson (ed.). London: Wiley-Blackwell, 32-52.

Van der Broek, R., Drijvers, H.J.W & Versnel (eds). *Religions in the Greco-Roman Worlds*, 129. The Netherlands: H.S. Brill, E.J. Leiden, 361-390.

Van Gestel, J.P.J., et al.2002. "Risks of Ancient Practice in Modern Times". *Pediatrics* 110, No. 6, 32-52, 78-80.

Van Hoorn, G. 1951. *Choes and Anthesteria*. Leiden: E.J. Brill.

Van Sleuwen B.E. et al. 2007. "Swaddling: A Systematic Review". *Pediatrics,* 120, No. 4, 1097-1106.

Van Straten, F.T. 1981. "Gifts for the Gods". *Faith, Hope and Worship – Aspects of Religious Mentality in the Ancient World*. H.S. Versnel (ed.). Leiden: Brill.

Vekemans M. & Dohmen, B. 1982. "Induced Abortion in Belgium: Clinical Experience and Psychosocial Observations". *Studies in Family Planning* 13, 355-364.

Vorster, C. 1983. *Griechische Kinderstatuen*. Hesse aus Hamburg, Köln: Selbstverlag.

Weisner, T.S. & Gallimore, R. 1977. "My Brother's Keeper: Child and Sibling Caretaking". *Current Anthropology* 18, no. 2, 169-190.

Werness, H.B. 2007. *The Continuum Encyclopedia of Animal Symbolism in World Art*. New York: Continuum.

Wileman, J. 2005. *Hide and Seek – The Archaeology of Childhood*. London: Stroud, Tempus.

Woysch-Méutis, D. 1982. *La Représentation des Animaux et des êtres Fabuleux sur les Monuments Funéraires Grecs: de L'époque Archaïque à la fin du IVe Siècle av.* Paris: Lausanne: Bbiliothèque Historique Vaudoise.

Zimbardo, P.G. 2004. "A Situationist Perspective on the Psychology of Evil: Understanding how Good People are Transformed into Predators". *The Social Psychology of Good and Evil: Understanding our Capacity for Kindness and Cruelty*. A. Miller (ed.). New York: Guildford Press.

Zukow-Goldring, P. 2002. “Sibling Caregiving”. *Handbook of Parenting.* Vol. I: Part: *Children and Parenting.* M.H. Bornstein (ed.). New Jersey: Lawrence Erlbaum, 253-285.

Yardley-Matwiejczuk, K.M. 1997. *Role Play - Theory and Practice*. London: Sage.

# INTERNET SOURCES

Beazley Archive: www.beazley.ox.ac.uk/index.htm (1-06-2011)
Den Store Danske Encyklopædi: www.denstoredanske.dk (1-06-2011)
Dyabola: www.dyabola.de/en/indexfrm.htm?page=http://www.dyabola.de/ (01-02-2011)
Hyginus' Fabulae: http://www.theoi.com/Text/HyginusFabulae1.html (10-06-2011)
Inscriptiones Graecae – Attica II2: http://epigraphy.packhum.org/inscriptions/ (10-06-2011)
National Geographic (October 21, 2008): http://news.nationalgeographic.com/news/2008/10/081021-stonehenge-toy.html (01-03-2011)
Oxford Classical Dictionary: www.oxfordreference.com.ez.statsbiblioteket.dk:2048/views/BOOK_SEARCH.html?book=t111&authstatuscode=202 (1-06-2011)
Record of the Art Museum, Princeton University, 46, no. 1 (1987): http://www.jstor.org.ez.statsbiblioteket.dk:2048/stable/i291501 (6-6-2011)
Suda online: www.stoa.org/sol/ (23-05-11)
The National Archaeological Museum, Athens: www.namuseum.gr/wellcome-en.html (15-03-2011)

# NOTES

The references in the note system are governed by the following principle: When books and articles are referred to just giving general or supplementary information about a given theory used in the book (for example an evolutionary approach) or information about a specific theme (for example play), references will not come with a specific page number. As examples, see note 34 and note 209.

## Part 1: Approaches to childhoods in ancient Attica – introduction

1 Freud 1981.

2 Freud later discarded his own theory of sexuality in childhood and his theory of the Oedipus complex. The theory, however, resulted in an increased focus on sexuality in ancient Greek society, which ended in over-sexualized interpretations of material culture like the one-sided pederast interpretations of naked children/young males on vases. *Pederasty* has been a part of ancient Greek society, but one must leave the modern adhorrence behind in order to understand and perceive the ancient Greek world and its cultural traditions. The antique view of pederasty was different from our modern perspective, which must be understood when working with ancient Greek material culture.

3 Sommer 2012.

4 Ariès 1962, 33-48, 396. However he mentions that the Greek understanding of *paideia* could have compared to that of 'childhood'.

5 Ariès 1962, 48-59, 327-352.

6 Shorter 1975.

7 To mention a few: Cunningham 1995; Heywood 2001.

8 DeMause 1974, 1, introduces ancient childhood with this statement: "The history of childhood is a nightmare from which we have only recently begun to awake. The further back in history we go, the lower the level of child care, and the more likely children are to be killed, abandoned, beaten, terrorized, and sexually abused".

9 DeMause 1974, 51-54.

10 DeMause 1974, 1-73.

11 For example, Pollock 1983 in her thorough analysis has pointed to almost stunning evidence concerning problems for the 'first generation' of historians mentioned in this section. Pollock's work is an exemplary scholarly example of how important it is that systematic empirical evidence is the basis for theoretical inferences.

12 Pollock 1983, 263.

13 Pollock 1983, 262.
14 Beaumont 2012, 5.
15 Beaumont 2012, 3-7.
16 Lillehammer 2000, 9.
17 See an overview in Berk 2013.
18 Kamp 2001, 25.
19 By stressing *recent* it is meant that today's paradigm about evolutionary human development and childhood has traveled far from the classical Darwin approach. Today it is accepted and documented that culture, socialization (for example play), and many other environmental factors can influence the direction of evolution by affecting both genes and brains in 'epigenetic' ways. For example which genes are to be 'turned on', and which that should be 'turned off'. See Bjorklund & Pellegrini 2002; Gottlieb 2007; Pellegrini et al. 2007; Konner 2010.
20 In this publication we distinguish between the words *oikos* meaning the private/family and the *polis* the public part of life.
21 In order to avoid a reification it must be said that models are constructs and do not 'exist' as such, they are just like geographical maps that help captains to navigate. This model can be helpful in the understanding of the complex two-way *intermediary* relationships between children and society/culture. In this model one is free in principle to take the part of departure at every level.
22 'Framing' does not mean 'determine'. The framing concept allows for many but not infinite ways to react on a specific condition.
23 Cole 1996; Cole and Cagigas 2010.
24 An affordance is what is directly or implicitly expected of the child, thus indicating what is proper behavior and what is not.
25 Wileman 2005.
26 This important principle is in line with some childhood archaeologists. Just to name one: Baxter 2005.
27 A *chous* (pl. *choes*) is a type of *oinochoe*, which is a jug for wine. Miniature versions of choes are often found in children's graves and are associated with the *Anthesteria* festival, where children on the second day of this event (the day was called *Choes*) were allowed to drink wine.
28 Tomasello 2009; Sommer 2012.
29 Spartans were known for their warrior life style which influenced all parts of their culture including children's lives. Male children were taken from their mothers at the age of seven or earlier to be fostered in military camps and girls were sent to school to learn different types of sports. The Spartans believed children to be owned by the state and not by the parents. Athens had softer parenting methods as the book will describe later on.
30 Masten 2001.
31 Sommer 2012, 159.
32 Hrdy 2009.
33 Baxter 2005.
34 Bjorklund & Pellegrini 2002; Bornstein 2002; Cassidy & Shaver 2008; Howes and Speiker 2008; Hrdy 2009; Tomasello 2009; Konner 2010.
35 Weisner & Gallimore 1977.
36 Hrdy 2009; Tomasello 2009.

37 Examples such as: Alexandrakis 1988; Pomeroy 1997; Patterson 1998; Dillon 2002.
38 Slaves and slave children are only mentioned briefly due to the lack of evidence.
39 Howes and Speiker 2008.
40 Baxter 2005, 2.
41 Baxter 2005, 3.
42 It is fair to say, however, that Baxter 2005 in many ways convincingly makes use of the 'active child' perspective.
43 This concept has been proposed by Dencik, 1999, 12.
44 Golden 1990, 30.
45 For how everyday routines are the bases for cultural acquisition and socialization, see Sommer 2012, 89-92.
46 Argyriadi 1991.
47 Kamp 2001.
48 Smith 2010, 8-12, on different types of play. Smith divides "games" from "play" e.g. rule-governed games such as "board" games (e.g. knucklebones in antiquity). This division will not be made in this book since it would unnecessarily complicate the general picture of child's play and the child's world of play, with regard to a past society. Section 3 on children's play is meant to give a wide perspective on play in Classical Attica and not a theoretical discussion on variations of play.
49 Smith 2010, 9-10.
50 This may be evidence of idealized child's play; children played, but were never romping around or overly excited while playing, but controlled as expected by the Athenian society.
51 Wileman 2005.
52 Pl. *Leg.* I, 643b-c/Pl; *Leg.* VII, 794a-795b.
53 Baxter 2005, 2.
54 Baxter 2005, 2-3.
55 Oakley 2003, 178.
56 Golden 1990, 14-15; Golden 1985, 91-104. This is attested by the later philosopher Philo (20 BC-50 AD) who in *De Opificio Mundi* 36.105 writes of Hippocrates' seven stage division. Hippocrates was a well renowned physician and lived from 460-370 BC and was one of the most important researchers in life cycles, illnesses and medical science in the Classical period. According to Shapiro 2003, 85-111, and Foley 2003, 113-137, the understanding of maturation, adolescence and adulthood of a boy and a girl in Classical Greece differed. The girl was often seen as an adult and ready to marry between the age of 12 and 14, whereas the boy did not become an adult before he had served as *ephebe* in the Greek army. Men did not marry until they were in their late 20's or early 30's.
57 Demand 1994, 142-145. Ancient medical reports from Hippocratic doctors mention these stages separately when a case (a child patient) is described. These stages were used by physicians during the Classical period. It is not known if the stages were accepted outside the medical world, but, some of the childhood terms, e.g. *pais* and *paidion*, are used in other types of literature like poems and plays.
58 Shapiro 2003, 85-111; Foley 2003, 113-137.
59 Arist. *Pol,* VIII 1340b30; Arist. *NE* 2.1105a2; Pl. *Symp.* 222B; Pl. *AX.* 365B, 366D, 367A.
60 Golden 1990, 14-15; Golden 2003, 13-17; Xen. *Oec.* VII.24.

61 Schnapp 1997, 12-51.

62 Golden 2003, 13. Both Plato and Aristotle vary at times, both with each others and with their own works. For further interest: Kullman & Follinger 1997, 287-323, and French 1991, 13-29.

63 After Golden 2003, p. 15.

64 Beaumont 2012. She gives a very insightful analysis of the subtleties of age in ancient Athens, i.e. how it was presented in iconography and the written sources, and how age was culturally used and understood.

65 See Sommer 2012, 28-31, about this very influential position in developmental psychology and its status in today's theory.

66 Pl. *Leg.* VII, 792.

67 Pl. *Leg.* I, 643. It must be stressed that Plato's version is his idea of an ideal state.

68 Price 1978.

69 Beaumont 2003, 61; Sommer 2011, 152-153. The figurines are important in the understanding of children and nursing in the Archaic period, for instance the practice of swaddling can be identified on the clay votives.

70 Beaumont 2003, 69; Cohen 2007, 257-278; Golden 2003, 13-29.

71 Beaumont 2007, 68-69. The *Kouroi* and *Korai,* however, gradually disappeared in the 5$^{th}$ century BC, and from 490-440 no children were carved as round-sculptures. The focus was on mythological children on vases, like Heracles as a baby, which slowly ends from the third quarter of the 5$^{th}$ century. The mythological babies are replaced with ordinary mortal children in a domestic context.

72 Beaumont 2003, 65.

73 Lagia 2007, 298-299; Morris 1987, 57-71.

74 Beaumont 2007, 68-69.

75 Last part of the 6$^{th}$ century – first half of the 5$^{th}$ BC. See Crelier 2008, 242-245, for statistic graphs on child burials in the Kerameikos. Lagia 2007, 304-306.

76 Beaumont 2007, 67-68; Beaumont 2000, 39-51. From the second quarter of the 5$^{th}$ century childhood stages can be distinguished in vase painting. Four stages have been identified: 1) Infant age, 2) Young childhood aged 3-7, 3) Older childhood aged 7-13, and 4) Adolescence ca. 13-18 depending on gender. According to Houby-Nielsen 2000, 152, these stages are also visible in skeletal remains in the grave context.

77 Houby-Nielsen 2000, 163.

78 Beaumont 2007, 72-73.

79 E.g. the Parthenon-frieze from 435-30 BC.

80 Toddlers, youngers and older children are often shown playing.

81 Oakley 2009, 207-235; Burnett Grossman 2007, 309-323.

82 Beaumont 2003, 78-79.

83 Lagia 2007, 199-304. The two cemeteries studied are: Kerameikos and the Plateia Kotzia, both in Athens. Lagia suggests that the reason for this under-representation of juveniles (since the late Classical period) is a change in burial customs. The cause of a lack of children is more socio-historically based than a result of bad preservation or recovery. (Houby-Nielsen 2000, 163.) The reduction of child burials coincides with the appearance of relief-decorated steles showing and sometimes commemorating infants and small children. The burial customs occur simultaneously

with the increased depictions and descriptions of children in art and literature. Burial customs changed and children do not seem to have been given any formal burial.

84 Beaumont 2003, 79, fig. 15-17. Roman copies of Hellenistic sculptures of children playing with animals like a goose or a puppy.

85 Beaumont 2003, 78-79. The Hellenistic image of the sleeping Eros became popular in the Roman period and resulted in various copies of this type of sculpture both in bronze and marble.

86 Kaltsas 2002, 270-271; Golden 1997, 176-191. Golden argues that there is no increased sentimentality towards children in Hellenistic times and ascribes the increased focus of children in art to a new Hellenistic style tradition. He uses mostly written sources to come to this conclusion and does not analyze the material evidence (which is the case with most of his work).

87 Beaumont 1998, 71-93. The change in attitude towards children is, according to Beaumont, witnessed in mythology through the representation of infant goddesses.

88 Sommer 2011.

89 See Beaumont 2012.

90 Tomasello et al. 2005.

91 Bretherton & Munholland 2008.

## Part 2: The care and socialization of infants and young children

92 Alexandrakis 1988, 79, Xen. *Oec.* VII, 12-31, who tells us that the most important work to an Athenian mother was the labor of nursing and training her children.

93 Alexandrakis 1988, 79; Pl. *Leg.* VII, 794; Xen. *Oec.* VII, 12-29.

94 Alexandrakis 1988, 80.

95 Kaltsas 2002, 184 fig. 363, several steles with saddened mothers exist.

96 Foley 2003, 133.

97 Xen. *Oec.* VII, 6.

98 Foley 2003, 120; Xen. *Oec.* VII, 6.

99 Neils & Oakley 2003, 3, fig. 1.

100 *Inscriptiones Graecae* II2 10650.

101 Golden 1990, 136-140. Other steles with grandparent inscriptions have been found, which may indicate that grandparents and grandchildren were closely connected. The inscriptions are found in the online database 'Inscriptiones Graecae'. Examples of such epitaphs: IG II2 3453 (great grandmother), 5673, 7195, 7393 (grandmothers) etc. It is *almost* always grandmothers that are mentioned in the inscriptions, and not grandfathers. Grandchildren were known as *paides paidón*.

102 Eur. *Bacch.* 1302-1326.

103 Eur. *Or.* 462-465.

104 Golden 1990, 136-140.

105 Shapiro 2003, 85-111. Some steles exist with father/daughter iconography, but they are rare.

106 Kaltsas 2002, 155, fig. 304. Perhaps, another example is found on a stele from around 410-400 BC, the girl in the middle may be the daughter of the deceased man, yet she is identified as a maid servant in Kaltsas 2002, 145, fig. 279 (he gives no specific reason for this identification). Yet, the girl may be the daughter, since the hair style looks too elaborate for a slave girl and she also makes a sentimental gesture by holding the man's hand as though she is saddened by his death.

107 Shapiro 2003, 106.

108 E.g. Shapiro 2003, 107, fig. 24.

109 Shapiro 2003, 105.

110 Arist. *Pol.* I.1259a38-b18.

111 Arist. *Hist. An.* VIII. 1158b11, 1163b15. Aristotle's view on fatherhood and the honor of such an institution may lay in his utopian idea of an ideal state. However, one could imagine that his ideas are in close connection to his own father's untimely death, and the acceptance into the School of Plato, where he was treated like a son of Plato. These two father-related episodes in his life may have created an over-fixated idea of father-honor and a view of fatherhood as being a teacher-apprentice relationship, which he had with Plato.

112 Golden 1990, 102.

113 Shapiro 2003.

114 Eur. *Fragment* 500N, 952N. Hyg. *Fab.* 8.

115 Golden 1990.

116 Shapiro 2003, 85, suggests that Athenian artists were "quite selective in the imagery of contemporary family life and parent-child relationships that they chose to represent". Family motifs were not popular until after the Peloponnesian war, and especially father/child-imagery was not seen (see Introduction).

117 Lamb 2004.

118 Gettler 2010.

119 Bornstein 2002.

120 Golden 1990.

121 Ar. *Thesmo.* 502-519

122 Theophra. *Char.* 20.5-6; 7.10.

123 Theophra. *Char.* 2.6; 5.5.

124 Golden 1990. Another example is seen in the *Iliad*, Book 6, where Hector kisses his little baby son Astyanax during the battle, showing care towards his son and future heir. The child is initially frightened by the crest of Hector's helmet, but greets his father happily. Human beings in principle are relatively 'morally open'. Therefore every culture has to develop sets of proper conduct – normative rules. In doing so many behaviors are deemed 'out'. Moralists, in order to induct societal order, often refer examples of bad behavior. But in order to 'work' they must have some correspondence with reality and must not have been taken out of the blue air. This point is used here in reference to the proposition that some ancient Greek fathers (how many we do not know) were devoted to their offspring.

125 Sommer 2012.

126 Arist. *Hist. An.* VIII. 1161b16 & IX. 1166a8, 1168a23.

127 Stern 1989.

128 Arist. *NE.* 1161b22-23.

129 Golden 1990, 100.

130 Ariès 1962, 33-48, 396; DeMause 1974, 1-73.

131 Hrdy 2009

132 Arist. *Hist. An.*, VIII, 588, especially the first week was critical. No precise estimation of the child mortality rates of ancient Athens has been conducted.

133 Golden 1990, 83; Garland 1985, 77. The ancient Greek word for untimely used on steles was *aôros.*

134 Golden 1990, 83-85. The arguments for this lack of interest are built on written sources mainly from Plato. He claims that most men treat their business responsibilities carelessly, including that of children. However, it should be stressed that Plato mostly shows negativity towards children, seeing them as inferior beings. It was also Plato that suggested the swaddling of children until age 3, which illustrates that he probably did not have much interaction with children, and not much understanding of them.

135 Kimball 2007, and this is sometimes why infanticide is practiced.

136 Hrdy 2009, 283.

137 LeVine 1977, 15-27.

138 Scheper-Hughes 1987a.

139 Dasen 2008. These rituals also exist however, in developed cultures e.g. in modern Christian societies, where burial costums and the idea of heaven resemble the ancient and traditional beliefs of afterlife. Garland 1985, 82, suggests that child cremations found in the southwestern part of the Athenian Agora may be those of prematurely or perhaps even exposed infants.

140 Golden 1990, 85. One could make an analogy to the Old Testament's idea of "Gods will".

141 DeMause 1974, 1-73.

142 Manson 1975, 117-150.

143 Doumanis 1983.

144 Konner 1975, 99-129, e.g. the Kalahari Desert San-tribes.

145 Hrdy 2009; Tomasello 2009.

146 Bjorklund & Pellegrini 2002, 225-226.

147 For example, the developmentalist Fogel, 2004, writes in his article "The History (and Future) of Infants": "…love and protection for them has been found in artifacts and documents from Ancient Egypt (2000-100 BC) and Greece (800-200 BC)", 735.

148 Perhaps these steles are not a product of the rivaling artistic program displaying idealized aristocratic family values through funerary art after the Peloponnesian War, but may instead show increased attention towards children as individuals. See section two on individual child steles (often depicted with toys and/or pets).

149 Golden 1990, 84.

150 Demand 1994, Hippocratic doctors mention a series of diseases often caught by infants and children especially.

151 Observed on several choes during empirical data collection in Athen, April 2011.

152 Van Hoorn 1951.

153 Johnston 1995.

154 Neils and Oakley 2003, 265. The pig was a protective figure in Spartan culture, but not necessarily in Athenian society. Werness 2009, 328-329, tells that the pig is associated with Demeter cults, where piglets were sacrificed to the goddess to ensure protection.

155 Demand 1994, 142. It was mainly Hippocrates and later the Hippocratic doctors, who created increased attention towards child illnesses.

156 Golden 1988, 159.

157 Golden 1990, 86. Aristotle notes that mothers may love their children even though they expose them and also miss them afterwards (Arist. *Pol.* VIII 1159a28).

158 Scheper-Hughes 1987b, 14.
159 Vekemans & Dohmen 1982, 355-364; Moseley et al. 1981, 276-279; Golden 1990, 88.
160 Pollock 1983; Johansson 1984.
161 Golden 1990.
162 Patterson 1985, 104
163 Golden 1990, 87.
164 Patterson 1985, 104-105. There are different ancient Greek words for child-murder, infanticide and exposure. Greek terminology suggests that the ancient Greeks did distinguish between the exposure of children, child-murder and harm.
165 Garland 1985, 77-88.
166 See Patterson 1985, 112, for the literary evidence of the exposure of children. The evidence comes from Arist. *Pol.* VII, 16 and Pl. *Resp.* 460c, but also from the mythological and theatrical world (comedies). There is no material evidence of child exposure in Classical Attica except for skeletons of babies found in the Athenian Agora that may perhaps have been exposed.
167 Johansson 1985, 117, based on a quote from Hes. *Op.* 376-81.
168 Polyb. 36.17.
169 Kimball 2007; Johansson 1984, 487-502.
170 Tomasello 2009.
171 Zimbardo 2004.
172 Sommer, Pramling & Hundeide 2010, Part II (by Hundeide), 101-5.
173 Scheper-Hughes 1992.
174 Sommer, Pramling & Hundeide 2010, Part II (by Hundeide).
175 Hrdy 2009.
176 Howes and Speiker 2008.
177 Table 1 is based on various written and iconographic information about the people that can be expected to be in the *oikos*.
178 This estimation of the number of grandparents is, in most cases, probably too high. In accordance with Golden 1980, because of a shorter average life span than today, many adults did not reach the age where they usually became grandparents.
179 Golden 1990.
180 For further interest see Golden 1990.
181 Hrdy 2009; Tomasello 2009.
182 Kaltsas 2002, 210-231; Charlier & Raepsaet 1971, 589. Examples of such votive commemorative reliefs can be seen in the section about the sacral world of the child, where several votive reliefs have been found at the Brauronia.
183 Shapiro 2003, 96-98.
184 Kaltsas 2002.
185 Kaltsas 2002, 183, fig. 362.
186 Dillon 2002, 134; Neils & Oakley 2003, 258. An estimation of slaves in the ancient Greek society suggests that an average household had three to four slaves, and wealthier families had more, while the poorer families had less. However, the estimation of 100,000 slaves to serve a population of around 30,000-45,000 male citizens (of Athens) indicates that only the poorest had no slaves.
187 Golden 1990, 124-125.

188 Cahill 2002; Trümper 2011.
189 Trümper 2011, 32-52.
190 Howes and Speiker 2008; Tomasello 2009; Hrdy 2009.
191 Sommer 2012, 145.
192 Hrdy 2009. Multiple carers and alloparents can e.g. be: Grandparents, other members of a clan, community, society, family or household and siblings.
193 Tomasello 2009.
194 Hrdy 2009.
195 Hrdy 2009, 184.
196 Hrdy 2009, 241.
197 Konner 2010, 442-45.
198 As well as grandmothers' presence in art and the previously mentioned epitaphs.
199 Poehlmann 2003.
200 Golden 1990.
201 Demand 1994, 2-5.
202 Golden 1990.
203 Hrdy 2009 206-207; Golden 1990.
204 Diner 1965 27-43. This may resemble a socially and culturally advanced version of matriarchal societies.
205 Fildes 1986, 21; Golden 1990, 146-148.
206 Kaltsas 2002. Slave children may be seen on various grave steles, yet the identification of *slave children* is difficult since adult slaves were in general depicted as smaller than their master/mistress and may therefore not be children but slaves with inferior status. More research on this topic is needed.
207 This is, however, with the exception of slave wet nurses and pedagogues. Interestingly, epitaphs to slaves erected by owners do not exist (to our knowledge) with the exception of those for wet nurses. This may indicate that a slave was, in general, not a person to whom one should get attached. Nevertheless, strong attachments might have been created to those who reared the child.
208 Therefore adults and sometimes older children have to 'give' caring and nursing while the child has to 'receive'. Interestingly the American word 'caregiver' is used in this regard.
209 Fogel 2004.
210 Cassidy and Shaver 2008.
211 Rotbaum et al. 2000.
212 We believe the woman is the mother because of her fine clothing, something a slave or nurse would not wear.
213 Fildes 1986; Golden 1990.
214 The earliest known feeders are housed in The British Museum, some being from the Helladic period. The feeding bottles look like small wine jugs and are made of terracotta.
215 Fildes 1986, 20-22.
216 LaCaille 1950. Feeding-bottles can be traced back to prehistoric times and appear all over Europe, including France and England. Fildes 1986, xxviii, comments that the earliest feeding vessels are found in Egypt, Cyprus and France and date to 3000-1000 BC, but in Greece, the first feeding vessels appear in the Protogeometric/Helladic period. Most feeders are found in children's graves.

217 Kern 1957; Bartsokas 1978; Neils & Oakley 2003, 265.

218 Example of an earlier feeding-bottle can be found at the Kerameikos Museum in the Phaleron Group Exhibition. The feeder dates to approx. 700-675 BC and is made of terracotta with black ornamentation.

219 The Benaki Museum, inv. no. 22477.

220 Bartsocas 1978.

221 Lys. I, 9-14.

222 Fildes 1986, 174-176. Fildes 1988, 1-32. When mortal children in mythologies were breastfed by their mother they often suffered a horrible fate, like Astyanax in Polygnotus' Iliupersis (Paus. X. 25.9). One of the most important ancient stories of children nursed by an animal is the prehistoric Roman myth of Romulus and Remus. However, also in Greek mythology divine children are breastfed by animals (e.g. Zeus), which underline their unusual heritage and destiny. These mythologies were created before the Classical period but might have influenced nursing customs.

223 Beaumont 2012.

224 Sutton 2004, 345, pl. 17.14. Berlin-Staatliche Museum, inv. no. F2395.

225 Sommer 2012.

226 Baxter, 2005; Beaumont 2012; Wileman 2005.

227 Stern 1985.

228 Stern 1985.

229 Stern 1985.

230 Hrdy 2009.

231 Fildes 1986, 3-36, e.g. the Isis cult where nursing female deities are frequently represented. Bonfante 1997, figurines of nursing women are found in the Mycenaean period and called "divine nurses". Neils & Oakley 2003, 225, fig. 25: In the Hellenistic period statuettes of nursing women rarely appeared in the material record, thus it was not a popular motif. However, figurines of nursing mothers are more frequently found in Etruscan art, and in the south of Italy and on Sicily – perhaps indicating another more positive view of breastfeeding and other feeding traditions.

232 Fildes 1986, xxviii.

233 Xen. *Oec.* 21-25. Sor. *Gyn.* II, XIII (XXXIII), 21-24 (On Milk): A later source Soranus of Ephesus (1st-2nd-century AD) writes about the nourishment of breast milk and how to test the quality.

234 Hippocrates II, 10-32 (Dentition).

235 Pl. *leg.* VII, 788a-790b.

236 Arist. *Pol.* VII, 1336a2-24, 1336b36.

237 Wileman 2005, 20, evidence of wet nurses goes back to ancient Egyptian times and contracts for wet nurses have been found on papyri from Roman Egypt.

238 Hrdy 2009, 206.

239 Fildes 1986, 21-22.

240 Neils & Oakley 2003, 321.

241 Fildes 1986, 21. Golden 1990, 146-148. Grave steles erected to freed nurses exist and one bears an inscription which mourns the death of a beloved nurse.

242 Fildes 1986, 17.

243 Cassidy and Shaver 2008.

244 Fildes 1986. Perhaps the milk was used in feeding-bottles for the infant to suckle instead of the breast.

245 Bonfante 1997, 174-188.

246 Bonfante 1997, 20.

247 Wileman 2005, 21.

248 Fildes 1986, 25, suggests that bottles were used to wean the child from the breast, and were therefore not used on infants. Bonfante 1997, 184, a worn female body symbolized poverty and slavery, while an aesthetic youthful body illustrated aristocratic living.

249 Monrad 1936, 39-40.

250 Rüfel 1984, 35 fig. 19. The Agora Museum, Athens, inv. no. PI18010.

251 The potty stool is included in the book, although dated to the Archaic period because of its uniqueness.

252 Based on our measurements.

253 Lynch and Papadopoulos 2006, 7.

254 Lynch and Papadopoulos 2006.

255 Neils & Oakley 2003, 240.

256 Neils & Oakley 2003, 240 fig. 41. The British Museum, London, inv. no. 1910.6-15.4. Cat. no. 5 p. V.

257 Van Hoorn 1951.

258 Neils & Oakley 2003, 241 fig. 42.

259 Hoffmann 1997, 147. The kylices are attributed the Sotades-painter. Sotades also painted scenes of immortality, for which he is most known. Yet, he has also made other cups showing women in a domestic context, and domestic scenes may have been a favorite theme on his stemless cups.

260 Neils & Oakley 2003, 240; Rüfel 1984, 28-38.

261 Boardman 1995.

262 The buyer may have been from the middle-class or upper-middle-class and not of aristocratic descent since the elite mostly used metal vases instead of the cheaper painted terracotta vases. If this is true, then the domestic scenes should be placed in the context of the upper-middle-class or the middle-class and not in elite-households. This may indicate that elite-mothers did not nurse their children themselves, but middle-class mothers did. Yet, the fine clothes of the mothers on the painted terracotta vases may indicate that the mothers came from the elite, but may also show that middle-class mothers also wore fine clothing? If vases with domestic scenes were private orders then they may have been ordered either by a person from the upper-middle-class or from the elite, who may have been satisfied with a domestic scene on a cheaper painted terracotta vase.

263 Lynch and Papadopoulos 2006.

264 The Athenian red-figure lekythos is today located in the Staatliche Museum, Antikensammlungen 2209 in Berlin.

265 Lynch and Papadopoulos 2006.

266 Sommer 2011, 152; Neils & Oakley 2003, 223-225, fig. 21-23; Price 1978, *kourotrophoi* with swaddled infants also come from the Archaic period.

267 Moss and Solomon 1979.

268 Neils & Oakley 2003, 223 fig. 20.

269 Ammerman 2007, 144-147. This is also seen in e.g. Etruscan and later south Italian cultures. Garland 1990, 81-83; Kaltsas 2002, 191. On some steles the infant wears a cap.

270 Neils & Oakley 2003, 185, fig. 26, shows infant twins swaddled the same way as on fig. 13.

271 Sommer 2011, 153, las on the Ampharete stele, fig. 5.

272 Van Gestel et al. 2002.

273 Pl. *leg.* VII, 789e.

274 Arist. *Hist. An.* VII.

275 Soranus *Gynaecia* II, 15

276 Dasen 2008, 50.

277 Sommer 2011, 152-157.

278 Neils & Oakley 2003, 3.

279 Sommer 2011, 156.

280 Soranus *Gynaecia* II; Arist. *His. An* VII.

281 Dasen 2008.

282 Sommer 2011, 156.

283 Van Gestel et al. 2002, 78-80.

284 Triandis 2001.

285 This does not mean that individuals were not greatly admired in ancient Attica, for example being a winner in sport and war. The point was that such individuals did not violate the fundamental rules. On the contrary they showed that they in a perfect way lived up to them.

286 Franco 2005.

287 Berk 2013 is an example of a widespread international standard textbook in child development. Here today's 'state of the art' is presented. Interestingly there is only one short reference to swaddling. The underlying message is that the topic is nearly not worth mentioning in contemporary developmental psychology.

288 Van Sleuwen et al. 2007.

289 They were probably also made from various materials such as leather, bone, wood and metals, which have unfortunately not been preserved.

290 The Benaki Toys Department, inv. no. 12.

291 The Benaki Toys Department, inv. no. 1093. Several owl-rattles are housed at the British Museum; London, and can be found at the Museum's online database. The owl-rattles are of similar size and shape indicating standardized production and design.

292 The rattle originates from Cyprus and dates to the Classical period. Rattles were mainly made in Cyprus and in Attica, indicating two distinct craft centers, like the feeders. Rattles from Cyprus are included to show the varieties of shapes and sizes of ancient Greek rattles. This is not possible by using only Attic rattles.

293 For various types of owl-rattles, see Beazley Archive "rattles" or the British Museum's database.

294 Berk 2009; Sommer 2011, 147.

295 Neils & Oakley 2003, 265 fig. 69.

296 Neils & Oakley 2003, 265.

297 Sommer 2011, 147.

298 Van Hoorn 1951, 64, no. 38, pl. 295.

299 Gopnik, et al. 1999.

300 The painter of the *chous* must have witnessed such play-scenes in everyday life to have portrayed with such accuracy. However, the artist did not of course think of child developmental issues, but may just have painted a happy play episode between brother and sister, this being an idealized version of the brother-sister relationship and/or a natural everyday episode in the ancient Greek *oikos*.

301 Field 1990.

302 Rutter 2008. Studies made in Romanian orphanages show that children can die, become severely brain damaged or mentally ill if not stimulated and activated by adult caregivers, which is also described in Sutton-Smith 1986, 29.

303 Pl. *leg.* VIII, 793e-794a.

304 The previously mentioned Ariès 1962, 33-48, 396; DeMause 1974, 1-73.

305 Pellegrini 2011.

306 Lawton 2007, 45-50; Van Hoorn 1951; Sommer 2011, 155, on active and crawling toddlers.

307 Neils & Oakley 2003, 285, e.g. fig. 96.

308 Van Hoorn 1951; Neils & Oakley 2003, 285, e.g. fig. 96.

309 Neils & Oakley 2003, 327.

310 Van Hoorn 1951. Several types of these choes with crawling and exploring toddlers have been found, all connected to the Anthesteria-festival.

311 Tomasello et al. 2005.

312 It should be stated that we do not consider this and other *choes* to be a 'photograph' of a real toddler boy and therefore not necessarily a snapshot of a past 'real episode'. However, in our Developmental Childhood Archaeology approach one must, in order to be open to new insights, be 'reflectively creative', but always with grounds in empirical data. But we are arguing and proposing interpretations and not pursuing absolute answers. However, since several of exactly this type of *choes* with the crawling toddler have been found, we may conclude that this image was either highly idealized (which may also have some ground in real observed situations) and/or actually a 'window' into the world of the ancient Greek toddler boy. Since these crawling-toddler-boy scenes are primarily of domestic and not mythological character, one could suggest that the episodes are real.

313 Bjorklund & Pellegrini 2002.

314 Neils & Oakley 2003, 237.

315 Shapiro 2003, 85-112.

316 Baxter 2005.

317 Sommer 2011, 157. Further iconographic evidence of active infants/toddlers on *choes*, see Van Hoorn 1951.

318 Zukow-Goldring 2002, 253-256.

319 We do not know the exact number of children in ancient Greek families. However, aristocratic families probably had fewer children than the middle-and lower-class and especially poor families. As mentioned earlier, the ideal picture of elite families was that of a small family, but this class was also criticized for its extensive use of infanticide.

320 Golden 1990, 118.

321 Cox 1988, 377-395; Cox 1997, 105-129, both articles focus on sibling feuds in connection to inheritance practices, and build on Freudian ideas of sibling rivalry. They do not deal with the

earliest years of child life. The articles are based only on literary evidence mainly from oratory sources. Golden 1990, 115-140, also deals with sibling relationships.

322 Dunn 2004.

323 Rogoff 1990.

324 Zukow-Goldring 2002. Weisner & Gallimore 1977, 169; Cicirelli 1994, 9. In non-industrialized societies, the term 'sibling' varies greatly and may be defined as certain types of blood kin, and is not only based on genealogy. Since it is not possible to "see" other types of siblings in the material culture, then "siblings" in the book correspond to brothers and sisters in genealogy (same parents).

325 Weisner & Gallimore 1977, 169.

326 Golden 1990, 128.

327 Cicirelli 1994, 10. In non-industrialized societies sibling care-giving allows parents to fulfill necessary work roles for family survival and maintenance. It also serves as a backup system in case of the death of parents. In modern societies it is often practiced to give parents "time off" to do other non-child-related activities.

328 Van Hoorn 1951, several choes exist with depictions of children/siblings playing together.

329 Van Hoorn 1951, 72, no. 12, fig. 507.

330 Neils & Oakley 2003, 275, fig. 83.

331 Kaltsas 2002, 155, fig. 307.

332 Pl. *leg.* VIII, 793e-794a.

333 Perhaps siblings looked after each other when playing outside (and inside) the household. Older siblings did perhaps take care of their younger siblings.

334 Weisner & Gallimore 1977, 177; Cicirelli 1994, 7-20.

335 Pl. *leg.* VIII, 793e-794a.

336 Weisner & Gallimore 1977, 169. Zukow-Goldring 2002, 278-279.

337 Zukow-Goldring 2002, 266.

338 Weisner & Gallimore 1977, 172. Zukow-Goldring 2002, 256-258.

339 Zukow-Goldring 2002, 274.

340 This may also be the case with nurse and slave care-giving: The child in the care of multiple caregivers get a complex and differentiated socialization and upbringing. This type of complex socialization also happens in modern societies, where children are together with multiple caregivers in daycare institutions.

341 Weisner & Gallimore 1977, 176.

342 Weisner & Gallimore 1977, 177.

343 Cicirelli 1994, 10.

344 Cicirelli 1994, 7-20.

345 Golden 1990, 123. It is not known whether this information is correct. Further research on the layout and social space of domestic houses is necessary to conclude if boys were restricted to the female sphere in the *oikos*.

346 Cox 1997, 105-129.

347 Golden 1990, 128-129. Soph. *Ant. & Soph. El:* Literary examples of sibling love can be seen in Sophocles' two tragedies about Antigone and Electra. Antigone loves both brothers despite their war against each other, and she ends up dying for burying her one brother against the will of the

new king of Thebes, (Creon). Electra's mother, Clytemnestra, kills Electra's father and his mistress for having sacrificed her first daughter. Electra saves her younger brother by sending him to the island of Phocis, for later to return as an adult, reunite with Electra and kills Clytemnestra as revenge for his father's death.

348 'Sacral socialization' is a term created by co-author Maria Sommer in order to explain the influence on the child of being a participant in sacral rites-of-passage and other recurrent religious rituals.

349 Berliner and Sarré 2007; Boyatzis 2005; Gallagher 2007; Rosengren, Johnson and Harris 2000.

350 Golden 1990.

351 Neils 2003, 143-145. Mothers would sacrifice clothing to Artemis to ensure a quick and easy delivery of the child.

352 Neils 2003, 143.

353 Dasen 2011, 297, 301.

354 Golden 1990, 23.

355 Arist. *His. An.* VII, 12, also mentions that amphidromia means "running around". The hearth of the house was also considered the heart and center of the *oikos*.

356 This knowledge of the *amphidromia* is built on a later Byzantine source (10[th] century AD) The Suda, which was written by the author Suidas. Suda online, "amphidromia".

357 Dasen 2011, 303.

358 Suda online, "dekatê".

359 Neils 2003, 144.

360 Dasen 2011, 305.

361 Neils 2003, 144.

362 Demand 1994, 122-126, depictions of women in child labor exist, but are not frequent. Oakley 2003, 186, fig. 28; Neils & Oakley 2003, 222 fig. 19: A stele with such a motif is housed at the National Archaeological Museum, Athens, inv. no. 749, and another at the Harvard University Arts Museum – Arthur M. Sackler Museum, Cambridge, MA.

363 Neils 2003, 145, fig. 6.

364 Andoc. I, 125-127: In Andocides' speech *On the Mysteries* it is mentioned that the father claims legitimacy of the child by placing his hand on the altar during the *Apaturia*.

365 Neils 2003, 145. When boys reached the age of fourteen they were once again registered in the phratry, where they sacrificed a lock of hair to illustrate their attainment of manhood.

366 Neils 2003, 144, fig. 5.

367 Van Hoorn 1951.

368 Dasen 2011, 312. Neils 2003, 147-148, fig. 66: *Choes* also show scenes of drunken men, who may have participated in the drinking contests during the Dionysian festival, and not all scenes are pleasant child-depictions.

369 Neils 2003, 146, these cakes are depicted on *choes*.

370 Neils 2003, 145.

371 Golden 1990, 42.

372 Neils 2003, 149. There exists more than one type of swinging-ritual called *Aiora*: "On the second or third day of the *Anthesteria* Festival, boys and girls participated in a swinging-ritual which is referred to in some of our sources. The ritual involved swinging over fumes from a vessel on the

ground, but its purpose and meaning are unclear. It was connected in some way with Erigone, the daughter of Icarius, legendary Athenian inventor of the process of making wine." Beaumont 2012, 83: To see more about *Aiora* and about this ritual, including boys and girls.

373 Shapiro 2003, 104, fig. 18a-b.

374 Dillon 2002, 69-70. Callim. *Aet.* Fr. 178.I-5Pf.

375 Neils 2003, 149. Hyg. *Fab.* 130.

376 Golden 1990, 46.

377 Neils 2003. Dillon 2002, 37-72.

378 Brulé 1987, 179-283; Golden 1990, 46-48; Neils 2003, 150- 153.

379 Dillon 2002, 37-72. Young girls could e.g. serve as: *Arrephoroi*, female servants at the midsummer festival of *Arrephoria*, and weavers of Athena's peplos; *kanephoroi,* young female servants known as basket-bearers, who served several goddesses, e.g. Artemis and Athena; *aletrides,* so-called corn-grinders served by upper class girls, who grinded corn for sacral cakes; and *arktoi,* young female servants, and so-called 'she-bears' in the sanctuary of Artemis Brauronia. Common for these girls was that they were all around the age of 7, unmarried and virgins. Some positions were only held by upper class girls and only for a selected few, while other roles were carried out by lower-class girls too. The common term for these girls was *parthenoi.* These ritual roles will not be treated further, since the age-group of the initiated girls lies outside the book's selected age-group i.e. 0-7. However, the cult of Artemis Brauronia and the Arktoi will shortly be dealt with, since girls may have been initiated into this cult at an early age.

380 Ar. *lys.* 642-647.

381 Brulé 1987, 250-251. Iconographic evidence on ceramic vases however, only shows older (adolescent) girls dancing as bears, and it is not certain that the scenes actually shows the she-bear dancing ritual.

382 Vorster 1983, 331, 345; Bobou 2010, 33-44.

383 Demand 1994, 122-126.

384 The Brauron Museum inv. no. 1171.

385 Various fragments of statues of children holding balls are found at the Brauron Museum.

386 The Brauron Museum inv. no. 1168.

387 Lawton 2007, 41.

388 The Brauron Museum inv. no. 1150.

389 The Brauron Museum inv. no. 1151.

390 Bobou 2010, 40.

391 Kaltsas 2002, 131-145, 209-233. Several dedicatory votive reliefs have been found around Attica, which indicates that other gods/goddesses were used as family protectors.

392 Bobou 2010, 33.

393 Kaltsas 2002, 270-271.

394 Babou 2010, 35.

395 The Brauron Museum inv. no. 1196.

396 Sommer, et.al. 2010.

397 Rawson 2011.

398 Vorster 1987, 249-259.

399 The Brauron Museum, inv. no. 1160.

400 Bobou 2010, 36.

401 Babou 2010, 40. Around 80 statues of children have been found in the sanctuary.

402 The Brauron Museum, inv. no. 1164.

403 The Brauron Museum.

404 Kaltsas 2002, 271, fig. 566.

405 Babou 2010, 40.

406 The artistic representations of children on grave steles and in the sculptural record are very standardized, showing children with the same types of objects, e.g. pets and toys. The representations are often cute and childish, but also built on the adult's idea of ideal child behavior and activities. This standardizing and idealized trend is a general trait in Classical Greek art, and is also seen in adult sculptures and statues. However, representations on vases, especially choes, do show varying scenes of child's play and activities.

407 Babou 2010, 37.

408 Pl. *leg.* VII, 794a.

409 Babou 2010, 42-43.

410 Babou 2010, 42.

411 Van Hoorn, 1951. Several choes depict uncontrolled playful behavior.

412 Lawton 2007, 41-43

413 Lawton 2007, 43-50.

414 Morgan 2011, 463.

## Part 3: Young children's play and toys

415 Lillehammer 2000, 22.

416 Sutton-Smith 1977; Smith 2010, 24; Pellegrini et al. 2007.

417 Pellegrini & Bjorklund 2004.

418 Fisher et al 2011.

419 Smith 2010, 21. The concept of "original sin" (humans born as sinners) resulted in the strict training and discipline of children.

420 Sommer & Bak 1981.

421 Konner 2010, 500.

422 See, Bjorklund & Pellegrini 2011, Konner 2010.

423 Smith 2010, 24.

424 Brulé 1987.

425 Bjorklund and Pellegrini 2002; Konner 2010; Pellegrini, et al. 2007.

426 James 2009.

427 Smith 2010, 27.

428 Piaget 1945.

429 Cole 1996.

430 Beaumont 2012.

431 Sommer 2012; Tomasello 2009; Bornstein 2010.

432 Smith 2010, 30-31; Sylva et al. 1976; Petersen 1988.

433 Sheridan 2001.

434 E.g. Golden 1990.

435 Beaumont 2012, 129.

436 Spin tops are seen on vases but always in an adult context, showing that even adults did play games.

437 Beaumont 2012.

438 Golden, 1990; 2003. Words are symbolic tools invented to give meanings to phenomena that exist in the actual world. If, for example, a specific phenomenon is real, then a word will be created to name it, thus making it communal and 'talkable'. Thus, an event that does not occur or is not 'worth' talking about will not be named. So, the mere presence of the word 'play' in the Classical Greek language indicates that play occured, was observed, and was also possible to talk and even write about – just as Plato did. And although he probably did not invent the word, it had probly been used more or less frequently in common conversation.

439 Golden 1990, 53.

440 Sommer 2011, 151; Golden 1985.

441 Pl. *leg.* VII, 794a.

442 Pl. *leg.* VII, 794a-795a.

443 Pellis and Pellis 2011.

444 Pl. *leg.* I, 643b-c.

445 Yardley-Matwiejczuk 1997. Berk 2013.

446 The discussion is ongoing and is often heard between biology, psychology and anthropology. Discussions are often one-sided: Biology versus sociology, nature versus culture, environment versus inheritance. A recent developmental evolutionary research paradigm now convincingly argue that biological, neurological, mental, and sociocultural levels are highly interdependent (Bjorklund and Pellegrini 2002). For example, will enriching play environments make specific neurons grow and expand in children's brains. Exposure to long term stress will on the other hand make hypothalamus and the frontal lobes shrink. In addition, the Classical evolutionary 'blue-print' idea that culture and environment has no 'immediate' influence on genes has been challenged as well (Gottlieb 2007).

447 Berk 2013.

448 Konner 2010, 675.

449 Bjorklund & Pellegrini 2011.

450 Harris 2000.

451 Tomasello 2009.

452 This may probably be the correct answer since Plato's works feature the idea of an ideal state, where citizens (including children) should act according to idealized and modeled behavior.

453 Pl. *leg.* VII, 794a-795a.

454 He probably also meant proper gender behavior e.g. boys should practice male jobs and girls the work of females.

455 Typology and chronology has not yet been fully established, thus Elderkin 1930 has tried.

456 Argyriadi 1991, 13.

457 Argyriadi 1991, 11-18.

458 Argyriadi 1991.

459 Argyriadi 1991. The word may derive from the word '*Kouros*' and therefore mean 'moulders of boys/men', however, only female dolls have been found so this is unanswered.

460 The identification of production centers is built on the large number of doll-findings in specific areas like Attica, Corinth and Cyprus. No clay analyses have been made, and the production-center identifications may therefore be questionable.

461 Higgins 1967, 6-24; Argyriadi 1991, 11. Argyriadi suggests that some dolls may be older (Neolithic), but she refers to terracotta figurines, and not to actual jointed-dolls. In this book these dolls are not treated, since they are most likely not toys, but votives or apotropaic figurines and are dated outside the Classical period.

462 Higgins 1967, 25-56; Argyriadi 1991, 14. Bell-shaped dolls from the Geometric period were known as *daídala*, and are not only children's toys, but were also connected to a Hera/Zeus-cult. Coldstream 1977, 202, argues that the Boeotian bell-shaped figurines are dolls and not idols. It must be stressed that the identification of early dolls as being playobjects and not sacral objects or idols is uncertain. This is the case with many dolls from before the Archaic period. However, dolls found in children's graves are most commonly identified as toys, also in the Classical period. Breitenstein 1941; Riemann 1940. These bell-shaped early types of dolls can be found at numerous museums in Greece and in other countries e.g. the Kerameikos Museum inv.no. 961; the National Archaeological Museum, in the Geometric vase collection; the National Museum of Copenhagen inv.no. 3887.

463 Other production centers are suggested in Argyriadi 1991, 11-18. See also: Elderkin 1930, 459 for further information on these early doll types.

464 Neils & Oakley 2003, 268. Archaic dolls are almost always from Corinth, and it has not been possible to locate an archaic doll from Attica during our collection of empirical data in Athens, April 2011. The archaic doll on fig. 31 is also from Corinth, and is included to give an example of dolls older than Classical dolls.

465 Elderkin 1930, 461.

466 Eumaros was a painter and the first to be mentioned in written sources (Plin. *HN,* XXXV, 56). He gender-divided his figures, so females were painted with white paint and males were red.

467 Two other seated dolls are housed at the National Museum in Copenhagen inv.no. 760. They are a pair that were found together, probably in a child's grave, near Athens.

468 Both dolls are housed at the Benaki Toys Department.

469 Argyriadi 1991, fig. 14 in her Catalogue.

470 Neils & Oakley 2003, 267, fig. 72.

471 Neils & Oakley 2003, 256, fig. 59a. Stanford Museum (Center of Visual Arts) inv. no. 17410.

472 No comparative chronological studies of ancient Greek dolls exist.

473 Argyriadi 1991, 12; Elderkin 1930. Dolls of various materials have been discovered e.g. dolls made out of bone, wood, alabaster, cloth, marble and ivory, but terracotta clay is the most frequent material.

474 Hellenistic dolls in Attica are rarer than dolls from the Classical period. It has not been possible to locate a Hellenistic doll in Athens during our collection of empirical data. A Hellenistic doll from Tanagra in the National Museum in Copenhagen, is unique and can therefore be seen on fig. 36.

475 Elderkin 1930, 462.

476 This has been suggested by Elderkin 1930, 464.

477 This is witnessed in the expression of the sacral and ritualistic tradition.

478 Neils & Oakley 2003, 307, fig. 124. The Harvard University Art Museum, inv. no. 1961.86. *Cat. no. 36, XXII.*

479 Breitenstien 1941, 28 fig. 266 pl. 29: This type of doll can be found in several Greek museums, but one is also housed in the National Museum, Copenhagen, inv.no. 1639. Layne 2008, 27. However, the interpretation of the doll being a toy is probably most correct since it is quite clear that the girl is playing wich, not sacrificing the doll.

480 Neils & Oakley 2003, 265, fig. 68.

481 Neils & Oakley 2003, 265. The doll on the stele can also be interpreted as a votive offering to Asklepios. However, the doll could also have functioned as a toy before the offering as e.g. in the Artemis Brauronia cult. Cult votives (dolls) may have been used as play objects, before they were sacrificed to the goddess. Sutton-Smith 1986, 27, claim that in some cultures the distinction between sacral and real life objects does not exist. Sacral objects were also used as practical objects, i.e. as a play object before becoming a votive. This is also attested by Argyriadi 1991, 16, who mentions that the static dolls on steles may be another type of doll, which are identified as *ex-voto*, and are perhaps placed in graves as apotropaic votives to protect the child in the Afterlife.

482 Pl. *Leg.* VII, 643b-c.

483 Matwiejczuk-Yardley 1997, 15-60.

484 Bjorklund & Pellegrini 2002.

485 Neils & Oakley 2003, 168, fig. 8.

486 Kaltsas 2002, 167, fig. 331.

487 This close-up of the hole on fig. 42 is on the Classical attic doll in fig. 33.

488 Doll nudity may perhaps be connected to the new sculpture tradition introduced by Praxiteles with his naked statue of the Knidian Aphrodite in the 4th century. However, since naked dolls may have existed before the introduction of nude Goddesses and the fact that dolls are most probably not representations of goddesses; this is probably not the case.

489 However, the dolls portrayed on steles may perhaps not be toys that girls normally dressed and played with, but could be of the *ex-voto*-type as mentioned earlier. This can perhaps explain why dolls on steles are not wearing clothing, and therefore why the dolls on steles do not correspond with the doll-type found in some graves. Children may have been buried with different types of dolls, both play objects and votives (*ex-voto*).

490 Reilly 1997, 156.

491 Oakley 2003, 182, fig. 21. The reason why the toy roller has survived is probably because it was made of bronze. The most common material for carts was either wood or clay, both of which have perished with time.

492 Oakley 2003, 182, cat. 122. The Princeton Art Museum, inv. no. y1986-87. *Cat. no. 39 a-b, XXIII.*

493 Oakley 2003, 182.

494 Van Hoorn, 1951, 15-16. However, it has also been proposed that push carts were connected to the Dionysiac walking cart.

495 Klein 1932, 13-14.

496 Fig. 44: Van Hoorn 1951, 68, no. 73, pl. 509. Fig. 45: 62, no. 20, pl. 182. Fig. 46: 64, no. 38, pl. 295. All in the National Museum in Athens, inv. no. 1742, 1223, 1267.

497 For more examples of these choes: See Van Hoorn 1951.

498 Layne, 2008, 26.

499 Since no wheeled horses from the Classical period have been found, two older toy horses have been included here in order to give an impression of what the Classical toy horse may have looked like (if it existed).

500 The Kerameikos Museum, showcase 5-6.

501 Neils & Oakley 2003, 266, fig. 70.

502 These types of wheeled horses from the Roman era (often dating to the 1st-century AD) are e.g. housed at the National Museum in Athens and the Agora Museum. Examples of other wheeled animals from this period exist, such as roosters. Also wheeled animals from the Byzantine period exist.

503 Neils & Oakley 2003.

504 The Nat. Mus. Athens, inv. no. 1040.

505 Neils & Oakley 2003, 271; Layne 2008.

506 Neils & Oakley 2003, 273.

507 Harcourt-Smith 1929, 217-219.

508 Oliver 2003, 23-24.

509 In the National Museum, Athens, the New Exhibition.

510 Neils & Oakley 2003, 270, fig. 77.

511 The Benaki Toys Department, inv. no. 1098.

512 Beazley Archive "3407, Berlin, Antikensammlung, F2549". The Berlin, Antikensammlung (Schloss Chalottenburg), inv. no.F2549. *Cat. no. 51 a-b, XXIX.*

513 The National Museum, Copenhagen, in the Dionysos-festival collection. Numerous knucklebones have been found and are housed in museums in Greece and Europe.

514 Neils & Oakley 2003, 278-279.

515 Neils & Oakley 277, fig. 85a-b.

516 Neils & Oakley 279; Layne 2008, 24. For example, to the Artemis and Hermes cults, but also to the Pan and Nymphs-cult in Delphi, where over 23,000 knucklebones were found in the Pan cave. The initials would either be those of children's forenames or be initials of mythical persons like Herakles, Archilles, etc.

517 Neils & Oakley 2003, 279, fig. 85a & b.

518 Neils & Oakley 2003, 277 fig. 85 a & b and fig. 87.

519 Neils & Oakley 2003, 278, fig. 87.

520 The Benaki Toys Department, inv. no. 13.

521 Individual correspondence with Dr. Maria Argyriadi from the Benaki Toys Department.

522 Neils & Oakley 2003, 264, 269 fig. 76; Murray 1985, 45 fig. 66.

523 Thomas 1984; Hindman 1981.

524 Individual correspondence with Dr. Maria Argyriadi from the Benaki Toys department. The Benaki Toys Department, inv. no. 2722. The excavation information clearly states that the altar is found in a child grave and was a toy.

525 Pl. *Leg.* VII, 643b-c.

526 Pl. *Leg.* VII, 643b-c.

527 Ar. *Nub.* 878-81, 375.

528 The Benaki Museum, the Ancient Greek Collection, inv. no. 31077. Several of these pigs are housed in this museum.

529 The Benaki Museum, the Ancient Greek Collection, inv. no. 31054 & 31079.

530 Pl. *Leg.* VII, 643b-c.

531 Neils & Oakley 2003, 264-282; Layne 2008, 31.

532 Tanner 2001, 265.

533 For a sacral interpretation of animals with children, see Beaumont 2012. 78.

534 Woysch-Méautis 1982, 23-79.

535 Woysch-Méautis 1982, 39-53.

536 Neils & Oakley 2003, 307.

537 Neils & Oakley 2003, 308 fig. 126, the Apollonia-stele from 100 BC is another example that shows a girl with a living dove. The girl is petting the bird, while it gazes at her from the top of a pilaster. The stele is from the Hellenistic period, but is influenced by Classical proto-types.

538 Fig. 60: Kaltsas 2002, 146-47, fig. 281. Fig. 61: The National Museum, Athens inv. no. 3661.

539 Tanner 2001, 265.

540 Neils & Oakley 2003, 280, fig. 91.

541 Neils & Oakley 2003, 280, fig. 92.

542 Beaumont 2003, 78, fig. 14; Kaltsas 2002, 271, fig. 566.

543 Many of these types of statuettes, some with animals, are found at the Artemis sanctuary in Brauron. The statuettes are of votive character and are therefore to be placed in a sacral context. Yet, they may still show what type of animals children played and were associated with, also in this sacral and feminine sphere.

544 These types of statues are also found in e.g. Delphi.

545 Woysch-Méautis 1982, 53-60.

546 Neils & Oakley 2003, 307.

547 This type of dog is also seen in votive statues e.g. at Brauron Museum inv.no. 1161.

548 Kaltsas 2002, 144-171, 180-207.

549 The National Museum, Athens, inv. no. 3249.

550 The National Museum, Athens, inv. no. 748.

551 Beaumont 2000; Beaumont 2012.

552 Van Hoorn 1951, 64, no. 41. fig. 288.

553 Van Hoorn 1951, 123, no. 476, fig. 235.

554 Van Hoorn 1951, 119, no. 438, fig. 324.

555 The Kerameikos Museum, showcase 10.

556 Van Hoorn 1951, 123, no. 478.

557 Woysch-Méautis 1982, 61-64. Hares are also seen on votive statues of children e.g. from Brauron (displayed in the Brauron Museum).

558 Neils & Oakley 2003, 286, fig. 98.

559 Woysch-Méautis 1982, 67-73. Van Hoorn 1951.

560 Van Hoorn 1951, 33-49.

561 Van Hoorn 71, no. 98, fig. 354.

562 Woysch-Méautis 1982, 73-76.

563 This probably has something to do with the fact that written sources are made by men, who probably did not engage in child contact or observations. Children and the world of children probably did not interest male philosophers.

564 Yet some toys could have been created by children themselves. Ar. *Nub.* 878-81, 375, in Aristophanes' play *Clouds*, a man called Strepsiades notes that his small son produces miniature baby houses, boats, go carts of leather and frogs carved from pomegranates. Yet the play also states that the father buys a toy for his son from the great toy maker Diasias, which indicates that well-renowned toy craftsmen, *coroplasts,* existed in the Classical period.

565 See the "time and energy budget"-argument in Pellegrini & Bjorklund 2011, 297.

566 Smith 2010, imaginary play without the use of toys may have been the earliest type of play in the development of homo-sapiens, and may be panhuman.

567 Kavanaugh 2011.

568 Kavanaugh 2011.

569 Hirsh-Pasek & Golnikoff 2008.

570 Beaumont 2012, 92.

571 Neils & Oakley 2003. Iconographic evidence on choes suggests for example that girls also used toy rollers/carts, which normally were believed to be boys toys. However, boys are never seen playing with dolls. Most often there is gender-specific play on choes, but exceptions do occur.

572 Konner 2010.

573 Toy weapons for boys may have existed, but were perhaps made of wood and therefore not preserved.

574 Smith 2010, 95-98.

575 *National Geographic*, October 21, 2008. Perhaps a toy was found in an infant grave near the Stonehenge. Miniature figurines from the Neolithic era found in child graves are today interpreted as toys, and toys are therefore among the oldest artifact-groups in the world.

576 Ghosh 1990, 326: Including tools and cult figures of stone. The earliest toys were animal figurines made of flint-like stone.

577 Perhaps the yoyo from China is even older.

578 Cooper & Sutton 1999. Children who are affected by abuse e.g. physical, sexual and mental, do not always play or have either aggressive or reserved play behavior. Sommer 2011, 152: Not all children in Classical Attica had a joyful childhood with play, and children such as child slaves, child laborers and poor children may have had too hard a life to play.

579 As evident in Ar. *Nub.* 878-81, where the boy makes toys of various types, not being societally important (yet perhaps a bit gender specific?).

580 Neils & Oakley 2003.

581 Neils & Oakley 2003, 271.

582 Konner 2010.

583 Grimm 2000.

584 Piaget thought that primitive reflexes were the only starting point for the newborn. Freud's newborn was totally determined by the Id, having no cognitive competences whatsoever. Social learning theory saw the newborn as a 'tabula rasa'. Despite these differences, they adhered to the *zeitgeist* that the environment was the sole developer.

A subsequent paradigm shift has – often on the basis of empirical studies – discarded such views stemming from the grand developmental era. Sommer 2012. Chapter 1.

585 Spelke and Kinzler 2007; Baillargeon 1994.

586 Karmiloff-Smith 1995.

587 Gopnik, Meltzoff & Kuhl 1999.

588 Golden 1990, 55. Eustath. *Il,* 1111.24. Poll. 9. 112, cf. Pl. *tht.* 181A.

589 Opie and Opie 1969.

590 See overview: Pellegrini 2011.

## Part 4: Conclusions and perspectives

591 Golden 2003.

592 See article by Dipla & Paleothodoros 2012.

593 Dipla & Paleothodoros 2012, 220, 228.

594 Beaumont 2012, 208.

595 For example, Golden 1990, 2003. Golden also (and mostly) built his conclusion on written sources.

596 Priviously-mentioned sources, such as Plato and Aristotle.

597 About adult perspectives versus children's perspectives on children's lives, see Sommer, Pramling Samuelsson & Hundeide 2010.

598 Childhood sociologists are highly critical towards the universal top-down theories of developmental psychology, but they have overlooked that this has been long gone in psychology as well. After the so-called paradigm shift in the 1970s much more contextual and cultural approaches have been emerging. This book adheres to theorizing and research after the paradigm shift. See discussion, critique and the alternatives in, Sommer 2012. Chapter 1.

599 In the registration, analyses and interpretations, in this work a classic archaeologist and a developmental psychologist have been cooperating from the very beginning. Despite a fruitful learning of each other's disciplines, there has been rather sharp role divisions. This has been done to prevent the psychologist from establishing himself as a sciolist archaeologist, and visa versa.

# INDEX


## A

Achilles 36
Active child 84-85
Active meaning-making child 26
Activity theory 114, 141
Adult vs child perspectives 154, 190
Affordance 168
Agora 38, 70-71, 74, 132-133, 173-174, 177, 187
Ainsworth, Mary 57
Aiora swinging-ritual 93, 181-182
Aletris 94
Alexandrakis, Dimitris 169, 171
Alloparenting 29, 60-63, 85, 89, 151, 155
    three criteria 61
Ammerman, Robert 178
*Amphidromia* ritual 54, 56, 91, 101, 151, 181
Ancient Greek society 'a culture of toys' 140, 145
Andocides 181
*Andron* 89
Animal figurines 111, 131, 189
    bird 61, 83-84, 100, 132-136, 138-139, 143, 152, 188
    dog 120-121, 132-133, 135-139, 152, 154, 188
    dove 99-100, 121, 126-127, 131-135, 188
    duck 133, 138, 139, 159
    pig 54, 79, 81, 100, 130-131, 133, 139, 152, 173, 188
    rabbit 138
    turtle 131, 152
Anthesteria Festival 36, 71, 83, 92-93, 101, 125, 151, 168, 179, 181
Antiphates 97
*Apatouria* three-day festival 92
Aphrodite 68, 131, 134
Apollo 97
Apollodorus 62
Archaeology-psychological approach 39
Archaic Greek society 36
Argyriadi, Maria 122, 169, 184-187
Aries, Philippe 18, 167, 172, 179
Aristophanes 50, 94, 131
Aristotle 35, 38, 48, 50-51, 76-77, 91, 106, 150, 170, 172-173, 190
    age stages 35
    view on fatherhood 172
*Arrephoroi*, female servants at the midsummer festival of *Arrephoria* 94, 182
Artemis 36, 90-92, 94-97, 99-101, 111, 119-120, 151
Artemis Brauronia sanctuary 94-95, 99
Artifacts 149, 152-153
    'ideal wing' 149
    'realist wing' 149
Asklepios 186
*Astragalos* 128
Astyanax 54, 172, 176
Athena 92, 94
Attachment 63, 68-69, 150, 175

## B

Ball 126
    games 126
    sports 145
Bartsokas, Christos 176
Basic trust in others 58
Baxter, Jane 20-22, 29, 30, 33, 168-169, 176, 179
Beaumont, Lesley 20, 22-23, 66, 109-110, 153-155, 168, 170-171, 176, 182-183, 188-190
Berk, Laura 178, 184
Berliner, David and Sarré, Ramon 181
Bjorklund, David and Pellegrini, Anthony 63, 112-113, 146, 168, 173, 179, 183-184, 186, 189
Bobou, Olympia 182-183
Bonfante, Larissa 176-177
Bornstein, Marc 168, 172, 183
Bottom-up theory 155
Bowlby, John 57
Boyatiz, Chris 181
Boys 58, 89, 97
    future roles of 26
    sacral rituals 101, 111
    school start 60
    too many 56

Brauron 94, 98, 100, 119
Brauronia 39, 94-95, 97, 99, 100-101, 120, 151, 174, 182, 186
Breast milk production 69
Breastfeeding 64-69
  process 67
*Brephos* 34
Bretherton, Inge and Munholland, Kristine 171
Brulé, Pierre 181-183
Burial customs 170-171, 173
Burnett Grossman, Janet 170

## C

Cadmus 48
Cahill, Nick 175
Care 28
  defined 28
  emotional 28
  physical 28
  planning/organizing 28
  social 28
Cassidy, Jude and Shaver, Phillip 168, 175-176
Charlier, Marie-Thérèse and Raepsaet, Georges 174
Child development 178
Child perspective 71
Child statues 101
Child's socialization into culture 31
Child's world, A 21
Childhood 17, 34
  a social construction 18
  architects 26
  history 18-19
  in ancient Attica, study 480-300 b.c. 17
  makers of 25
  sentiments 18
  teleological enlightenment belief 19
Childhood archaeology 19
  a schism in 153
Childhood architects 145
Childhood sociology 155, 190
  major problems 155
Childhood stages in vase painting 170
Children 17
  ancient horrible treatment 18
  and age in contemporary Europe 34
  aristocratic and upper-middle classes 17, 63
  Hippocrates' seven stages 169
  in ancient Attica 34-35
  in ancient Greek household 150
  in art 34, 36
  on vases 36-37
  safety precautions 71
  sentimentalized 37
  slaves 63
  statues 100-101
  the world of 105
  words for children in the Classical period 34
Children's cultural acquisition and socialization 24
*Choes* (*chous*) 26, 32, 36, 54, 70-72, 82-83, 85- 86, 88-89, 92- 93, 101, 108, 110-111, 122-123, 125, 137-140, 143, 151, 168, 173, 179, 180- 181, 183, 187, 189
Cicirelli, Victor 180
Circulation of children' phenomenon 58
Classical period: dating of 480-300 BC 37, 117-120
  ideal concept of 'the perfect family' 56
Clytemnestra 181
Cohan, Ada 170
Cohan, Ada and Rutter, Jeremy 22
Cole, Michael 168, 183
Cole, Michael and Cagigas, Xavier 168
Coloplasts 115, 189
Community of minds 141
*Constructions of Childhood in Ancient Greece and Italy*, Cohen 152
Contextualism 23
Cooperative breeding 29, 60, 151
Corinth 38, 117, 119
Cost/benefit balance of raising a child in the Classical period 56
Cox, Cheryl 179-180
Crawling 83-84
  toddlers 179
Creon 181
Cross-socialization 89
Cultural differences and panhuman similarities 24
Culturally attuned affordances 25
Culture 24
  collectivistic 77
  individualistic 77
  levels of 24
  material 38-39
  as surplus energy 115
Cunningham, Hugh 167
Cyprus 38, 64, 79, 178

## D

Darwin, Charles 106, 168
Dasen, Véronique 173, 178, 181
Deaths of close relatives 141
Dedicatory statues 100
Dehumanization 57, 150
  labels 57
*Dekatê* 56, 91, 101, 151, 181
  ritual 91

Demand, Nancy 169, 173, 175, 181-182
DeMause, Lloyd 18-19, 53, 167, 172-173, 179
Demeter 101, 119, 173
Dencik, Lars 169
Derevensky, Jeffery 21
Developmental Childhood Archaeology 17, 19, 23, 149, 154, 179
Developmental psychology 23, 38, 144, 155
*Dexiosis* (farewell handshake) 59
Diasias 189
Dillon, Matthew 169, 174, 182
Dionysos Festival, 71, 187
Dipla, Anthi and Paleothodoros, Dimitris 190
Divine Nurses 176
Dolls 11-12, 26, 30, 38-39, 41, 68, 106-107, 109-123, 130, 135, 142-144, 146, 151-152, 186
- *aidala* 185
- as adult females 121
- Classical period 117-120, 185
- connected to 'rites-of-passage' rituals, 110, 120
- doll makers, coroplasts 115
- ex-voto 185
- in ancient Greek history 115
- in Classical Athens 113
- nudity 186
- of various materials 185
- on steles 186
- production centers 115, 116, 119
- the archaic 116-117, 119

Doumanis, Mariella 173
Dunn, Judy 180

## E

Early Archaic period (Ca. 700-580 BC) 36
Early ontogenetic cognition – a recent paradigm 144
Echinos 91-92
*Eileithyiai* 90, 101
Electra 180
Embeddedness 24
Ephebe 169
Epigenetic 168
Erigone 93, 182
Erikson, Erik 21
Estimation of slaves 174
Eternal triangle (person-object-person) 80-81
Euempolos 47
Euripides 48-49, 150
Evolutionary development and childhood 168
Evolutionary theory 29, 53, 63, 106, 110
Exposed newborns 55-56
Exposure of children 174

## F

Fahlander, Fredrik 12, 22
Family 59 (see also *Oikos*)
- the family of Antiphates 97
- the family of Lycoleon 97

Father 48, 150
- a mild version of father/son-relationship 49
- affiliation in children 51
- and child 48
- as the patriarchal *Kyrios* 48
- farewell handshake 48
- Greek 172
- in the care of 50
- recent research 50
- respect for 48
- role of 50
- swinging-ritual *Aiora* 93

Fawn, the 138
Feeding bottles 54, 64-65, 67, 115, 175, 177
Feeding traditions in ancient Greece 69
Female gender socialization 30
Festival of Anthesteria 92, 168
Fetching game 135-36
Fildes, Valerie 63, 175-177
Fischer, Kelly 183
Fogel, Alan 173, 175
Foley, Helene
Fragile toys, the material evidence 143, 178
Framing 25
Franco, Patricia 178
French, Valerie 170
Freud, Sigmund 17-18, 21-22, 63, 85-86, 106-107, 141, 167, 179, 189
Freudian theory 17
Functionalism 23
Functions of sibling care-giving 180

## G

Gallagher, Sally 181
Games 31-32, 92, 101, 111-112, 114, 126, 128-129, 135, 142, 145, 152, 169
- Tug-of-war' games:
- *Helkystina* 145
- *Dielkystina* 145
- *Ephelkystina* 145

Garland, Robert 178
Geometric period 116
Gettler, Lee 172
Ghosh, Arun 189
Girls 34, 89, 97, 110, 113
- future economic burden 55

future roles of 26, 60, 121
giving dolls to 113
in role play 113, 122
sacral roles of 182
statues of 99-100
the ritual life of 94, 101, 107, 111, 120
Golden, Mark 21, 34, 50, 55, 58-59, 62, 85, 90, 169-176, 179-181, 184, 190
Gopnik, Alison, Meltzoff, Andrew and Kuhl, Patricia 190
Gottlieb, Gilbert 168, 184
Grandchildren, *paides paidón* 171
Grandmother 47-48
hypothesis 61
Grandparents 61, 151, 171, 174
Graveyards, cultural place of grief 47
Greek 'pederast' interest in young boys 17
Groos, Karl 106
Grubbs, Judith Evans and Parkin, Tim 22
*Gynaikonitis* 60

## H

Harcourt-Smith, Cecil 187
Hector 172
Hellenistic period 37
Hewlett, Bonnie 47
Heywood, Colin 167
Higgins, Reynold 185
High child mortality 51, 53
ancient Greek 52
attentiveness towards infants 53
coping with grief 52
fear that a child might die 54
medical explanation 54
ritual practices 52
social support 52
spiritual beliefs and fatalism 52
Hippocrates, 176
Hippocratic three stages 34
Hirsh-Pasek, Kathy and Golnikoff, Roberta 189
Hoop 129-130
Houby-Nielsen, Sanne 170
Howes, Carollee and Speiker, Susan 168-169, 174-175
Hrdy, Sarah Blaffer 60, 168, 172-176
Human beings as morally open 172
Humans 63
Hyperthermia 77

## I

Iconographic ambiguity 151-152
Iconographic evidence 40
status as 153-154
Idealized and desired ways to live 153
Identification 114
Imaginary play, the functions of 140-141
In the eye of the beholder 98
Individual in ancient Attica, the 178
Infanticide 40, 51-57, 141, 150, 160, 173-174, 179
Infants 40, 52, 54, 57
activation of 81
affect attunement 67
as passive moldable organisms 77
basic trust in self and others 67
burial customs 52
cultural beings from the beginning 80
feeding tradition in Classical Greece 64
house burials of 53-54
internal 'working models' 40, 60
introducing to the goddess 91
mind-reading 83
minds of 80
nurtured and cared for 53
physical world of 144
pointing 80
statues of 94-95, 99
with depressed mothers 81
Intentional act 80
Intentional expressions 40
Interdisciplinarity, a call for 155-156
Interpretation of choes with the crawling toddler 179
Interpretative perspectivism 154

## J

Johnston, Sarah 173

## K

Kaltsas, Nikolaos 171, 174-175, 178, 180, 182-183, 186, 188
Kamp, Katherine 21-23, 111, 155, 168-169
Kavanaugh, Robert 189
Kerameikos 170, 176, 185, 187-188
Kern, J.H.C. 176
Kimball, Samuel. A. 173-174
Kleisthenes 36
Knucklebones, *astragalos* 128-129, 187
Konner, Melvin 32, 168, 173, 175, 183-184, 189
Korbi, Jill 21
*Kore* 36, 115, 119
*Kouros* 36, 185
*Kourotrophos* 36, 37
*Kroatala* (castanet-like instrument) 117-118
Kullman, Wolfgang and Savine Föllinger 170
Kylix 72-74, 81

*Kyrios* 48, 60, 91, 101
the father of the household 150

## L

LaCaille, A.D. 175
Lagia, Anna 170
Lamb, Michael 172
Lawton, Carol 179, 182-183
Layne, Jaime 186, 188
*Lekythoi* 36
Leto 97
LeVine, Robert 173
Lillehammer, Grete 21, 105, 168, 183
Lycoleon 97
Lynch, Kathleen, and Papadopoulos, John 71, 74, 177
Lysias 65
Lysistrata 94

## M

Macro-level 25
Male and female roles in Classical Greek culture and society 98
*Mammothreptos* 62
Marriage squeeze 55
Masten, Ann 168
Material evidence 38
care items meant for children 38
grave gifts for children 38
grave steles with children 38
vases, scenes of play, potty training, adult-child interactions and children in motion 39
votive offerings and gifts to the Gods 39
votive reliefs, families with children and grand-children 39
McNiven, Timothy 39
Meaning 24
Mediating 25
*Meirakion* 34
Melisto-stele 120-121, 133, 135
Michalitsi (northwestern Greece) 123
Miniature toy altars 90, 130, 141
Mnesagora and Nikochares 132-133
Mnesikles 123
Monrad, Svenn 69, 177
Morgan, Janett 183
Morris, Ian 170
Mortal children in mythologies 176
Moseley, Dianne 174
Moss, J. and Solomon, H.C. 177
Mother 45-48
ancient Greek upper class 150
biological 45
centricity 50, 69
Motherese 60-61
Motherhood 28
joys of 74
Mothers 173
in various classes 177
Mourning 55
Multiple attachments 29, 57, 151
Multiple care 29, 60
givers 180
Multiple carers and alloparents 175
Multiple-caring relationships 60-61
Mutual eye-to-eye contact 73
Mythological babies 170
Mythology 153, 171, 176

## N

Neils, Jenifer and Oakley, John 21
*Nèpios* 34
*Neuróspasta* 115
Non-humans 57
Number of children in ancient Greek families 179
Nursing women 176
Nymphs 115, 187

## O

Oakley, John 169, 170-171, 173-174, 176-181, 185-189
Object exploration and object play 145
distinctions of 145-146
Observation of preverbal infants and toddlers 40
Oedipus complex 17, 167
Oikos 24, 26, 28-29, 36, 40, 45, 50, 54, 66, 67-68, 70-71, 73- 75, 82, 88-91, 93, 101, 150-151, 174, 179-181
and the *polis* 168
Classical Attic family and household 141
family unit 57-62
Opie, Iona and Opie, Peter 190
Orestes 48

## P

*Paideia* 167
*Paidion* 34, 169
Painted vase scenes as 'frozen here-and-now episodes' 39
*Pais* 34, 169
Papadopoulos, see Lynch
Parental investment theory 53
Parents 26, 63, 85
Parkin, see Grubbs

*Passé-boule* 88, 126, 143
Patterson, Cynthia 169, 174
Pedagogue 26, 35-36, 48, 58-60, 79, 84, 141, 151, 175
Pederast 17, 23, 167
Pediatrics (discipline of) 54
Peisis 97
Pellegrini, see Bjorklund
Peloponnesian War 25, 36, 37, 172, 173
Pentheus 48
Persian invasion 36
Pet 132
  relationship with 133-134
  group of birds 133-134
Phenomenology 23
*Philia* (affection) 49-51
Philo 169
Phormiskos 129
Physical education and competition in sports 145
Piraeus 48-49, 135-136
Plague epidemics 36
*Plangónes* 115
Plateia Zotzia 170
Plato 33-35, 38, 68, 76-78, 81, 88, 100, 102, 106, 111-112, 114, 121, 130-131, 139, 145, 152, 173
Play 30, 32, 86, 141, 169
  a primary child-driven activity 33
  a universal activity 151
  age, an inverted U-curve 112
  ancient Greek words for 111
  and brain development 109
  arguments for, in ancient Attica 110-111
  as early sacral socializer 141
  as practice to adult life 106-107, 112
  as pure pleasure 107
  emotional states of 32
  fantasy 32
  gender socialization 112
  gender specific 142
  humor 32
  in activity theory 107-108, 114,
  in Freudian theory 107
  in humans 105, 108
  in Piaget's theory 107
  in the *oikos* 88
  infancy period (0-2 years) 108
  language 32
  object 32, 145
  peer- 86
  physical activity 32
  Plato 112, 114, 121
  preschool period (3-6 years) 108
  pretend 32
  recent research 109
  role and fantasy, Plato 35
  role play 86, 108, 112-115, 121-122, 140-142
  sacral 90
  same gender 88
  solo- 144-45
  superfluous energy theory 106
  toddler period (2-3 years) 108
Play-scenes in everyday and the painter 179
Poehlmann, Julie 175
*Polis* 90, 92, 168
Pollock, Sandra 19, 167-168, 174
Polytheistic 39, 102, 151
Pomeroy, 169, 171
Potty stool 25, 28, 38, 40, 69-75, 177
  ancient 70
  high chair 71-74
Potty training 69-70
Praxitiles 186
Price, Theodora Hadzisteliou 170, 177
Production centers 185
Protective amulets 54
Psychological interpretation of body language 40, 72-73, 80, 83-84, 98

## R

Rattle 11-12, 40-41, 54, 64, 70-72, 78-81, 142, 144, 150-151, 178
  attention attractor 80
  club-shaped 78
  owl- 78-79, 178
  pig- 79
Rawson, Beryl 182
Recent developmental evolutionary research paradigm 184
Reilly, Joan 186
Religion 90
Reproduction-control 62
Rites and sacral activities 90
Roles of mother/father 50
Roman orphanages studies 179
Rosengren, Karl, Johnson, Carl and Harris, Paul 181
Rotbaum, F. 175
Rousseau, Jean-Jacques 106
Routines 27
  customized behavior 27
  functions of daily 27
  pure ritualization 27
Rühfel, Hilde 177
Rutter, Jeremy 179

## S


Sacral interpretation of animals with children 188
Sacral purposes and meanings 132
Sacral socialization 90, 97, 100-102, 130, 151, 181
Sacral toy objects as practical objects 186
Sacral world
  invented by adults 141
  of the child 102
Scheper-Hughes, Nancy 173-174
Schnapp, Alain 170
Self-socialization 130, 151
Sentimentalized mother-and-child scene 74
Sentiments 45-46
Shapiro, Harvey 48, 169
She-bear 94, 101
Sheridan, Mary 183
Shorter, Edward 18, 167
Sibling
  care 87, 88-89
  definitions of 180
  love, examples of 180-181
  relationship 85, 89
  rivalry 179
Siblings 85-86, 151
  new paradigm 86
  old Freudian one-sided theorizing 86
  older siblings 86-87
  playing together 88
SID (Sudden Infant Death) 77
Slave children, identification 175
Smith, Peter 169, 179, 183, 186-187, 189-190
Socialization 29-31, 126, 141
  approach 22
  definition 31
  explicit and implicit 31
  sacral 31
  self- 30
  *tabula rasa* 29
  to make social 30
Socio-historical impacts visible in the material evidence 36-37
Sommer, Dion 31, 162, 167, 168, 169, 170, 172, 175, 176, 182
Sommer, Dion, Pramling, Ingrid and Hundeide, Karsten 174, 190
Sommer, Maria 12, 162, 171, 177-179, 181, 183-184, 190
Soranus of Ephesus 76
Sotades-painter 177
Sparta 19, 27, 55, 168, 173
Spartan children 168
Spelke Elizabeth and Katherine Kinzler 190
Spin top 126, 184
Steles 17, 23, 36- 39, 41, 45, 48, 51- 53, 59, 63, 68, 75-76, 82, 88-89, 100, 111, 120-123, 126, 132- 135, 139-141, 143, 149-151, 154, 170-171, 173, 175-176, 178, 183, 186
Stern, Daniel 172-173, 176
Sully, James 107
Sutton, Robert 176, 179, 183, 186, 189
Swaddling 12, 41, 54, 75-78, 91, 150, 170, 173, 177-178
Sylva, Kathy 183


## T


Taking care of animals in childhood 139
Tanner, Jeremy 188
*Teknon* 34
Teleological principle 35
Theokles 132-133, 135
Theophrastus 50
Time 27-28
  and energy budget-argument 189
  historic 27
  ontogenetic changes in human lifespan 28
To be slim – a female ideal 68
Toddler 82, 84, 98-99
  on *choes*, vases and steles 82
Tomasello, Michael 168, 171, 173-175, 179, 183-184
Too many mouths to feed theory 56
Toy altars 90, 130, 141
Toy rollers and push carts 71, 88, 123-125, 134, 186, 189
Toys 140, 151
  created by children 189
  cultural functions of 140
  definition of 143
  developmental functions 144
  in early history 189
  investment in 140
  part of economic system in ancient Attica 142
  similarities between ancient and modern 142
  the oldest artifacts created by man 142
  types of 152
Toys and play 32-33, 130-131
  structured by adults 33
  used by young children 33
Triandis, Harry 178
Trümper, Monika 175


## V


Van Gestel, Josephus Petrus 178
Van Hoorn, Gerard 173, 177-181, 183, 186-188
Van Sleuwen, Bregje 178
Vekemans, Marcel and Dohmen, Brigitte 174
Vorster, Christiane 182-183
Votive statue of an infant/toddler boy 98

## W

Weisner, Thomas and Gallimore, Ronald 168, 180
Werness, Hope 173
Wet Nurses 28, 41, 58, 60, 62, 64, 68-69, 141, 150, 175-176
Wheeled horse 11, 123, 125-126, 142, 152, 187
Whistle 129, 152
Wileman, Julie 69, 110, 115, 119, 145, 168-169, 176-177
Women in child labor, depictions of 181
Words as symbolic tools 184
Woysch-Méautis, Daphné 188

## X

*Xenoi* (friends) 58
Xenophon 45

## Y

Young children 90
    active participants in religious rituals 90
Yoyo 127-128, 142, 151-152, 189

## Z

Zeus 92, 140
Zimbardo, Philip 174
Zone of proximal development 86
Zukow-Goldring, Patricia 179-180